AF632174

THE MONEY TRAP

THE MONEY TRAP

GRAND
FORTUNES
AND
LOST
ILLUSIONS
INSIDE THE
TECH
BUBBLE

ALOK SAMA

MACMILLAN

First published in the United States 2024 by St. Martin's Press,
an imprint of St. Martin's Publishing Group
First published in India 2024 by Macmillan
an imprint of Pan Macmillan Publishing India Private Limited
707 Kailash Building
26 K. G. Marg, New Delhi 110001
www.panmacmillan.co.in

Pan Macmillan, The Smithson, 6 Briset Street, Farringdon, London EC1M 5NR
Associated companies throughout the world
www.panmacmillan.com

ISBN 978-93-6113-433-3

Copyright © Alok Sama 2024

The moral rights of the author have been asserted.

The views expressed in this book are the author's own and the facts reported by him have been verified by the publisher to the extent possible. The publisher hereby disclaims any liability to any party for loss, damages or disruptions caused by the same.

All rights reserved. No part of this publication may be reproduced, stored in or introduced into a retrieval system, or transmitted, in any form, or by any means (electronic, mechanical, photocopying, recording or otherwise) without the prior written permission of the publisher. Any person who does any unauthorized act in relation to this publication may be liable to criminal prosecution and civil claims for damages.

5 7 9 8 6 4

This book is sold subject to the condition that it shall not, by way of trade or otherwise, be lent, re-sold, hired out, or otherwise circulated without the publisher's prior consent in any form of binding or cover other than that in which it is published and without a similar condition including this condition being imposed on the subsequent purchaser.

Designed by Meryl Sussman Levavi

Printed and bound in India by Thomson Press India Ltd.

FSC www.fsc.org
MIX
Paper | Supporting responsible forestry
FSC® C010615

For my parents, in fond memory

Novelists don't usually have it so good, do they, when something real happens (something unified, dramatic and pretty saleable), and they just write it down?

—Martin Amis, *London Fields*

CONTENTS

PROLOGUE

Brain Damage

Someone wants me out of the way. Someone desperately wants me out of the way. I don't know who and I don't know why, but I am about to find out.

I step out of my office onto Grosvenor Street, turning my trench coat collar against the gray and chilly morning. Walking briskly, I cut across on cobblestoned Avery Row, the type of Dickensian alley one associates with dark acts and clandestine liaisons. A house of ill repute was the highlight of Avery Row in the eighteenth century, but these days people visit to satisfy cravings of a more banal variety. The brothel has been displaced by a Starbucks.

I walk past two of my favorite blue plaques in London. Separated by two hundred years and a wall, these are the former homes of Jimi Hendrix and George Frideric Handel. I imagine Hendrix jamming "Purple Haze" and Handel conducting "Hallelujah," one high on LSD, the other on Jesus. I've never tried either, I get high just walking by.

My destination—Claridge's—is where you might take mum for high tea on her eightieth. I admire the imposing red brick façade, traverse the white marble Art Deco lobby, and request a table for four in the Foyer lounge. A Chihuly chandelier dominates this impressive room, its strands of tubular glass spiraling outward like Medusa's serpentine hair. Churchill lived at Claridge's after his ejection from Number 10. I picture him in the Foyer, jowly and scowling, dipping a cigar in his cognac, a lion licking his wounds while others drink tea and eat cake. But I am not here to smoke cigars or eat cake, nor do I feel like a lion. I am not a predator; no, I am the prey. An hour prior, I had received a message instructing me to be in the lobby at 10 A.M. I had asked my company's general counsel to join me. If there was going to be a revelation, I wanted Brian as a witness. Besides, I could use a friend. I send him an agitated message. Where are you, buddy?

Two men approach, both medium height and middle-aged. One is bald and svelte. In tight black jeans and a fitted black turtleneck, he could pass for a salesman at the nearby Armani store. He stretches out his hand, introducing himself as Avram, the former Mossad officer I've been communicating with on Signal using disappearing messages. I've had him checked out, he's for real. He knows someone who can identify my tormentors, but his source insists we meet in person. Would I be willing to pay for Avram and his friend to fly from Tel Aviv to London? I agreed, reluctantly.

Avram's smile does not reach his reptilian eyes. He seemed nicer online, but doesn't everyone?

His companion (burly, square-jawed, sports a military crew cut) introduces himself as James. The name, like his baggy tweed jacket, doesn't fit. *Why didn't you pick a debonair Hebrew name, like Lior or Ziv?* "James" looks like a shabbily attired policeman, the antithesis of his slick companion. According to Avram, James is also ex-Mossad and has the answers I need.

While waiting for Brian, we chat about the weather and their flight from Tel Aviv. Both order black coffee, which seems in character. Out of respect for the setting, I request Claridge's Blend tea with milk and sugar. The portly waiter (white jacket, black bow tie) nods approvingly, and asks if I would like scones with clotted cream and jam with my tea. I decline politely, shaking my head in disbelief. The incongruence is disorienting, like a Tom Clancy thriller set in Downton Abbey.

I ask why they chose Claridge's.

"Close to your office. And only tourists come here, nobody will recognize you," says Avram, with the vulpine air of a man who thinks of everything.

I don't tell him we could safely remain incognito in any neighborhood establishment open to the general public. The investment community I inhabit confines itself to private clubs (5 Hertford, George, Harry's Bar) where we willingly submit to the tyranny of dress codes and pay hefty annual dues for the privilege of paying even heftier prices for food and drink. He is right about the tourists, though.

Brian finally arrives. Genial and languid, he looks lawyerly in his dark suit and tie, but the puffy face and bloodshot eyes suggest he just rolled out of bed. I know he arrived from San Francisco the previous night.

The spy currently known as James takes charge. He stands and requests we hand over our mobile phones. Brian turns to me for guidance. It seems a tad dramatic, but I shrug my shoulders and nod. James switches the phones off, and places them on a console table some twenty feet away. *Maybe he doesn't realize the new Series 3 Apple Watch can do most things an iPhone 8 can?* Knowing more than a Mossad agent makes me feel smug.

"I have bad news," says James, now seated, looking grave. It triggers a distant memory. An avuncular cardiologist on Harley Street peering over his reading glasses pronouncing what felt more like a sentence than a diagnosis: I have coronary artery disease.

I cross my arms and brace myself.

"There is conspiracy to remove you from your job," James announces, leaning back, expecting a reaction. As if he'd told me Elvis was in the building.

I exhale deeply and nod impatiently. I wake up every morning and wait to be punched in the face. A thuggish spy telling me there's a conspiracy is as useful as that waiter offering scones with clotted cream and jam.

James pulls an iPad from his briefcase and places it on the coffee table in front of us. He starts to display a set of photographs.

The first shows a white stucco-fronted end-of-terrace Victorian house. A black wrought iron fence and yew hedging define the property line, a hawthorn tree frames the entrance. The gray door is open, stepping out is a tall woman wearing a stylish yet practical fitted red coat. Oversized sunglasses ride jauntily on her forehead, pushing back her dark brown hair. With her is another woman, about twenty, wearing a blue denim jacket, black track pants, and white trainers. She is holding a leash, on it a golden retriever, its creamy coat glistening in the sun, staring directly at the camera as if guided by a canine sixth sense.

It is my home, my wife, Maya, our daughter, Alya, and our dog, Ellie.

More photos of the three walking up Argyll Road, cutting through Holland Street, all the way to Kensington Gardens, where Ellie is released. More shots—Maya stepping into a dark blue Jaguar sedan, arriving outside an apartment block I recognize as her parents' home in Dulwich.

An evil eye has transformed the idyllic into the eerie. But there is more. A transcontinental change of scene. Me stepping out of a faded red brick prewar apartment block. I am outside my home in San Francisco's Presidio Heights. It is a foggy morning, and I am wearing a navy blue hoodie, black T-shirt and track pants, gray Allbirds wool runners.

As creepy as this is, I examine the photo critically. *Am I trying too hard?*

A camera tracks me walking down nearby Sacramento Street and entering a café I recognize: the very hip As Quoted, where the decor is as white as the clientele, the staff dress like orthodontists, and alarm bells clang if your dietary habits threaten the animal kingdom. I emerge with what looks like a large cup of coffee but I know is actually a turmeric latté with a dash of coconut sugar.

Avram and James watch me intently. Brian is wide awake now, mouth hanging open like a goldfish.

"I am sorry, I know this is difficult. I want to prove you I have access to information," said James.

I lean forward and nod vigorously.

"I need you pay me $200,000 as retainer. Within four weeks, I give evidence who is behind this. As success fee, you must pay me $1 million."

"How did you get these photos? Did you take them?" I ask.

"You pay me and I get answers," he responds. "But you need know some things I do illegal in many places. So you cannot use what I give in court of law."

"I can't be involved with anything illegal. Neither can my employer," I tell him.

He shrugs.

"Can you at least give me some idea who is behind this?" I ask.

"Not right for me to say now. I will find and deliver you proof," he answers.

I take a deep breath and sink into the couch, shoulders slumped. I have no right to expect their sympathy, nor do I expect them to know I've just been orphaned. But I'm scared. Someone wants to damage me. I experience an emotion I'm not familiar with: I feel sorry for myself.

"Why are they doing this to me?" I finally say.

Avram and James exchange glances, unsure how to react.

"You control billions of dollars," says Avram, finally.

Control? This is the grand illusion. I can barely control my bladder. Money doesn't give you control, it buys you a nicer coat. But I know what they mean. The ageless cliché. Money and power and what people do for it. The stakes are high. My intrepid boss Masayoshi Son has launched his gargantuan $100 billion SoftBank

Vision Fund. We are nearing what John von Neumann, on his deathbed in 1957, called an "essential singularity beyond which human affairs as we know them cannot continue."[1] Neumann believed gods were necessary but had lost their glory, and the only candidate to fill this void was technology. *Deus ex machina*—god from the machine—was finally here, and Masa Son's ambition is to be its high priest. A priest armed with one hundred billion blessings.

I've had enough. For these two strangers, I am nothing more than a mark. "James" could be the creep surveilling my family, a mercenary operating on the edge of the law. My impulse is to flee, but then I realize I'm expected to pay for their coffee.

I settle the bill and leave, but cannot handle the idea of returning to an office that might be bugged. It feels like it's about to rain, but these days I always feel like it's about to rain. Regardless, I decide to walk home, a forty-five minute journey that takes me through Hyde Park. The precipitation is the typical English drizzle, not forceful yet dominating, while the majestic trees in London's Royal Parks reveal their kaleidoscopic fall glory.

I am on the phone, oblivious.

My first call is to my lawyer, Mark MacDougall. It is early on the East Coast, but I promised Mark I'd call right after the meeting. He answers immediately, listens patiently, then asks an unlawyerly question.

"You feeling OK?"

I confess to being shaken up.

"That's understandable, Alok," he responds. "If it makes you feel better, we'll have your house swept."

In a few hours, a geek squad will examine every nook for listening devices, check all electronic equipment for signs of malware, and declare my home exorcized.

"But here's what I want you to think about," Mark continues.

He pauses. "Somebody wants to catch you with your pants down, and the best they could do was pictures of you buying coffee. We have nothing to hide. Keep your head high and do your job. We'll get through this."

No Mark, it was a noncaf, alkaline, Ayurvedic beverage—but maybe this isn't terribly important.

I walk along the Serpentine and stop at the Lido to pick up a coffee—real deal, no gut-cleansing flimflam—and pause at the plaque. I know what it says, I've read it before: IN PROUD MEMORY OF CAPTAIN J. O. COOPER, KILLED IN THE GREAT WAR, AGED 20. . . . HE SPENT HIS BOY'S DEAR LIFE FOR ENGLAND. A grieving father's tribute. *How did the son die? A twenty-year-old captain?* There's a story here. I see stories everywhere, stories I want to write.

Out of habit, I stop by the waterside Isis sculpture. This is just past the Lido, across the path from the Diana Memorial Fountain. I saw a black swan here once, gliding gracefully in the lake, almost within touching distance. I think of the mastermind who commissioned this stakeout presented with pictures of my dog chasing squirrels, and I laugh out loud. Comedy surrounds me, though sometimes it is as elusive as a black swan.

The next call is to my wife.

Maya is surprisingly calm. She listens patiently, then asks a question that makes me smile. "Did you try the scones at Claridge's?" But then she concludes on a sobering note.

"I hate this. You need to get out of there. It's horrible what this job is doing to you."

She is right. My Apple Watch screams panicked notifications—elevated heart rate, need more sleep, not enough steps, a vicious circle of gratuitous data creating an escalating, enervating, enveloping angst. Something is going to break very soon.

Part I

1

BORN TO RUN

Dr. Shiv Gupta laughed. It was the indulgent laugh of an older man who has heard something that reminds him of his youth.

With his shiny scalp and round rimless glasses, Dr. Gupta looked like Gandhi but ate more food, wore more clothes, and had a quirky sense of humor. He taught statistics at Wharton and started his introductory lecture by asking students to consider that the average American has one breast and one testicle.

Dr. Gupta was on a personal visit to Delhi and seeing me at the request of my father, a scholarly gastroenterologist who evidently felt he needed help guiding a prodigal son.

It was the winter of 1983, and we were seated in the Cafe at St. Stephen's College, where I was pursuing a BA in mathematics. "Cafe" was pronounced to rhyme with "safe." Nobody knew why. It sounded cool, I guess? On the table was the Cafe's signature fare of runny scrambled eggs loaded with fried onions and chopped tomatoes, mincemeat cutlets, and thick white toast dripping with butter, which we washed down with milky Lipton black tea. I didn't smoke out of respect for Dr. Gupta, but normally this would be followed by soulful drags on a Classic Filter Kings cigarette, the butt held between thumb and index finger like Amitabh Bachchan in *Deewaar.* Around us everyone was smoking. The Bihari communists in khadi kurtas favored filterless *beedis*, a wannabe hipster in faded Levi's flashed a packet of duty-free Marlboros.

The source of Dr. Gupta's mirth was my response to a question that makes every twenty-year-old bristle.

"So what do you want to do with your life, young man?" he asked, leaning back in his wicker chair, which crackled in protest as he shifted his weight.

"I'm working on solving Fermat's last theorem, sir. I think I can do it," I responded, while pushing back my thick, black, and regrettable bouffant.

I was referring to Pierre de Fermat's scribbles in the margins of a 1637 edition of *Arithmetica*, an enigmatic riddle not solved until 1993. Cracking Fermat was the nerd's equivalent of being the first to climb Everest—a thrillingly original journey of the mind culminating in a mountaineer's pleasure of seeing a view no person has seen before.

The problem with solving thorny math problems, as with planting flags on snowy peaks, is it doesn't pay the bills. And while Neumann's beautiful mind gave us game theory, it also calculated the optimum height for apocalyptic explosions over quaint wooden Japanese houses. All the reasons my concerned father had asked Dr. Gupta (himself a mathematician) to counsel me.

"I spoke to your professor. He told me you appealed your grades even though you had the highest marks in the university?" he inquired.

"Yes. I had a different way of looking at the convergence of Fourier series. They probably didn't understand," I responded, dismissively.

I wasn't trying to be ironic, probably why Dr. Gupta laughed—this time louder, rocking back and forth in his wicker chair. Which, out of sheer terror, now burst into a loud salvo of crackling.

"Do you have any concerns about America, son?" he asked.

How would I know? All I had to go on was well-read library copies of *Time* or *Life,* or anodyne Hollywood films like *What's Up, Doc?* that made it past overzealous censors. That and the music of Dylan, Paul Simon, and Springsteen.

"I'm not sure, sir," I responded. "There's this Bob Dylan song, about a boxer who could have been a world champion. They put him in jail because he was black."

When Dr. Gupta leaned forward, even his traumatized wicker chair was subdued.

"It's not easy, son," he said, with the weight of a wisdom reluctantly acquired. "You have to change. Dress like them, act like them, speak like them. Some people even change their name. You know, every Friday, I take a small group of Indian students out for dinner. We eat pizza and share a bottle of red wine. That's what I look forward to every week. Sometimes I wonder. But then I come to Delhi and I feel sad. Look what they've done to this country! Maybe you can be happier here, but what will you do?"

He had a point. Ours was an India suffocated by the Fabian socialism of Nehru and his successors. You needed a permit to open a *paan* shop, and in Hinglish, as in French according to George W. Bush, there was no word for "entrepreneur." Everything was broken in this stifling License Raj. There were no jobs, no safety net, electricity was intermittent, and (in India's repressed society) sex even more so. Springsteen had the last word. If you grew up in India in the seventies or the eighties and were fortunate enough to be educated, "tramps like us, baby we were born to run."

Dr. Gupta suggested my background was a good fit for an MBA in finance at Wharton. I think he meant math skills rather than smoking weed—presumably he was unaware of my regular partaking—though with hindsight both seemed equally relevant.

"Fermat's conjecture has been there three hundred and fifty years, it will wait for you. You can always get a PhD later, any university will give you a scholarship. Americans are scared of mathematics, we're good at it. But the MBA will give you more options," he argued persuasively.

■

The 1984 fall term at Penn had begun. The canopy of trees framing Locust Walk was a dazzling palette of orange, red, purple, yellow, and every conceivable shade of green. I'd never seen anything like it. Leaves in Delhi were either green or brown, everything was simpler.

I was a walking cliché as I strolled down Locust Walk that glorious afternoon, a brown bespectacled mathematician who followed cricket and read books. The hair was shorter, but I still struggled with Vs versus Ws. (Even today, Vest Willage is confounding.) As I looked around, chronically bewildered, someone slipped me a pamphlet. Some guy named Michael Milken was speaking at 6 P.M. in Penn's convention hall.

Milken was about forty, medium height, in nondescript business attire, neither imposing nor charismatic. The occasional wisecracks ("back then a hundred million was real money") seemed stilted and didn't age well, but this crowd loved it. "He makes over a billion a year," someone whispered. So what if he didn't look like Tom Cruise or move like Jagger? We were in the "greed is good" decade, when Reagan's America said no to drugs and yes to money with no appreciation for the irony.

Like me, Mike was a skinny, nerdy, twenty-one-year-old quant jock when he came to Wharton. His research demonstrated that a diversified portfolio of bonds rated below investment grade represents great value because the higher yields systematically offset losses from higher default rates. Buying these "junk bonds" was the equivalent of being a guaranteed winner if you consistently bet red at the roulette table.

In making this claim, Milken challenged a sacrosanct finance tenet—the efficiency of markets. According to this elegant hypothesis, smart traders ensure any anomalies disappear in nanoseconds, so that market prices always represent the collective wisdom of all participants. If you believed the wonks, the market was an omniscient artificial intelligence. It is a nihilist view of investing, the implication being that blindfolded monkeys throwing darts at a newspaper's financial pages could match Wall Street's finest. But Milken proved them wrong, all those eggheads who win Nobel Prizes for economics. That, as much as all the cash he made, was impressive—like cracking Fermat's last theorem.

Milken's work had another appealing dimension. Buying high-yield bonds wasn't a lucrative trade that made you money at someone's expense. Milken created a $9 trillion capital market, democratizing access to capital for small and midsized American (later global) companies, even countries. Not that I cared that much about small and midsized American companies, it just felt nice to see finance as an equalizer in this loaded game of capitalism.

All of which made Milken a hero. If my younger self had studied the classics, I would have recognized a Greek tragedy in the making. Because heroes have flaws, frequently fatal. Five years later, after a trial that epitomized eighties excess, Milken would be indicted for racketeering and securities fraud. I didn't see that coming. All I saw was a man flying higher than Dr. J in the Spectrum.

■

Investment banking isn't money for nothing. "Busy" means working sixteen hours a day on weekdays plus another sixteen on weekends. I didn't mind. Like every other immigrant, I wasn't here for a rest cure. I was twenty-three and newly wed, needed that green card, wanted those microwave ovens and color TVs.

Morgan Stanley was a fortunate landing place, avoiding the scandals that plagued most of its peers thanks to a risk-averse culture. When I joined, it was primarily an investment banking business, a patrician white-shoe franchise with an enviable roster of blue-chip clients, a genteel Aston Martin compared to the muscular Porsche that was the cultish Goldman Sachs. My colleagues came from a world of green quadrangles, majestic spires, and lacrosse sticks. They were friendly enough, but their social lives transitioned seamlessly from Yale secret societies to Greenwich country clubs. And beneath the cultivated simplicity that is the hallmark of American aristocracy was an impressive work ethic and formidable IQs. I couldn't outsmart these people, maybe not even outwork them.

I remembered Dr. Gupta's advice—dress like them, act like them. A nice salesman at Barneys told me blue worked best with my skin tone. The nice salesman was Black and nattily cloaked in blue and sold me a blue suit I couldn't afford and I discovered credit card debt and felt very American.

"As far back as I can remember I always wanted to be a banker" said nobody I ever met. Only slick gangsters in movies feel that way. Most of us could just as well have been lawyers or accountants. I once pulled an all-nighter to prepare a selling memo for an IPO just so my boss would have it on his desk the following morning. The memo was on my chair when I came in. No acknowledgment for effort, just a typo in the appendix circled in red.

While the pressure to generate fees was relentless (ABC, Always Be Closing), what we sold wasn't used cars or condos. It was good old-fashioned problem solving. A bank needed capital to satisfy new regulatory requirements without diluting its owners. A cable company's business was damaged by the 1990–91 recession, and required debt restructuring. A US phone company stymied in its domestic growth wanted to venture overseas.

In 1993 Morgan Stanley's influential strategist Barton Biggs pronounced that he was "maximum bullish" on Asia. I volunteered for a tour of duty, starting with setting up the firm's capital markets business in Hong Kong, then establishing our investment banking business in India. Not quite a ticker-tape return to my homeland, but my parents were happy to see more of me.

CEO John Mack's office asked if I had any use for a recent addition to the Morgan Stanley board—former defense secretary and later vice president Dick Cheney. His connections could be useful in sourcing government business, like privatizations, so I invited Secretary Cheney to join me in Delhi. I was told his schedule needed to be "spaced out," since he was recovering from a recent cardiac episode. Which meant four meetings a day, but the unsmiling (even to the hotel staff) Secretary Cheney seemed fine spending the intervening time with me. With a calm and unsettling lucidity, he was surprisingly forthcoming about his paranoid worldview, including the unfinished business of "taking out Saddam." Secretary Cheney was also on the board of Procter & Gamble, which had recently and embarrassingly lost $157 million dabbling in exotic financial instruments, and he had many questions about derivatives.[1] And so it came to be that over a leisurely South Indian breakfast of steaming *idlis* and spicy *sambhar* in Delhi's Oberoi Hotel, I found myself lecturing Dick Cheney on weapons of mass (financial) destruction.

He invited me to join him for dinner at the US ambassador's residence. On the drive back to our hotel, I commented on how effusive the ambassador (a career diplomat) had been about Morgan Stanley.

For the first time in two days, the unsmiling Secretary Cheney smiled.

"I suspect he wants a job when he retires, Alok," he responded.

Of course. Everyone wants a piece of that Wall Street action.

In my time at Morgan Stanley, I did deals for consumer product companies in Cincinnati, media companies in London, internet companies in Germany, conglomerates in Hong Kong, telecom operators in Australia, hotel companies in India, and banks in China. I saw the world—the depressing banality of a Holiday Inn in Saginaw, the creepy weirdness of karaoke bars in Seoul, the stunning sophistication of Le Bristol in Paris. At age thirty-three, after an exhilarating and exhausting journey, I earned the coveted brass ring and became a managing director.

■

The madness began on August 9, 1995, when shares of Netscape, creator of the first internet browser, more than doubled on their first day of trading. The lead underwriter for the Netscape IPO—Morgan Stanley.

Over the next five years, the NASDAQ rocketed eightfold, while venture capital funding increased over ten times. Fortunes were made for those who got in early, among them an upstart Japanese entrepreneur named Masayoshi Son. Few had heard of him, but his $100 million Yahoo! investment in 1996 became worth over $30 billion. By 1999, he claimed to own 7–8 percent of all publicly listed internet properties,[2] and for a brief period became the richest man in the world.

Being an investment banker then was more lucrative than at any time in history, even more so than the eighties. We relocated to London in 2000, me still with Morgan Stanley, and bought our first home. A six-story Georgian terraced house—with a microwave oven and four color TVs—in tony Kensington, with J. K. Rowling as our neighbor, a Porsche 911 and an equally predictable Mercedes SUV in the underground garage.

Which should have been awesome, except it wasn't. The key to banker smugness was knowing nobody made more, except maybe movie stars and football players, but they had actual talent so that was fine. Now we watched enviously as kids whose start-ups went public became billionaires overnight, and traders doubled their money daily betting on internet stocks. How can you feel like a winner when nobody around you wants to play the thankless yet vital role of being a loser? And if making money was so easy and no longer cool, why suffer seventy-hour three-country work weeks? It was depressing.

■

In April 2000, on one of my rare days not traveling, my colleague Martin tapped on the glass door of my office seeking help with a client he smilingly described as "difficult."

Martin was an experienced banker, and I wondered why he thought I might do better. I understood when he told me the client's name—Nikesh Arora. It is strange how even the statistically accomplished assume there's a reasonable chance that two among over a billion Indians might know each other. It is even stranger that in my world they usually do, for the community of Indian professionals lurking in the money corridors of New York, London, or Hong Kong is indeed incestuous.

"Sure, happy to help. I've met Nikesh. Briefly, cocktail party a few weeks ago," I told Martin, but warned him that Indians are frequently like crabs in a bucket.

Nikesh was a senior executive at T-Mobile, the mobile affiliate of German telecommunications giant Deutsche Telekom. I emailed to reintroduce myself, and we arranged to meet for lunch at Nobu, located on the second floor of the trendy (well, at the time anyway) Metropolitan Hotel in Mayfair.

I arrived early and seated myself at a table next to the picture windows overlooking Hyde Park. As always at Nobu, I marveled at Boris Becker's broom closet acrobatics, which culminated in a ruinous paternity lawsuit. I was relaxed about this meeting. "CEO impact," aka "impressing powerful men" (it was mostly men) is a core skill for investment bankers. For me this meant listening more than talking, avoiding pitch books or taking notes, never selling. They came away impressed you let them impress you. Women—and Nikesh, as I would discover shortly—were more demanding. They expected insight.

I saw Nikesh stride in purposefully. He was tall, his bearing upright, a prominent dimple on his chin the defining feature of his Bollywood good looks, covert flecks of gray around his temple suggested we were roughly the same vintage. The fitted black suit and crisp white shirt exuded power. Not wearing a tie (in the City an accessory as essential as stockings for women) suggested cultivated nonchalance. His aura complemented the wardrobe in radiating charismatic self-confidence. I could slide into a room and disappear; I preferred it that way. When Nikesh walked into a space, he owned it; you felt his intimidating presence.

"So I gather you met Martin?" I asked, smiling, once he was seated.

"Lightweight," he said, shrugging dismissively. "Didn't add anything."

Poor Martin, never had a chance.

Over the signature Nobu fare of yellowtail sashimi with jalapeños and miso-marinated black cod, we then played the game of twenty questions typical of encounters among Indians of my generation.

"Are you from Delhi, Nikesh?"

"Yes! You too, right?"

Back and forth, like a baseline rally at Roland-Garros—what school, what college, what did your parents do, when did you leave India—and so it goes until we're able to pigeonhole each other in the postcolonial hierarchy of India's English-speaking educated minority. Fortunately, the Venn diagrams of our respective lives had a comfortable overlap. Our roots were middle-class—which in India meant ceiling fans rather than air-conditioning. We both attended high school in Delhi, following which Nikesh trained as an engineer. Like many of our peers, we arrived in New York in the mid-eighties with $500 of American Express Travelers Cheques and started a life where an off-peak three-minute phone call to India was our biggest indulgence.

Our relationship developed. We treated our preteen daughters to a Taylor Swift concert at Wembley, though we missed the opening act. Some kid named Justin Bieber. We made an ideal golf pairing, Nikesh's "grip it and rip it" style complementing my deliberate mode. He invited Maya and me to his fortieth birthday celebration in Morocco, and we started an annual tradition of vacationing together with our respective families over the New Year's holiday.

Nikesh got me in a way few people did. "You have to understand that for Alok everyone is a *chutia* unless proven otherwise," he once said among a group of friends. (A *chutia* is a mildly derogatory Hindi insult, not nearly as offensive as a literal translation might suggest.) It was an observation delivered without judgment, a harsh yet satisfying moment when someone recognizes an uncomfortable truth about you. My cynicism was not rooted in people's lack of wealth or status. Intellect, or lack thereof, had something to do with it, but it ran deeper. In this world I inhabited, everyone, myself included, was trying to be something they were not—act richer, be cooler, seem nicer, behaviors most evident at those tedious charity auctions where people raise their hand compulsively but only because everyone is watching. *(I prefer my good deeds done Oscar Wilde–style. Anonymously, then have somebody find out.)*

■

When I met him, the Arora rocket ship was warming up. This guy didn't need to pretend, he was cool. As a banker, I saw the commercial opportunity, for every CEO is a potential fee payer, and at a personal level I admired his intellect and drive.

Nikesh was the founding CEO of T-Motion, a "mobile internet service provider." In this era of dial-up modems, 2G wireless networks, and Nokia feature phones (the iPhone came five years later) accessing the internet via a handheld device was futuristic yet predictable. My team recognized this, and it was why Martin was trying to build a relationship with Nikesh.

I helped Nikesh refine and facilitate—introductions to private equity players, for example—his plan to launch a "mobile virtual network operator" (MVNO) delivering on his mobile internet vision. (MVNOs lease capacity from existing operators rather than building a wireless network. Cable companies typically offer mobile service in this fashion.) But fate intervened in the form of Google, then an exciting Silicon Valley disruptor with no international presence.

Nikesh's job interview was conducted by Google cofounders Larry Page and Sergey Brin over a tour of the British Museum, where these pharaohs of our time walked past the statue of Ramesses the Great and compared the Google search algorithm to the Rosetta Stone.

Silicon Valley founders frequently struggle to evolve beyond their coding roots, and Nikesh gave Larry and Sergey exactly what they needed—a military-style execution capability. Googlers preoccupied with spacey goals like "Don't be evil" were introduced to earthy concepts like accountability and budgets. All performance metrics skyrocketed, and by 2014 Nikesh was based in Silicon Valley as Google's chief business officer with a reported annual compensation of $51 million. An astounding number, even more so at the time, but his compensation was tied to results, and Nikesh objectively delivered for Google shareholders. Besides, when someone pays $10 million for Damien Hirst's pickled shark or $69 million for Beeple's NFT, it is a reminder that in a free market, for art or for talent, monetary value is whatever the next bidder is prepared to pay.

■

The first time I saw him was at Nikesh's wedding.

It was the July Fourth weekend in 2014, and the venue was Borgo Egnazia, a faux-fortified resort in Puglia on the site of an ancient Roman settlement. The pearly white weathered stone walls, a church with a bell tower, and a central piazza all combined nicely to reinforce the Mediterranean *borgo* vibe. The whimsical

Arabian-style arches seemed out of character, as if the architect confused the boot of Italy with Moorish Andalusia. It was a pleasing package, exotic and exclusive, with a nearby seaside championship golf course completing the luxe resort experience.

The glamour quotient was raised by Nikesh's friend Ashton Kutcher, a savvy venture investor (Spotify, Airbnb, Uber) in his own right, and his wife Mila Kunis. Under a moonlit Adriatic sky, a turbaned Ashton, accompanied by the *prima ballerina* from the San Jose Ballet, led a raucous dance number set to the Bollywood hit "Singh is Kinng." A titillating wardrobe malfunction, à la Janet Jackson at the 2004 Super Bowl, added some unexpected spice to the performance.

The welcome party at Borgo Ignazia was at the beach club. The theme was all white, ambient house music played in the background, overhead drones captured photos of the notable and the fashionable mingling under the setting sun. My daughter Alya and my son Samir had both flown in that morning from New York, which made this a family reunion of sorts.

As I scanned the scene, my eye settled briefly on an Asian gentleman, elegantly attired in a white lounge suit, standing slightly removed from the others. He looked trim and sprightly, but his receding hairline and the wrinkles that appeared when he flashed his expansive smile gave away his age, likely mid- to late fifties. His head appeared modestly oversized for his physique, giving him the wizened appearance of Yoda, a comparison I later learned he was fond of making. There was a quiet stillness to his bearing, standing erect with arms dangling rather than crossed or hands in pockets.

He kept to himself, unusual in a wedding setting where festive intermingling was the norm. *Perhaps he doesn't know anyone, maybe a language thing?*

There was soon a sign that this was not merely a shy party guest. Every so often, someone would glide toward the man and bow deferentially. He would reciprocate gracefully, his accompanying smile giving the formal greeting the warmth of a bear hug. Only the big hitters approached him, among them the CEOs of Google and Deutsche Bank, the editor of the *Financial Times,* the founder of an Indian telecom empire. Ashton Kutcher introduced himself like an adoring groupie.

This must be Masayoshi Son.

SoftBank's $20 million investment in Alibaba (the Amazon of China) was now worth at least $50 *billion.*[3] The greatest venture investment ever. Alibaba was preparing for a September IPO, which would give Masa flexibility to realize his monumental profit. In this world, where your worth is measured by your last deal, his status was exalted.

I wasn't surprised to see him, for I was privy to what few knew. Nikesh had impressed Masa in engineering a commercial deal that allowed SoftBank-controlled Yahoo! Japan to use Google's search technology to power the Yahoo! Japan portal. After a thwarted attempt to merge Sprint and T-Mobile, Masa realized he needed the execution capability and global connectivity Nikesh offered. The two had met a couple of weeks previously at the Four Seasons in Beverly Hills and agreed that Nikesh would join SoftBank as its president in one of the most lucrative compensation deals of all time—a $73 million annual pay package.[4]

They also made a compact. Masa committed that Nikesh would succeed him as CEO of SoftBank. Based on Masa's announced life plan, this would be when Masa was "in his sixties." His sixtieth birthday was only three years away.

I saw Masa once more that weekend, playing in a golf outing organized for guests. Apart from Nikesh and Masa, the group included hedge fund legend Stanley Druckenmiller and tech private equity mogul Egon Durban.

Nikesh and Stan are big men, both towering over Masa. With a wide backswing that took the club well past parallel while keeping both feet firmly planted on the ground, Masa generated enough clubhead speed to keep up with them. Even at a distance, I sensed the intense concentration—like a Jedi energy field—as he lined up a shot. When he nailed a putt, there was no demonstrative high five or loud exclamation, just a barely perceptible fist pump.

On the golf course and in the investment world, the Force was strong with this man. You underestimated him at your own peril. Still, I wondered. Financial markets routinely emasculate Jedis who challenge their omniscience. Like Milken, Masa was a visionary and an iconoclast—a hero. But heroes have flaws. Thirty years on, I understood this, I understood hubris.

2

I TOOK A PILL IN IBIZA

It began with a pill.

Pacha is the mecca for Ibiza clubbers, and that night master blaster DJ David Guetta was the caliph. The setting for Pacha is unlikely, even tacky. The neighborhood has the feel of a decrepit US suburban strip mall, complete with a sprawling parking lot across the street. The building itself is a cavernous warehouse. A Costco logo might seem in character, but what you get instead is an entrance flanked by faux palm trees, with a giant neon sign flashing Guetta's message of universal love. F*** ME, I'M FAMOUS. Once inside, more dazzling signage, T-shirts worn by a few, and pink psychedelic phallic objects wielded by many combine to drill the slogan into your brain. A message as loud as the techno beats, as ludicrous as it was ubiquitous. *FMIF.*

It was a few days after Nikesh's wedding. Maya and I, along with a small group of friends from London, had joined Nikesh and Ayesha (his wife) in Ibiza. Our day had been long, starting with a boat in the blazing sun out to Formentera for lunch on the beach at the retro shack Juan y Andrea, where we washed down seafood paella with rosé before dipping into the turquoise water. The evening began with dinner at the voyeuristic Cipriani, where Paris Hilton and her entourage of beautiful people eyed each other with carnal fascination. And then the dénouement at Pacha, where the action begins after midnight. At 1 A.M. there was still no sign of our famous and eager-to-copulate headline act.

My friend Jonty, a burly former South African army officer who escorted Nelson Mandela off Robben Island, must have noticed my stifled yawn. He put his arm around me and whispered in my ear, in his hoarse Afrikaner accent. "You need this, mate," he said, pressing a tiny pill into my hand. "Let's ditch this VIP lounge horseshit, let's get down there and rock."

Jonty's energy was uplifting, and Ibiza that kind of place. Brandishing a fluorescent pink F*** ME, I'M FAMOUS baton and sporting a black *Eyes Wide Shut* mask, Jonty parted the sea of gyrating bodies and led me to the promised land in the middle of the arena. The molly began to kick in, the volume of those pulsating techno beats cranked up in my head. First gradually, then suddenly.

Am I missing something? Someone read my mind and handed me a fluorescent pink baton. Wielding a stick seems to activate a dormant Neanderthal gene, and the F*** ME, I'M FAMOUS logo weaponized the tool in a way only Freud could explain. I felt like the empowered ape in the opening of *Space Odyssey*, at one with the sea of primates on the dance floor, all of us jumping up and down, banging an invisible nail with our pink phallic hammers.

I have a hallucinogenic recollection of being dragged away at some point in the morning, pink baton still in hand. Nikesh invited us to his terrace suite at the Ibiza Gran Hotel to watch the sunrise, as one does after a night out in Ibiza. We stretched out on the recliners on the terrace, overlooking the marina and Ibiza's fortified Dalt Vila old town in the distance. It was past 5 A.M., and I was fixated on the early morning hustle on the marina. Fishermen, I assumed, grinding out a living while the *bon vivants* at the Gran Hotel were tucked under their silky Frette bedsheets.

"Alok," asked Nikesh, "do you think you could go back to your old life, work sixty hours a week, on the road all the time?"

Something in his tone jerked me out of my musings. Conversations with Nikesh were like chess games, you had to think a few moves ahead before speaking. Not easy in my current state.

"I'm not sure man, been there, done that," I said.

We both smiled knowingly.

Back in our hotel room a short while later, the seed Nikesh had planted was germinating.

"I think Nikesh might offer me a job," I told Maya.

"Seriously? You would consider that, working for a Japanese bank?" was her incredulous reaction.

"It's not a bank," I said, amused at her predictable reaction. We had been together thirty years, and she is my life hack, her upright intelligence and dazzling smile always shining a light into my darkest corners. (She does occasionally spout irritatingly kitschy clichés like "you are what you are"—I mean, what the fuck else would you be?—but when your favorite Stones track is "Paint It Black," her kind of luminosity is existential.) Maya had never been a fan of Wall Street, always urging me to trade the money for a simpler life. She had turned down Wharton herself, opting for a degree in arts administration and a job at the New York Philharmonic that had the incidental benefit of elevating my standing in the cultural Dow Jones.

I explained what SoftBank and Masa Son were about, a unique combination of global telecom operator and racy technology investment company. Its name came from its origins as a software distributor—a "bank for software." Masa wasn't even Japanese, he was Korean, as well known in Silicon Valley and Wall Street as he was in Tokyo, where the company just happened to be headquartered.

"Maybe worth thinking about, I know you're restless," she responded wearily, but now ready to hit the bed.

■

I thought about it a lot, sitting on my terrace. *Unless stated otherwise, I'm always thinking about something a lot. Like the toe hang on my putter or inflated used-car prices. Frequently something darker, occasionally something deeper. It's exhausting.*

I had left Morgan Stanley some time ago, the Zegna suits and Hermès ties hanging in my closet like sloughed-off skin from a prior incarnation.

Investment bankers are like martlets—birds without feet, condemned to a life of continuous flight. Many self-destruct, while others get shot. The fortunate ones glide to a gentle reincarnation; only a precious few seem to fly forever. But while in flight, all are driven by the irresistible power of money.

The communication of my first bonus—my "number"—was a moment of drama. No appointments were scheduled, but everyone knew it was D-Day. I was at my battle station, hunched forward, squinting intently at my clunky Bloomberg screen, when my colleague Michael tapped on my shoulder.

"Vincent wants to see you in his office," he explained.

Vincent was the handsome soft-spoken Harvard-educated suspender-wearing Frenchman who ran our department. I'd never met anyone with a hyphenated last name. It was intimidating. And Vincent's was preceded by an aggrandizing "de" suggestive of European nobility. He would invite every team member to join him at a small round mahogany meeting table in his office. Two large windows normally overlooked bustling Forty-Eighth Street in Rockefeller Center, but the blinds were drawn and lights switched off, a small brass lamp on his adjacent mahogany roll-top desk the only source of light, the green lampshade casting a weblike shadow on the ceiling and wall. It felt medieval, like a candlelit rent-collection routine Vincent's feudal ancestors might have imposed on hapless French farmers, except the flow of funds was reversed.

He solemnly asked me to take a seat and handed me a piece of paper, on it—well, all I noticed was my number. One hundred and ninety thousand dollars. *Merci énormément, monsieur.*

That first bonus hitting my frequently overdrawn Chemical Bank account was a curious high, a cocktail of self-affirmation and gratitude blended with shocked disbelief. If my account had been accessible online, I would have hit refresh multiple times. I bought Maya a Bulgari gold bracelet, which she thought flashy and never wore. My indulgence was six tailored shirts from Saks —a buy-five-get-one-free promotion—all two-toned and monogrammed with French cuffs. The absurdity of a brown dude who should be fixing your computer dressed like Hollywood royalty was yet another joke I didn't get.

The paychecks got bigger, many times bigger, but greed took over when poverty ended. Over a decade later, when my London boss (a jovial and burly Bostonian we called the Gorilla) communicated my biggest ever number, he asked why I wasn't smiling. For when it comes to bonuses, every banker is unhappy in his or her own way. A common gripe is that you could make more elsewhere, which was the case with the Gorilla and me. Another is when you just know the schmuck next door made more. And then there's the simmering status anxiety of lacking nothing yet always wanting something—a co-op with a nicer view of Central Park, a house closer to the water in the Hamptons, flying first class but craving a NetJets card.

Does it ever end? I asked one of my mentors. With his steely blue eyes, close-cropped hair, and trousers that always seemed an inch too short, Brad looked like an ex-marine. He wasn't, but he was a first-through-the-door kind of action figure you wanted to follow.

Over a glass of wine on one of our many Cathay flights in and out of Hong Kong, I asked Brad what powered our hard-charging boss, a Wall Street legend who wore black silk suspenders festooned with yellow dollar signs and looked less like a banker than an actor trying to play one.

He turned his head sideways, his laser eyes boring into mine.

"Alok, for him it's a game of whoever has the most when they die, wins." The laser eyes switched off abruptly, like a Jedi lightsaber, and he turned away.

A warning, but he would never present it that way. The choices were mine to make.

I bought Maya an expensive trinket after every bonus. She accepted with the joy of someone who preferred I do the dishes. Meanwhile, the early morning flights and late night phone calls wore me down, until it finally sank in. I'd seen enough money but not enough of my children. This Tantalusean hamster wheel would keep on turning: there would always be a nicer home, a faster car, eventually a bigger plane.

I should have walked away, but I didn't. Nobody does; nobody walks out of the money trap. Instead, I did the one thing a martlet can never do. I slowed down. That and the implosion of the internet bubble meant I was doomed. My biggest client was European cable operator NTL (later Virgin Media). NTL had a market value approaching $100 billion in 2000, and printed fees of over $100 million for Morgan Stanley. In 2002, it filed for bankruptcy.

They come for you when the bonus pool is tight, when there's too many mouths to feed. The partners who are your friends and neighbors, the mentors you look up to as older brothers. *I took it personally, wouldn't you?* But then I forgave them. Because on Wall Street, self-pity, like lunch, is for wimps. Besides, I would have done the same. Because people like that are the only people here.

■

It was now 6 A.M. in Ibiza. On a whim, I decided to call my twenty-one-year-old firstborn. From age ten Samir could checkmate my king within fifteen moves while playing *Call of Duty,* and had now blossomed into a fountain of worldly wisdom. A few weeks earlier in the gym, he had eyed my withering arms critically, and handed me a pair of dumbbells I could barely lift.

"Biceps are the male cleavage, Daddy you need to do something about your arms," he pronounced.

Samir was a rising senior at Yale College. His main interest wasn't finance, his inspiration more Jerry Maguire than Jamie Dimon. That summer he was interning at the Raine Group, a boutique advisory firm with links to William Morris Endeavor, the leading global talent agency. Raine's biggest investment banking client—SoftBank.

It was late in New York, but he kept long hours and answered immediately.

"Dude, we were clubbing all night, insane," I volunteered, not without a hint of pride.

At an absurdly inappropriate age—he claims he was eight—I had initiated Samir into *Lebowski* fandom. His first email address was theminidude@hotmail.com, and we've called each other "dude" ever since.

"You were what? Dude, where are you?" he asked.

"In Ibiza, with Nikesh," I responded.

"Nikesh? I've been listening in on calls with Masa Son and him. Is Mummy with you? I know what goes on there, please don't tell me my mother was doing drugs."

"No, no, dude, wacky place, though, it was the F*** ME, I'M FAMOUS party . . ."

"It was what?"

"Never mind, another time, tell me about Nikesh and SoftBank."

Samir was staffed on a deal SoftBank was evaluating. No reveals, but his message was unequivocal.

"Dude, I think they need someone like you. And they're doing seriously cool shit. I think you should do it."

He was replaying what his senior colleagues might have said, but his main point was that SoftBank was primarily a telecom company. The transformation to investment management required building out its in-house deal machinery, which was the opportunity for me.

Doing "seriously cool shit," presumably substantial and complex technology deals, as a principal at SoftBank was intriguing. After leaving Morgan Stanley, I had cofounded an India-focused investment business in partnership with the Dubai government. Right idea, terrible timing. The financial crisis destroyed Dubai's finances, and the business never scaled to my expectations.

Plus it was an exciting time to be a technology investor. Three years prior (in 2011) venture capitalist Marc Andreessen's "software will eat the world" clarion call summarized a fresh wave of innovation. Facebook and Twitter had gone public recently and Alibaba's IPO was scheduled for September. Ubiquitous fourth-generation wireless networks and smartphones were enabling new business models like Uber to transform sclerotic industries like transportation, while Netflix was upturning the media business from linear to on-demand. The action was moving to the cloud while everything, even love and sex, was being disrupted. It all pointed to a repeat of the late nineties internet boom, my headiest phase as a deal junkie.

I missed that buzz, but only in the way a reformed addict might occasionally crave a fix. But being an empty nester creates a void in every parent's life. I used to feel sad, looking at pictures of their younger selves that no longer existed. I had had no time for them, and now they were gone. Would doing something to impress my kids, or at least one of them, help me hold on? The bar to get Samir's respect was high. Doing drugs in Ibiza did not make the cut. One-armed push-ups and working for SoftBank seemed to do the trick.

■

Lunch the following morning was poolside at the Gran Hotel. As anticipated, Nikesh asked to have a private chat.

We walked around the courtyard pool in our shorts, linen shirts, and sunglasses, nursing glasses of rosé, while he laid out Masa's vision to dominate global telecom and his own thoughts on technology and media investing. The numbers were impressive: with the ability to monetize its Alibaba stake, SoftBank possessed balance sheet firepower even the flagship funds for the largest private equity firms could not match—over $50 billion, more with leverage.

"I can't outsource deals to investment banks. I need someone I can trust in the room who represents SoftBank," he said. "You're one of the smartest guys I know, but there's plenty of smart people out there. Integrity and experience, tougher to find. I could use your help, buddy."

"I like the idea of us working together, Nikesh, I think we'll have fun," I said, and meant it. "Maybe as much as yesterday," I added, laughing. Rollicking Ibiza clubs were a lot like rambunctious bull markets. "But I'm not sure I can handle it. If it didn't involve working with you, I wouldn't consider it. And in any case, I need time to untangle myself from my business."

I proposed a flexible consulting arrangement, prepared for him to insist on outright commitment to an opportunity most would grab. But he agreed, perhaps himself unsure what was in store.

■

Later that evening, Maya and I departed Ibiza for London.

I'm in a reflective mood on flights, perhaps a legacy of frequent air travel in an era without Wi-Fi and with minimal inflight entertainment. I'd never really got Ibiza, but evidently without the magic pill—ecstasy, molly, MDMA, E, or if you're not into the whole brevity thing, methylenedioxymethamphetamine—Ibiza would be just another Mediterranean island with stony beaches and overpriced restaurants. It's not just Ibiza, psychedelics apparently unlock much of what goes on in Silicon Valley, and it goes beyond Musk and his reported use of ketamine.[1] Looking for a mental edge, Spencer Shulem, CEO of start-up BuildBetter.AI, uses LSD regularly and suggests pressure from venture investors has everything to do with it. "They don't want a normal person, a normal company. They want something extraordinary. You're not born extraordinary," he says.[2] *An extraordinary admission, Spencer—I hope you build a better AI.*

I was neither a Valley founder nor a millennial raver and drugs don't feature on my menu—unless you count ibuprofen, which I take regularly in anticipation of needing ibuprofen—but that pill reminded me how much I missed the absence of constriction and camouflage. In college, the highlight of my typical day was a communal male bonding ritual of sharing meticulously rolled joints with an acknowledgment of "This is good shit, man" after every puff. Our dealer was a sleazy hairy Sikh who ran a local dry-cleaning shop, and as for what he plied us with, I have no clue. It looked suspiciously like goat shit, and there's a reasonable chance it was. We were stoned, but in a weirdly lucid way, listening to Bob Marley and creating a better world while frequently laughing uncontrollably.

Those were good times, man, that really was good shit.

3

THE AIRPORT TEST

New York was my introduction to the land of the free and the home of the two-car garage. In 1984, an MTA bus from JFK dumped me into what seemed like the scariest place on earth—the Port Authority Bus Terminal. It was Morning in America, according to Ronald Reagan, but it was dark there on Eighth Avenue. Almost forty years on, I can still see it, I can smell it. A scene from a Soviet Cold War propaganda film: the crowds, the vagrants, the grime, evocative of India's slums with the added dimension of a palpable hostility. I wasn't expecting Disneyland, but coming from India, I craved something better. I'm not sure what exactly, perhaps a more cosmopolitan and edgier version of Copenhagen? Except I'd never been to Copenhagen—I'd never been anywhere.

As a cricket-obsessed teenager, I would season every new bat diligently, preparing it to counter red rocklike missiles hurled at me from twenty-two paces. Which meant lovingly applying a coat of linseed oil, then beating the face incessantly with a wooden hammer, leaving visible scars. New York was like that for me—a knifepoint mugging in the East Village, racist slurs in Times Square, my red used Volkswagen Jetta stolen and eventually recovered uptown, bearing the loss of its wheels with admirable fortitude.

■

I was in New York at Nikesh's request. He had called three weeks after Ibiza and taken me through a complex deal involving two separate but related acquisitions in the Mexican telecommunications industry. After a brief compensation discussion, I proposed terms squarely in the Goldilocks zone, which he thought reasonable. However, he wanted me to jump through an additional hoop. A virtual interview with a senior member of the SoftBank management team, the man who was hitherto the vizier in the sultan's court—Ronald Fisher.

Ron Fisher was affable, avuncular, and almost seventy. He seemed none the worse for wear, due (as I later learned) to an impressive daily early morning exercise regime, typically sporting a bandana, culminating in meditative deep breathing. You won't find a nicer guy than Ron, but that smiling laid-back demeanor belied a rapier-like intellect, a sharp eye for detail, and unflinching loyalty to Masa. One of Ron's keys to preserving his sanity in the face of SoftBank's deal frenzy was a rigid observance of the Shabbat. Ron and I hit it off immediately, a relationship that evolved into warm companionship nurtured over frequent dinners, always involving a bottle of fine wine.

On our video call, we discussed a satirical blog post ("The Ten Year Itch") I'd written recently, which Ron had appreciated and forwarded to his son, an investment manager. The subject was India, and my thesis was that every decade an eager new crop of investment managers in New York gets excited about India for the same old reasons—the young population, an educated and growing consumer class, democracy, the infrastructure opportunity—and how this renewed enthusiasm coincides neatly with the global liquidity cycle and rising animal spirits in global financial markets.

Which led me to a question I'd always wondered about.

"Ron, you were by Masa's side through the internet bubble, right? What was that like?"

"Ha! Masa, well, he has his own way of thinking, Alok. I can't really explain it, when you meet him you'll know what I mean," he responded, laughing.

He paused.

"I think things will be different with Nikesh. I've never seen Masa take to someone like that. He won't do anything Nikesh doesn't agree with."

It was said without a quantum particle of resentment. I respected this about Ron, the humility and absence of ego.

At the end of our video call, Ron asked what it would take to persuade me to join SoftBank full-time. I said after meeting him I was favorably inclined. Ron Fisher was a person I wanted to be around. He had about him an air of contentment that made me less afraid of aging.

■

My experience with Mexico was limited to a weekend trip to Cabo for a niece's wedding and occasionally sampling Clase Azul Reposado tequila, both about as useful as watching Sergio Leone's spaghetti westerns in preparation for going to America. However, telecom mergers in emerging markets were in my sweet spot, courtesy of my years in Asia. Mexican billionaire Carlos Slim was being forced to divest a piece of his overweight América Móvil at the behest of the Mexican regulators. SoftBank was a potential acquirer,[1] and was simultaneously negotiating with another Mexican media conglomerate to purchase its telecom business, the end game being to merge the two acquired businesses and create a nationwide competitor to the dominant América Móvil.

The kickoff meeting between principals was held in a wood-paneled conference room in the law firm Cleary Gottlieb's plush headquarters on Park Avenue. The primary agenda was for Carlos Slim's bankers (Citigroup) to present the acquisition opportunity to us, with the América Móvil management team in attendance. They were selling, we were buying.

Through much of the meeting, Nikesh's distracted and intelligent eyes were glued to his oversized Android smartphone rather than the bankers' colorful pitch deck. He could have been playing Candy Crush for all anyone knew, but every so often he would raise his head along with his index finger and make an observation that cut through the arguments marshaled by the presenters with the destructive accuracy of *der Blitzkrieg* and the diplomacy to match. "You guys really think you can pack a hundred million subscribers into five megahertz of spectrum . . . your EBITDA margins are ridiculous, no operator does 60 *percent* . . ." and so it went.

It was an amusing spectacle, the first of many such encounters—Wall Street's finest reduced to stammering schoolboys when confronted by a trenchant examiner. I was relieved to be on Nikesh's side of the table.

At Morgan Stanley, I was surrounded by the quickest minds you'll ever meet. Despite over a decade of training with these professional sprinters, being in meetings with Nikesh felt like being on a track with Carl Lewis. His was the type of analytical mind you aspire to win in a lottery—or rent for over $50 million a year. Like me, he had a marrow-deep inability to suffer fools, gladly or otherwise, though our coping mechanisms were different. Mine was to sulk in silence while waiting for inspiration in the form of devastating irony. With Nikesh, if you showed up unprepared, your fate was outright defenestration.

Following the meeting, Nikesh asked me to listen in on a call (we were still at Cleary's Park Avenue offices) to negotiate terms for an acquisition of DreamWorks Animation for $3.4 billion.[2] The original DreamWorks was founded, with much fanfare, by the holy trinity of the media world—Steven Spielberg, former Disney Studios chairman Jeffrey Katzenberg, and Asylum

Records founder David Geffen. DreamWorks Animation, led by Katzenberg, was spun out as a public company to focus on animated content, its biggest hit being the *Shrek* series.

Immediately after the call, Nikesh invited me to join him for a short stroll westward to the Peninsula Hotel at the corner of Fifth Avenue and Fifty-Fifth Street. As much as I liked the Peninsula (great service, buzzing terrace bar, glass-enclosed indoor pool) I entered with a degree of trepidation that had nothing to do with the gargoyles adorning the imposing Gothic façade. The last time I stayed here was September 2001. But for a serendipitous schedule change, I would have been at the World Trade Center for a meeting at 9 A.M. on September 11. I was stuck at the Peninsula for three weeks, shell-shocked and aching to be home with my family in London, on perma-hold with British Airways, captive to their theme song, Delibes's "Flower Duet" from *Lakmé.* It's a pretty tune, but I detest *Lakmé.* Like many Indians, my attitude toward appropriation of our culture (like Ashton Kutcher's turbaned Sikh caricature) is indulgent bemusement, for we tend to revel in our intellectual and cultural superiority. But romanticizing the seduction of young brahmin maidens by colonizing British officers, as Delibes does in *Lakmé,* crosses a personal line I didn't know existed.

We were here to meet with Thomas Tull, the founder of Legendary Pictures (the Christopher Nolan Batman films, *Inception, The Hangover*) and co-owner of that essential billionaire accessory: a sports team, in his case the Pittsburgh Steelers.

The saccharine notes of the "Flower Duet" ringing in my ears, I followed Nikesh into Thomas's plush suite overlooking Fifth Avenue. He invited us to sit on a chintzy upholstered couch while he ensconced himself in a substantial leather armchair directly across from us. Thomas (in his forties, pleasant, tough-guy torso) seemed eager to deal with SoftBank, even more so after Nikesh informed him we were buying DreamWorks. Nikesh led the negotiations, I chimed in occasionally, within an hour we had an agreement to invest $250 million in Legendary Entertainment and create a joint venture to leverage Legendary's content in Asia.[3]

This was a trademark SoftBank deal construction—a minority stake in a US technology or media business with an accompanying partnership to exploit the investee company's intellectual property in Japan and frequently the rest of Asia. As early as 2000, Masa described this as his "time machine management" strategy, the idea being to "foster the global inclusion of superior business models found through its venture capital operations in the United States."[4] It was inspired by SoftBank's Yahoo! investment, which was accompanied by the creation of a Japanese joint venture between Yahoo! and SoftBank. Yahoo! Japan, eventually a public company, became substantially more valuable than its US parent.

Next was lunch with Vijay Shekhar Sharma, founder of Paytm, an Indian fintech start-up. The venue was the Sky Lobby on the thirty-fifth floor of the Mandarin Oriental on Columbus Circle, with a dramatic backdrop of northeast-facing Central Park views. The genial and earnest Vijay got the Arora treatment and didn't fare much better than the bankers, failing to convince us that his payment business could evolve into a broader financial services firm. I felt sorry for Vijay. He was vegetarian and the only lounge menu items that worked (fries and croquettes) involved potatoes. We passed on the deal.

(Four years later Warren Buffett's Berkshire Hathaway would invest in Paytm at a $10 billion valuation.[5] Vijay became a billionaire and no longer needed capital or sympathy. When Vijay and I reconnected, we reminisced about Nikesh, lost opportunities, and potatoes.)

That afternoon we made a drive-through acquisition while at the Raine Group's offices on Seventh Avenue—a streaming service called DramaFever,[6] offering serialized Korean drama to a global audience. Korean soft power (*Squid Game, Parasite*) is intriguing. No state-sponsored effort, even one that enlists the mind hackers at TikTok or Facebook, can rival pop culture to manipulate public perception to a nation's advantage. *Why has India, with its prolific filmmaking industry, failed so miserably to do this?*

■

I now got what Samir had been trying to tell me. We'd dropped some serious cash over a stroll across midtown Manhattan, and we were just getting started. Plus we now owned a piece of Batman. All of which felt empowering and very cool but also concerning. This may seem trivial, but one of my lessons—personal and macro—from the 2008 financial crisis is that while the absolute level of risk is always significant, the rate at which risk is accumulated is a better predictor of systemic risk.

At the time, Masa was all about his telecom strategy. He hoped to ride the smartphone revolution and create a global communications business by stringing together a chain of acquisitions, a strategy that Vodafone and others had pursued unsuccessfully. Despite the obvious economies of scale, in handset procurement for example, differences in regulatory regimes and technology made this global telco vision unwieldy.

Nikesh, by contrast, seemed less enthused about telecom and more interested in content (like DreamWorks and Legendary) that might be exploited in the digital world. At Google he had advocated acquiring Netflix in its early days. It was a brilliant idea; Netflix combined with Google's YouTube and its user-generated content would have been the ultimate digital media platform.

I wasn't convinced about either strategy. While nobody wants to be a dumb pipe, combining distribution and content has been a fool's errand for phone companies and their button-down CEOs. AT&T's acquisition of Time Warner Media (Ma Bell and Bugs Bunny in the same room) would eventually destroy $47 billion in value for AT&T shareholders.[7]

■

In a break between meetings at the Mandarin, I caught up with Alya. She was now a sophomore at Columbia College, studying ancient languages that brought dead worlds to life. Greek mythology was my Hector's ankle, but thanks to her I'd educated myself in Homer and Sophocles, much of which she'd read in the original Greek. Alya had no interest in SoftBank but was curious about what it was like working with "Uncle Nikesh," as she affectionately called him.

"I'd forgotten how quick he is. And it doesn't feel like work when we're together, it's fun," I responded.

■

The day ended with Nikesh hosting dinner at the sleek and minimalist Sushi Nakazawa in the West Village. Nakazawa-san is a disciple of the legendary sushi master Jiro Ono, the subject of the eminently watchable *Jiro Dreams of Sushi.* Nikesh's chief of staff, Jonathan "JB" Bullock, also a Google import, joined us for dinner. JB, a taciturn Cambridge-educated Brit, was immediately put on the spot by Nikesh.

"JB, what do you think, does Alok pass the Airport Test?" he said.

What the fuck is the Airport Test? Had I known, I might have prepared. Apparently Sergey Brin came up with the notion that for Google to hire you, you needed to be interesting enough for your colleagues to enjoy spending a few hours with you in case you happened to be stranded together at an airport. Wall Street was two-dimensional, acuity and hunger were enough, but Google wanted more. I liked it, and embraced the ethos as we built out the SoftBank team. One of my favorite recruits was Shu Nyatta, a Harvard-educated Rhodes scholar from Kenya who worked as a tech banker at J. P. Morgan, but was also rated among the hippest soul artists in the United States.

As for JB, he smiled politely at me and nodded respectfully to his boss. At that point we'd met for a few minutes and exchanged even fewer emails, what else could he do?

Regardless, I assumed I'd passed the test. Next step, the small matter of meeting with Masayoshi Son.

4

HAPPINESS FOR EVERYONE

Flying time was twelve hours, carrier British Airways, destination Tokyo. The flight number, apropos for a man on a mission, was BA007.

The head purser came by, a willowy middle-aged woman sporting a fitted navy blazer and a matching wide-brimmed hat. She delivered her perfunctory welcome routine, but sensing my bored disinterest, leaned over and whispered conspiratorially.

"You know, we have Sir John Major flying with us today."

Directly across, I saw the former British prime minister arranging his bags in the overhead storage bin.

"Ah, OK. He can join my mile high club," I said.

She looked at me, quizzically.

"Bradley Cooper, Emma Stone, Quentin Tarantino, Jamie Foxx, John Goodman. And Cindy Crawford, she was the best. Celebrities I've slept with on British Airways," I explained.

She tried to restrain a smile, but the dam of British reserve had been breached. Queen and country forgotten, she leaned back and broke into a fit of laughter.

"I'll make sure we make a note of that in your personal preferences, sir!" she said.

I considered staying in character and ordering a martini

(shaken, not stirred) but thought the better of it. In my younger days I could power through these overnight transcontinental flights, sitting or standing, a few units of alcohol easily assimilated. Now I needed a flatbed, an eye mask, noise-canceling headphones, an unobtrusive crew, no alcohol, and, on this occasion, a five-milligram dose of Ambien.

■

As a child, I was obsessed with Jules Verne's *Around the World in Eighty Days* and the miracle of the international date line. Foreign travel was a sci-fi adventure, a Boeing 747 as exotic as a Virgin Galactic spaceship. Morgan Stanley changed this. Investment bankers, like sharks, need continuous motion to stay alive, swimming in and out of client offices globally. One of my bosses had a test for us. Every time he visited a CEO's office, he would ask the accompanying banker for the restroom location. If you needed a receptionist to show the way, you weren't there often enough.

Tokyo was an occasional and unpleasant destination during my New York years. The twelve-hour jet lag was a validation of sleep deprivation as an instrument of torture, a disorientation captured masterfully by Bill Murray in *Lost in Translation.* My trips rarely went beyond connecting weakly and disconnecting promptly with staid Japanese telecom executives. Flying in from Hong Kong, my home base for much of the nineties, presented a different misery. HKG-TYO was one of the last international routes where smoking was permitted. It was five hours in a tin can with businessmen in brown suits blowing smoke rings while drinking Suntory whisky, the smell of stale cigarette smoke permeating every surface. That's a lot of baggage to overcome, even for a fine metropolis like Tokyo.

My attitude softened following a leisurely family holiday to Japan in 2004, when we experienced the sublimity of Kyoto in the time of *sakura.* The serenity was therapeutic, the *domo arigato* expressions of gratitude so infectious that I found myself bowing to the *Shinkansen* out of respect for its astonishing punctuality.

Over the years, I've come to associate a pleasing sensibility and eccentricity with all things Japanese. The surreal fiction of Haruki Murakami and Yoko Tawada, for example, defies all Western conventions of plot and structure. If cats are talking and it's raining fish, you do not question why, you calmly accept that it must be so.

I suspect my perspective suffers from the superficiality I find irritating about people who've seen the Taj Mahal, read Salman Rushdie, love chicken tikka masala, and think they know India. Regardless, my bar for unconventionality when it comes to all things Japanese is high.

Masa was a stranger to me, and no Walter Isaacson–caliber biographer had dug into his life. Among his rare media interactions, a *Harvard Business Review* interview caught my eye,[1] particularly Masa's endearing acknowledgment that living in the future comes at a price. As relayed by Masa, everyone thought he was "crazy," a moniker he wore as a badge of honor, his aspiration to be remembered as "the crazy guy who bet on the future."

What brand of "crazy" is Masa talking about? The heroes of Silicon Valley who bend the laws of physics to give us electric cars and reusable rockets frequently reduce themselves to buffoonery. And then there's Adam Neumann and Elizabeth Holmes, whose reality distortion fields can be as dark as their black T-shirts and turtlenecks.

Masa seemed to have no political or lifestyle distractions, and his claim to the overused "visionary" accolade seemed legitimate. He had predicted the mega-trends underlying what he calls "the Information Revolution," which he believes surpasses the Industrial Revolution as a multidecade transformational event. SoftBank started as a software distributor to ride the PC revolution of the eighties. The company then reinvented itself twice, surfing the even more potent internet disruption of the nineties and then again the smartphone wave starting in the late noughties. Web 1.0 was about accessing read-only pages on desktop computers, Web 2.0 allowed seamless interactivity on mobile devices. With his prescient investments in Yahoo! and Vodafone Japan, Masa bet on both iterations early and won handsomely.

But what makes him tick? The media seemed to accept the clichéd narrative of Masa's extraordinary drive resulting from a destitute childhood as the son of Korean immigrants. Hunger is a powerful motivator, as an immigrant I got that. But the world romanticizes the causal relationship between adversity and breakout success. That Nietzschean "that which does not kill you" cliché works only some of the time. Malcolm Gladwell, when he talks about "desirable difficulty" in *Outliers,* falls into this elementary logical trap of survivor bias. We hear stories about people who overcome childhood trauma and go on to form companies or run countries, but what about the orphans and dyslexics who spend their lives in obscurity or worse?

On SoftBank's website the stated corporate mission was "Happiness for Everyone."[2] A trite line you might see on a Disneyland billboard, so banal that it couldn't possibly be posturing. *Is this idealism the key to Masa? Could happiness for everyone actually be the business of someone's life? And what does happiness mean to a tech billionaire? Family, money, or gigabit broadband?*

On Wall Street or in the City, that question would provoke a cynical response. But this was a land of talking cats and raining fish.

■

"So, Nikesh tells me you are a smart guy," said Masa, smiling, as he invited me to take a seat across from him at his dining table.

While he was polite enough, this was a half-statement, half-question, the implication being I had a point to prove.

"Nikesh is very kind," I responded, also smiling.

The agenda had been set. I had one hour, -1— over lunch, to establish my credentials as a "smart guy" to a man widely regarded as a genius. Nikesh had teed it up, but now I had to make the swing.

Our lunch was scheduled for 11 A.M., which struck me as early, but this was Masa's preferred routine. Fortunately, my flight landed on time, and Fumiko-san, one of Masa's assistants, arranged for a car and driver to take me to the Conrad Hotel.

Tokyo has some fine hotels (the Aman might be the finest urban hotel anywhere) but the Conrad had the unassailable advantage of being in the same building as SoftBank. As with many high-end Tokyo hotels, the Conrad starts on a high floor. In this case, you checked in at the double-height lobby on the twenty-eighth floor.

SoftBank's office had a separate entrance, and at precisely 10:45 A.M., I found Fumiko-san waiting for me in the building lobby. She was slender and elegant, wore a printed dress, high heels, and a warm smile. She led me to an elevator intended for the exclusive use of Masa and his guests, where a security guard in a khaki uniform and a comical red postman's cap was holding the door open.

As we ascended, I noticed the highest floor was twenty-six. Since the Conrad reception was on twenty-eighth, I wondered about the twenty-seventh, perhaps a Murakami-esque parallel universe? I asked Fumiko-san. She looked at me, half-smiling, her expression typical of the Japanese when they encounter incomprehensible gaijin behavior.

"I don't know," she responded, in her lilting voice.

There's a reason I avoid talking to strangers; they seem to think I'm strange.

A young man in nondescript corporate attire (dark suit, white shirt, red tie) was standing by at the elevator bank on twenty-six. He bowed and smiled radiantly as I exited.

"Welcome to SoftBank, Sama-san," he said. "I am Tanaka. I hope you had a nice journey."

The effervescent Tanaka-san was Masa's chief of staff. He seemed to bounce rather than walk, repeatedly bowing along the way, as he escorted me to Masa's dining room. Once there, he asked me to remove my shoes and wait, assuring me Masa would arrive shortly.

Before he departed, I asked him about the twenty-seventh floor. His smile disappeared, and he made an audible hissing sound, a sucking in of air between lips and teeth, while rubbing his head.

"I don't know Sama-san, I am so sorry."

Masa's private dining room overlooked scenic Hamarikyu Gardens, with Tokyo Bay beyond. Water and greenery below, blue sky above, a combination always pleasing to the eye.

The dining room covered a third of the floor, much of the space given to an exquisite traditional Japanese garden, each bonsai a work of art, all an integral part of this surreal meal experience. An open pavilion overlooking the indoor garden displayed what I later learned was Masa's priceless Japanese calligraphy collection. The dining table was a traditional horigotatsu, low to the ground with recessed floor beneath, a concession to inflexible gaijins unable to countenance sitting cross-legged.

Masa made his entrance at exactly 11 A.M., punctual like the *Shinkansen.* I bowed to him, my deference genuine. A private lunch with Warren Buffett once fetched $19 million in a charity auction.

I'd seen Masa at a distance in Puglia, but the two things that struck me at close quarters were his movement and his wardrobe. Sprightly, in his late fifties, he shuffled rather than walked, feet barely leaving the ground. He wore a maroon cashmere sweater under a brown woolen blazer, despite the temperature set at what felt like a suffocating 25°C (77°F). (This took some getting used to. With the thermostat set in the mid-twenties, we would frequently wear T-shirts while he wore his olive-colored Uniqlo ski jacket.) I was in full executive battle attire, including the risible pomposity of a well-worn monogrammed shirt with French cuffs. My internal temperature already elevated by adrenaline and caffeine, I requested Masa's permission to remove my suit jacket, and laid it down by my side on the mat.

We took our seats, legs tucked under the table. Masa had invited me to sit with my back to the open area with the interior garden, while he himself sat directly across, with the glass windows at his back. This was a breach from the formal North Asian protocol of the host always leaving himself, rather than the guest, exposed to a surprise attack. This was fine by me. I did not feel slighted, nor did I fear a ninja attack.

Masa's valet Kato-san, attired assassin-like in a black suit, white shirt, and skinny black tie, appeared suddenly, his movement a graceful glide, a streamlined Japanese version of Jeeves. Perhaps, like Jeeves, Kato-san read Spinoza in his spare time? Kato-san bowed and offered me a pour from an open bottle of Riesling, which he held in his right hand. In impeccable English, he asked if I'd prefer red wine, displaying a bottle of unopened red Burgundy in the palm of his left hand—La Tâche from Domaine Romanée-Conti.

I'd never sampled a La Tâche before, at over $5,000 a bottle out of reach for even the most inflated expense accounts. But this was not the time or the place for such indulgence. I declined, and instead followed Masa's lead, accepting a small pour of the exquisite dry Riesling.

Kato-san shimmered out, his entry and exit an impeccably executed stealth operation.

"So I had dinner with Satya last night," Masa said, smiling.

Satya? Nadella, I assume.

It was an icebreaker, but Masa said it as if he knew I played bridge on weekends with the Microsoft CEO.

"Yes, Satya is great!" I responded, spontaneously and enthusiastically. I'd never met him, nor did I play bridge, but if Son-san believed Satya Nadella was my buddy, so be it. I wasn't lying—to do so talking about Satya, which means "truth" in Sanskrit, would be shamelessly ironic. I had seen the guy on CNBC, and his stewardship of Microsoft was indeed great.

Masa beamed. Apparently, recognizing the greatness of Satya had elevated my legitimacy.

"Thank you for coming such a long way. I hope your flight was comfortable," said Masa, graciously.

"Son-san, thank you for seeing me, this is a great honor," I said.

He nodded politely as I told him a bit about my background, focusing on my years as a telecom and technology specialist through the boom-bust cycle of the late nineties and the early noughties. Since telecom was Masa's primary industry focus, I highlighted my experience creating China Unicom, privatizing Korea Telecom, and buying and selling phone companies in Asia and Europe.

"Son-san, we all admired you as an internet investor in the early days. How did you think about the internet then, and what would you have done differently?" I asked, trying to get him talking.

Kato-san reappeared, with the first of four courses. A clear soup to start, a pasta dish next, sea bass the main course, a mildly sweetened jelly for dessert. The portions were perfectly sized, the ingredients fresh, the sauces light, the flavoring subtle and refined.

"I hope you enjoy the food," he said, "I have a new Italian chef."

Once Kato-san glided away, Masa responded to my question.

"Well, the internet business model for me was all about platforms with theoretically infinite reach at zero variable cost," he said, and repeated for emphasis. "Infinite reach. Zero variable cost."

This was a succinct description of the disruptive power of the internet. Over the last twenty years, some of the most successful technology businesses have been "platforms" requiring minimal capital investment, creating value by promoting interaction between users. Such business models typically have strong "network effects." As the number of participants increases, the platform becomes more valuable to all users. Uber, later a SoftBank investee company, is a good example. As the number of drivers increases, waiting times come down and riding options increase, attracting more customers, which in turn attracts more drivers, creating a classic "network effect" or "self-enforcing flywheel." A "winner take most" dynamic is another characteristic of such business models, since at some point the platform becomes so entrenched it is virtually impossible for a competitor to displace it.

"I saw this very early, and I knew we had to invest so aggressively, a once-in-a-lifetime opportunity," he continued. "My only regret is I wish I had more money so I could have invested even more."

Hmm. This is like Icarus wishing he'd flown closer to the sun.

At its peak in February 2000, SoftBank was valued at almost $200 billion. When the bubble burst, SoftBank's share price and Masa's own net worth declined 95 percent, earning him a citation in the Guinness Book of World Records.[3] For losing the most money ever. An evisceration of $59 billion of paper wealth, a record that stood for over twenty years until Elon Musk surpassed it in 2022. (Though Musk recovered much of it in six months.) Any normal person would be tormented by the decision, deliberate or otherwise, not to cash in their chips. But for Masa, normal was the cruelest of insults.

"I wanted to invest in Amazon before the IPO," he said. "I met with Jeff Bezos, and we almost agreed on a deal. I wanted to invest $100 million at a valuation of $300 million. But my team told me we didn't have the money," he said, smiling wistfully. "Can you imagine? We could have owned maybe twenty percent of Amazon!"

I shook my head, awed by the prospect of what might have been. A 20 percent stake in Amazon would become worth over

$360 billion in 2024, roughly equal to the GDP of Colombia. *But would Masa have invested in Alibaba if he had owned 20 percent of Amazon?* I asked him.

"You know, I never thought of that. I don't think Jeff would have let me. Now I suddenly feel better!" he said, laughing loudly. His eyes vanished when he laughed like that.

"Son-san, you lost almost everything in the crash. How did that feel?" I continued.

He laughed again, this time leaning back and throwing up his hands. "You know, when I became the richest man in the world, I spent all my time worrying about how to spend my money. It was so much stress. And then the market solved my problem so I had nothing to worry about. All gone!"

"Yes, Masa," I said, veering into cautious impertinence as I switched from the formal Son-san to the diminutive. Something about sharing a glass of wine does that. "But you didn't lose everything. You were still a billionaire!"

We both laughed out loud.

"Yes, yes, I know, Alok. But I never worry about money, maybe this is also why people think I'm crazy. As a child I had nothing and I was so happy, if I lose everything I am still happy."

He paused, and added. "My goal is happiness for everyone. Nobody should be sad. I want technology to make people happy."

He started to talk about his latest, in this case literally, pet project. Pepper the robot, a humanoid with an "emotional engine," designed to be a companion for the aging in Japan. For a country with a population among the oldest in the world and the highest suicide rates, this seemed laudable.

I recalled seeing large posters in the lobby, promoting what looked like a cross between the *Star Wars* droids R2-D2 and C-3PO. *My golden retriever Ellie has a fine emotional engine, and she is warm, soft, and cuddly. Can a hunk of metal match that?* Regardless, Masa seemed serious about this happiness business.

I never heard him talk about religion, but his faith in technology was evangelical.

SoftBank's stake in Yahoo! was worth over $30 billion at its peak in 2000. A series of strategic blunders by Yahoo! management—including a missed opportunity to buy Google for $1 *million* in 2001—along with the implosion in internet valuations decimated the value of what was once the most valuable virtual real estate. SoftBank eventually sold its stake at a fraction of the peak valuation. SoftBank's Alibaba position, now worth $70 billion following the September IPO, raised similar concerns.

"Masa, are you considering selling Alibaba stock?" I asked.

That disarming smile disappeared.

"I will never sell Alibaba," he said adamantly. "This is the best investment in the world. You know they have over eighty percent market share in China, growing over twenty-five percent every year. Eighty percent! It is a fantastic company, fantastic. And anyone who thinks I should sell is stupid. Stupid, they don't understand."

I nodded instinctively while interrogating my instinct to agree to an opinion opposite to the one I held. Had Masa fallen forever in love with Alibaba? If so, like every other young technology company, Alibaba would not remain Alibaba forever. And then there was the risk posed by a capricious and autocratic Chinese regulatory regime.

Investment decisions require the cold detachment of a Mr. Spock, but Masa evidently viewed Alibaba with a dangerous combination of affection and reverence. Perhaps he had felt the same way about Yahoo! in 2000. And if he had, his estimated $20 billion opportunity loss (relative to selling Yahoo! at its peak) seemed to have made no impact on his thinking. And this was why Nikesh wanted me on the team and Samir thought "someone like me" was needed, because my Morgan Stanley training was old-school corporate finance.

The takeover of Vodafone Japan in 2006 rarely gets a mention in the Masa Son hit parade, but it tops anything else in his repertoire—a bit like Dylan's monumentally excellent yet bafflingly ignored "Blind Willie McTell." People assume Masa's comeback after the 2001 market implosion was all about Alibaba. While insanely successful, Alibaba was a modest punt at a time when Masa was in the Bill Gates wealth postcode. Moreover, his decision was based on Jack Ma's "strong and shining eyes" and a fuzzy plan that connected Western companies with Chinese suppliers. The Vodafone Japan deal, on the other hand, was executed at a time when SoftBank was tottering and required clear vision, extraordinary chutzpah, flawless execution, and a ton of cash.

As a segue into the subject, and knowing Masa's passion for golf, I asked if he was familiar with Vijay Singh, who came from modest Fijian roots to become the number one golfer at a time when Tiger was at his peak.

"Of course," said Masa. "He is fantastic, one of the best."

I told him Nikesh and I once spent a long weekend with Vijay, and I asked Vijay about the pressure of going head-to-head against Tiger. Which Vijay often did, and won.

"Alok, pressure was when I was a driving range pro in Fiji, trying to make a living hustling tourists for $100 a hole with $20 in my pocket," said Vijay, laughing, as we strolled down the fairway at the Stanford Golf Course in Palo Alto.

"Masa," I said, "your takeover of Vodafone was exactly like that. Like Vijay betting $100 with $20 in his pocket!"

With a smile extending all the way to his ears, his piercing black eyes sparkling, Masa wagged a finger at me.

"You are so right! So right!" he said. "That was crazy, but you know, sometimes you have to be crazy to win. You know who win in a fight between a crazy guy and a smart guy? The crazy guy always win! Always!"

He said it with profundity, but I didn't understand what he

meant, and it seemed rude to question him. Instead, I nodded and smiled politely.

He then told me his Steve Jobs story, clearly a favorite, one he had recounted in a Bloomberg TV interview with Charlie Rose.[4] In 2005, more than a year before the launch of the first iPhone, Masa made a crude sketch of a handheld device vaguely resembling an iPod, and took it to the late Steve Jobs demanding exclusive Japanese distribution rights for Apple's future "smartphone." According to Masa, a bemused Steve dismissed the drawing as ugly, and made fun of Masa's design aesthetic. Moreover, since SoftBank didn't own a phone company and Apple didn't have a product, what deal could they possibly agree to? Masa persisted, and Steve eventually relented, telling him, "You're a crazy guy, but I like you," and gave Masa an exclusive if and when he owned a phone company and Apple had a product.

"Steve was like Leonardo da Vinci, a technologist, but also an artist. So sad he is gone, he was my good friend."

We observed a moment of silence in memoriam. I could have pointed out that many in the Valley revere Apple cofounder Steve Wozniak more than they do Jobs because Woz was a coder, but that would be petty. For all his flaws, Jobs was indeed that rare combination of left brain and right brain, the Apple phenomenon as much about design integrity as superior technology.

"Steve thought I was crazy," he continued. "Everybody thought I was crazy. Vodafone thought I was so crazy, they even lent me money to buy the company from them," he said, laughing. "But I knew the iPhone would change everything. I proved all of them wrong."

On the strength of the Jobs handshake to deliver an indispensable futuristic device, Masa wagered $15.4 billion—almost four times the value of a diminished SoftBank—on Vodafone Japan.[5] He used 90 percent leverage, including $4.6 billion of financing from Vodafone,[6] to buy a company that bled subscribers and cash. Jobs kept his word, smartphones changed the world, and by virtue of being the exclusive Japanese purveyor of the iPhone, SoftBank engineered one of the great turnarounds in the history of the investment business. Its initial equity investment of circa $2 billion became worth almost $42 billion when the company went public in 2019.[7]

I summarized the takeaways from my meetings in New York with Nikesh. Airing doubts about buying DreamWorks or investing in the Batman franchise seemed pointless. Instead I laid out how Masa might engineer a sequence of deals to create a profitable business for SoftBank in the burgeoning Mexican telecom market.

The smile reached its widest, the eyes crinkled, and that finger wagged at me again. Now he was radiating warmth, even respect.

"Alok! You are so smart, so smart! Now I understand why Nikesh thinks so highly of you."

I hadn't said anything particularly insightful or original, but perhaps I made Masa feel I understood his brand of genius. And I made him laugh.

Suki-san, Masa's other assistant, walked in, sporting what I would come to recognize as her trademark brightly colored designer spectacles. Unlike the ebullient Fumiko-san, Suki-san seemed remote. Making her smile was a challenge, her lack of English proficiency made it tougher. But she controlled Masa's schedule, and being on her right side was paramount.

Suki-san's entry and exit matched Kato-san in stealth, her mission to deliver a suspiciously blank yellow Post-it note. As with many CEOs, this was Masa's prearranged cue that the meeting needed to end.

I had steered clear of discussion about titles or compensation, these were secondary. I wanted to get the measure of the man, and I liked what I saw. He was charming and funny and interesting and certainly passed my Airport Test. But there was more. While seemingly obsessed with grandiose visions of happiness for humanity, he connected with me at a human level. When he looked at me and smiled, it was like Nick Carraway meets Gatsby—he understood me the way I wanted to be understood, assuring me he had precisely the impression of me that I hoped to convey. And if copious servings of La Tâche were involved, happiness (or at least pleasure) for everyone was guaranteed.

"I hope you will join our family," he said, as we rose from our seats. I think he meant it.

"I know I can help you achieve your vision, Son-san. I hope you will give me the opportunity," I responded.

Masa personally walked me to the elevator bank, where Tanaka-san stood waiting. Tanaka-san seemed animated, his excitement barely suppressed.

"Sama-san, I went to the Conrad Hotel, I have answer for you. There is no twenty-seventh floor because the twenty-seventh and twenty-eighth is combined," he said, beaming proudly.

Of course. No parallel reality. A double height reception.

Masa was looking at Tanaka-san as if he were speaking Dothraki. Now embarrassed, Tanaka-san mumbled an explanation. While Masa looked on in polite incomprehension, I beat my retreat.

I turned my back on them and entered the elevator, and once inside pivoted toward them with a casual wave. Embarrassingly, I found both Masa and Tanaka-san bowing formally, hands on their thighs. I tried to switch gears and bow, but it was too late. The elevator doors were drawing shut.

5

STRAWBERRY FIELDS FOREVER

Some people start off on the wrong foot. I started off in the wrong seat.

I was back in Tokyo a few weeks later. According to Nikesh, my lunch with Masa had gone well. Masa categorized people as stupid, smart, or crazy, the last being the ultimate accolade reserved for himself and select others. Since crazy was unachievably aspirational and smart an equally high bar, I assumed I'd established I wasn't entirely stupid.

In what became a monthly routine, Nikesh had flown in from the West Coast, while I commuted on BA007 from Heathrow to Haneda, departing London on Monday morning, arriving in Tokyo at 8 A.M. on Tuesday, and after checking into the Conrad, reporting for duty to Masa's conference room on the twenty-sixth floor in Shiodome.

This handsome wood-paneled enclosure ran parallel to Masa's dining room and in theory enjoyed the same stunning views. Except the blinds were always drawn. Masa processed information visually, and he wanted graphic slideshows to facilitate every discussion; light and views were a distraction.

My eyes were drawn to a grainy black-and-white image directly across from Masa's customary seat at the head of the giant rectangular boardroom table. It was a life-size portrait of a grim-faced man in a loose-fitting kimono. With no external distractions, his virtual presence dominated this room. The receding hairline suggested middle-aged, though I later learned he died at thirty-one. The twin crests on the kimono and a ceremonial dagger under the waistband indicated a man of action. Perhaps a samurai? If so, not of high rank, given the scraggly garment and shoddy shoes.

The posture, with the right hand concealed under the fold of the kimono, seemed familiar. A regal warrior from another continent—Napoleon Bonaparte. In portraits, Napoleon is frequently portrayed with his right hand tucked inside his tunic. The matter has become the subject of speculation, even scholarship, among historians. Some say the gesture signifies the "gentlemanly restraint" associated with nobility. Others have an altogether more prosaic explanation—itchy fabric. A deformed right hand or the need to press down to alleviate chronic stomach pain have been offered as other plausible reasons.

As I looked closely at the image, a different icon came to mind, a favorite. I visualized the samurai in a cowboy hat, a hand-rolled cigarette hanging loosely from the lips, adding to the impression of languid insouciance. I imagined a poncho instead of a kimono, the right hand nestled on the silver snake grip of a Colt 1851 six-shooter, and the theme from *The Good, the Bad and the Ugly* began to ring in my ears. And then I understood. Across centuries and continents, the samurai, Napoleon, and Blondie posed liked this for the same reason. They just looked so fucking cool.

Hierarchy and protocol are paramount in Japanese business culture, and nowhere is this more evident than in the seating arrangements in meetings. In this—my first—meeting, I arrived with Nikesh and carelessly positioned myself directly across from him, next to Masa, who was enthroned at the narrow end of the rectangular table.

Masa peered at me over his reading glasses, his eyebrows raised.

"Ron will sit there," he said, pointing to my seat.

Mortified, I moved one seat down. Masa nodded approvingly. Evidently, the two seats on either side of Masa were for his prince, Nikesh, and his vizier, Ron Fisher. Physical proximity to Masa at his table was a sign of where you stood with him. Everyone observed, everyone remembered.

Keen to change the subject, I asked Masa about the photograph.

Curiosity was my redemption. Masa looked at me and smiled indulgently.

"That is Ryōma. He was a great man and a great warrior," he said.

■

Like Jean-Pierre Melville's beautiful assassin in *Le Samouraï*, Sakamoto Ryōma was a rogue samurai, a ronin with no master. He rebelled against the powerful nineteenth-century Tokugawa shogunate while advocating against feudalism and clamoring for the modernization of Japan. A 1966 best-selling novel, *Ryoma on the Move,* elevated Ryōma to cult status in Japan, portraying him as an idealist with bold dreams, a sense of humor, and the ability to get things done.

Masa embodied all these qualities. His goals were audacious, sometimes outrageous, and frequently, like Pepper the empathetic robot, tinged with idealism. As a telecom operator, he had to have a billion subscribers, as an asset manager it had to be a trillion dollars. Like Vodafone Japan, his acquisition targets were at times several times larger than his own balance sheet. His humor was infectious and self-deprecating. On the eve of a trip to London to meet Prime Minister Theresa May, I emailed Masa imploring him to dial down his "crazy," concluding my message with a smiley emoji. His response was punctuated with two smiley emojis. "But I am a little bit crazy!" he said. And Masa is certainly a man of action, and not just dealmaking. His relentless operational focus—a bit like Elon Musk sleeping on the Tesla factory floor—is perhaps his most unheralded quality. In one of our interminable "Sprint Network Discussions" Masa embarrassed Sprint's network team by identifying and proposing a fix for a blind spot in Sprint's network in downtown Houston.

A golfing incident in India showed me the extent of Masa's obsession with Ryōma. We were playing at the DLF Golf Club outside Delhi. Golfers are always tinkering with their equipment, in search of those elusive extra yards off the tee. I assumed Masa's driver would be the golfing equivalent of the mystical Hattori Hanzō sword wielded by Uma Thurman in *Kill Bill.*

I asked to have a look.

"It is a Ryōma driver," he said, smiling as he handed me the club.

Sure enough, it was branded Ryōma, a cartoonish image of a swashbuckling samurai on the sole.

On the eighteenth tee, after we had all hit our tee shots, I asked Masa if I could try his driver. It felt tinny, and the ball finished a disappointing fifteen to twenty yards short of my first drive. Masa now asked to try my driver, and sure enough, it traveled a good distance past his previous shot.

On my next trip to Tokyo I presented Masa with a brand-new Callaway driver, identical to mine. A few weeks later I asked him how he was getting on.

"I cannot bring myself to hit with another driver. I feel like I am being unfaithful to Ryōma," he said.

We both laughed out loud at his sheepish response.

■

It wasn't just his driver. SoftBank itself was stamped with Ryōma. SoftBank's brand logo—the horizontal double bars, ostensibly an equal (=) sign suggesting the SoftBank Group has an answer to the world's problems, is based on the banner of Kaientai, a trading company established by Ryōma.[1]

Many of Masa's favorite projects had elements of Ryōma-inspired idealism, none more so than SoftBank's relatively low-profile alternative energy business. Masa was among the first to visit Fukushima after the nuclear debacle and was so moved by the plight of the people that he declared to his board an intention to focus exclusively on alternative energy. A compromise was reached, and SoftBank Energy was created (under SoftBank Group), its mission to replace all of Japan's nuclear power with solar energy. Masa then reasoned that India gets twice as much sunshine as Japan, and the cost of construction is half, so generating solar power in India should be four times more efficient. The math isn't nearly as straightforward, but regardless, SoftBank Energy spread its wings and became one of the largest global generators of solar power.

Anything to do with energy in India got me interested due to a legacy of painful childhood memories involving blackouts and sleepless summer nights in suffocating sauna heat. Sensing my interest, Nikesh asked me to join the board of SoftBank Energy, and my first reaction was amazement at the sky-high return on equity for the Japanese solar projects. What should have been pedestrian single-digit returns were turbocharged by 90 percent leverage provided by Japanese financial institutions at subsidized rates. This was classic Masa. With creative financial engineering and low-cost Chinese solar panels, a staid low-margin project became a lucrative investment opportunity. With no additional cost to the consumer.

Apparently, happiness for everyone could be powered by leverage as much as by technology.

■

As Masa, Nikesh, and I strolled randomly down the streets of Ginza, the sleek and minimalist aesthetic of the Mikimoto storefront was irresistible. Mikimoto is to Tokyo what Tiffany is to

New York. A million iridescent crystal plates framed the giant two-story glass windows, while inside a circular chandelier covered the entire footprint of the store, like a bright white Venus encircled by a string of pearls.

We wandered in.

This was my first experience being with Masa in a public space, outside the confines of HQ in Shiodome. No agenda, just a random stroll after lunch. It was Nikesh's idea, and Masa had reluctantly agreed. As we approached the crowded sidewalks of Ginza, I understood Masa's hesitation. Pointed fingers, hushed conversations, stifled giggles, occasional clicks of ubiquitous smartphones—the cult of Masa came alive on the streets of Tokyo. (Tanaka-san told me later that Masa had more Twitter followers in Japan than Prime Minister Abe.) I assume being framed by two gaijin of a brown disposition added to the novelty of this rare Masa sighting.

Inside the Mikimoto store, the staff and sparse clientele were more discreet. We drifted aimlessly until Masa turned to us.

"You should get something for your wives," he said, smiling.

I might have explained Maya's cynicism about expensive trinkets, but I held back, for our relationship was still formal. As Nikesh started to engage with a salesperson, a tall, handsome Japanese gentleman, smartly attired in a fitted black suit and black turtleneck, appeared suddenly, like a hologram. *People do this a lot in Tokyo, is there a training program?* He bowed reverentially to Masa and perfunctorily to us, then held out his business card with both hands in a typically ceremonial fashion. He introduced himself as the store manager and took his place behind the counter.

He spoke to Masa in Japanese, I suspect some variation of "Son-san thank you for gracing us with your presence," then addressed all in impeccable English.

"You are our honored guests. We would like to offer you a 20 percent discount on anything you buy."

Mikimoto's offerings are Veblen goods. Like Hermès's Birkin

bags, they have negative price elasticity—the higher the price, the more people want the product. The irony of offering a discount to one of the most price-insensitive buyers in the world was striking. But it wasn't about the money. Mikimoto was making a statement: one Japanese icon's reverence for another.

■

Tokyo's fine restaurants rarely seat more than a dozen people, apparently the limit of an accomplished chef's attention. The decor is minimalist, the walls whitewashed, no background music, definitely no Wi-Fi, nothing to distract from meditative immersion in the food. The chefs, collectively with more Michelin stars than their Parisian counterparts, are frequently showmen as much as craftsmen.

A celebrated sushi chef told me he arrives at Tokyo's Tsukiji fish market at 4 A.M. for the daily auction, making sure his tuna was sourced from the right captain, with the proper technique for both killing the fish and laying down his catch. I asked him why I never saw female sushi chefs. His deadpan response—conveyed reluctantly by our embarrassed translator—is that a woman's senses were compromised at certain times of the month, and therefore female chefs could never guarantee consistency. The incident bothered me viscerally. *Was the dude serious?* For gaijin tend to be a constant source of amusement for the Japanese. Misogyny, a thinly veiled suggestion of racism, but the one thing I never questioned was the dedication to fish.

The core group on these culinary excursions was Masa, Nikesh, and me. Frequently, the restaurant was privatized. Ron Fisher would always join if he was in Tokyo. Members of Masa's Japanese inner circle were occasional attendees, among them the fascinating Nakamura-san, who always had a seat at Masa's table, his engagement vital on all things complicated. Nakamura-san looked like a brooding protagonist from one of Murakami's *Men Without Women* short stories—dark and trim, saturnine with watchful eyes, likely in his fifties, though the wrinkles suggested older. Fumiko-san and Suki-san both smiled demurely when I asked them about Nakamura-san. His karaoke skills were legendary, he was an accomplished golfer. And he played the trumpet.

I wanted to but struggled to bond with Nakamura-san, his limited English an impediment. But this changed when I asked him if he liked Miles Davis. Unable to find the right English words to express himself, he raised his hands as if holding a trumpet.

"Ta-ra-raaaa," he hummed loudly.

The first bar from "Concierto de Aranjuez."

"*Sketches of Spain!*" I exclaimed, referring to the Miles Davis album that features "Concierto" as the first track on side A.

None of my clever observations about tax-free spin-offs had made such an impact on Nakamura-san. I made the case for *Bitches Brew* and *Kind of Blue,* pointing out that familiarity with Rodrigo's original made it tough to appreciate Miles's version of "Concierto." He nodded, but regardless, every time I saw Nakamura-san, he would wrap his hands around an imaginary trumpet, close his eyes, and vocalize the opening bar from "Concierto de Aranjuez." Ta-ra-raaaa.

Another frequent companion was SoftBank's external counsel, Ken Siegel, a senior partner at the US law firm Morrison Foerster, commonly referred to by an unfortunate abbreviation—MoFo. Ken was in his sixties and had spent most of his professional career in Tokyo. He was fluent in Japanese and had carved out a lucrative niche for himself as Masa's go-to US lawyer. Ken was sharp, energetic, and intense, his lawyerly punctiliousness matching my own obsession with detail. We were an effective deal-execution team, exchanging meticulously crafted emails and becoming friends in the process.

Ken was a Japanophile, and I learned much from him. Through the Covid pandemic, as the world puzzled over Tokyo's low case rates despite being among the world's most congested cities, I was reminded of Ken's observation that one might spend an entire working day in Tokyo without touching anything other than personal possessions. I tried it, and managed to limit my tactile contact to my clothes, disposable chopsticks, and my indispensable range of Apple devices. Automatic doors, preset elevators, bowing rather than shaking hands, elaborate smart toilet seats, it all made sense. Japan's enviable life expectancy statistics suggest that serenity and minimal germ load rather than torturous cryotherapy and fasting might be easier paths to longevity.

■

Over dinner, our conversations generally focused on deals of the day, but sometimes, led by Nikesh, we played games. You might scribble down on a piece of paper your favorite animal, the folded scraps thrown into a common pile. Someone would read out the animal names, and you were supposed to guess who had picked what. I hated these games, the pressure to outsmart overwhelmed sincerity. Nikesh and I were like a married couple, quick to call each other out. When "Unicorn" (Valley speak for a start-up worth over $1 billion) came up, Nikesh immediately pointed the finger at me. "Typical Alok, trying to be clever." He was right.

When "favorite entrepreneur" was offered as a prompt, I was convinced Masa would pick the man whose raison d'être was redefining "crazy"—Elon Musk. Instead, he chose a measured and reclusive financial engineer who tinkers with tracking stocks instead of rocket thrusters—the wily media dealmaker John Malone, aka the cable cowboy. It was an intriguing choice suggestive of Masa's own appetite for financial alchemy, foreshadowing a later attempt at a colossal merger.

We were frequently invited to Masa's home. While there, we never encountered anyone other than Kato-san and his apprentice Akuga-san. Masa's home was a monument to tasteful refinement, every piece of stone, fixture, and artwork selected by Masa personally. (I won't say more out of respect for his privacy.) We had some fun times together in Masa's den, most of all our ping-pong challenge matches. When Nikesh beat Masa, he had a former Japanese Olympian instruct him. But nothing this coach taught Masa could counter Nikesh's unconventional loopy left-handed topspin. Masa had to satisfy himself by beating me, which was fine; I was happy just to be there.

■

Our evenings together ended early, frequently by 8 P.M., though the string of email messages that followed suggested that Masa's neural wheels spun late into the evening. Why risk sleeping when you might have a eureka moment at 3 A.M.? A rare exception was my first invitation to Masa's home. Sitting on his porch after dinner, overlooking his sprawling formal garden in the heart of Tokyo, he outlined the principles that became the basis for his prolific dealmaking.

"Singularity is coming" was his refrain, with artificial general intelligence to be the driver of a new cognitive Industrial Revolution.

In January 2023, ChatGPT reached one hundred million active users in two months, faster than Facebook, Instagram, TikTok, Spotify, or Netflix. But Masa spoke animatedly of such things almost ten years prior. When he did, I nodded earnestly, smiled politely, and buried my angular nose in the tulip-shaped wine glass to savor the earthy Burgundian aromas of La Tâche.

At the time I associated "singularity" with black holes, a state where the laws of physics no longer apply. To better understand Masa, I read Ray Kurzweil's *The Singularity Is Near.* Kurzweil described the mathematical power of accelerating rates of change and the implications for machine intelligence. Progressively cheaper computing power, combined with the declining cost of generating, transmitting, and storing data, would allow sophisticated machine learning algorithms to continuously train and "learn," eventually exceeding the human brain not just in processing power but in every cognitive function. This crossover point was "singularity"—a state John von Neumann predicted in the fifties, when a computer could do no more than solve elementary arithmetic problems and global digital storage capacity was barely sufficient for this book.

Some, like Elon Musk, believe that singularity is an existential threat to humanity. He gave the example of a self-improving AI that is tasked with picking strawberries, but gets better and better and plants and picks more and more until earth's entire land mass is strawberry fields.[2]

Strawberry fields forever don't seem scary. If I were Elon, I might have picked that icily malcontent machine named HAL to make the point. Regardless, Elon has a contingency plan—the colonization of Mars. His strategy to replicate earth's balmy temperature is to nuke Mars at its poles and create an atmospheric greenhouse,[3] as a collateral benefit offering redemption to Oppenheimer's tortured soul by allowing him to become a different incarnation of Vishnu. Not Shiva the Destroyer but Brahma the Creator.

Masa, on the other hand, is a fervent AI accelerationist. While Musk's Neuralink project seeks a Vulcan mind meld with machines to control them, Masa put his faith in benign companion humanoids with "emotional intelligence." Like Pepper the friendly robot.

■

The notion of a "time machine" was at the heart of Masa's investment philosophy from his early days as an internet investor. Not Wellsian science fiction or Einsteinian time travel, but transplanting proven tech business models from the United States to other markets with a time lag, usually with a tweak to adapt to local conditions. Thus Amazon was the inspiration for backing Snapdeal and Flipkart in India, and Coupang in South Korea. Uber was the model for backing DiDi in China, Ola in India, and Grab in Southeast Asia. (This time machine rarely works in the opposite direction, for SoftBank or others—a tribute to the Bay Area planetary system with Stanford University as its sun.)

Masa's parents ran a coffee shop in Tokyo when he was a kid. The business struggled to attract traffic, until Masa persuaded his father to offer free coffee. It worked. Customers came for the free coffee but frequently bought a relatively expensive pastry or croissant. (This is a classic B-school "loss leader" strategy, but impressive coming from a ten-year-old. Also not applicable universally—in India, we will gleefully grab our free beverage and bolt.)

In addition to cross-selling, the strategy promoted adoption; enough visitors became regular paying customers to more than offset the upfront cost of the promotion. Over the coming years, consumers from Bangalore to Baltimore would benefit from SoftBank's extraordinary munificence in the form of a free ride and/or a free meal, in some measure as a result of Masa's adolescent coffee shop experience.

In his eponymous book, the celebrated venture capitalist Reid Hoffman (PayPal, LinkedIn) calls this growth-at-any-cost strategy "blitzscaling." The goal is market dominance and the pricing power that comes with it: when you get there you crank up the profit engine. For Masa this meant an obsessive focus on 80 percent market share, an escape velocity threshold beyond which you became a price setter.

Blitzscaling works brilliantly for platform models like Amazon, Facebook, and Alibaba. Less so for businesses where the economics are local and the network effects nonexistent. That painful lesson lay ahead.

■

Beyond failed territorial ambitions and imagined ethnic supremacy, the former Axis powers of Germany and Japan have another thing in common—a peculiar penchant for communal nudity. In the spas of ski resorts in Germanic Europe, I have seen naked people I prefer not to have seen naked, and been naked around people I prefer not to have been naked around. Après-golf bathing in Japan posed a similar challenge.

Yoshimitsu Goto, chief financial officer of SoftBank Group, was our master of ceremonies on a steamy August morning at Yomiuri Golf Club. The genial and always formally attired Goto-san and I became kindred souls, speaking weekly to discuss Masa's latest ideas. Goto-san used a translator in all our meetings, but I insisted that his English was better than he let on, and this became our private joke. When I eventually departed SoftBank, Goto-san solemnly told me I was his "best non-Japanese friend."

On this day Team SoftBank, represented by Masa, Nikesh, Goto-san, and me, was playing golf with Team Mizuho. Mizuho was SoftBank's ardent financial backer, most recently leading a $19 billion financing that enabled the Sprint acquisition.

To my surprise, I was in a four-ball with Masa and the two senior Mizuho representatives, including the tall and urbane Yasuhiro Sato, chairman and CEO of Mizuho Financial Group, the holding company for Mizuho Bank. The CEO of Mizuho Bank was the fourth member. Protocol would dictate that Nikesh play in this game, but this substitution was no accident, rather a deliberate and graceful concession by Nikesh.

I half expected Kato-san to caddy for Masa, like the bowler-hatted valet Oddjob did for Goldfinger. But our caddies were all female, as is customary in North Asia, and dressed like beekeepers—loose-fitting light green tunics with matching trousers tucked into boots, heads covered with white scarves worn above peaked caps and tied around necks, leaving only eyes and foreheads exposed. I stared at my bare arms and stroked my exposed neck apprehensively.

Our bags were loaded onto driverless carts that crawled like centipedes along the paved paths lining the closely mown areas. Surprisingly unencumbered by their cocooning, the beekeeper caddies buzzed back and forth to the carts, grabbing clubs with uncanny anticipation. No yardages were provided, just a club, and after a few holes, you realized your role was limited to swinging. Inflight exhortations to the golf ball, celebrations, admonishments, these were all part of caddy duties.

After nine holes, we stopped. Not for a comfort break or drink but an elaborate Chinese luncheon, accompanied (predictably) by La Tâche supplied (predictably) by Kato-san.

Masa shot an impressive seventy-three that could easily have been a sixty-nine but for a few putts that, like financial markets, stubbornly refused to bend to his iron will. I played as well as I could, but he had me by six shots. Our opponents from Mizuho fared less well, but in the grand tradition of client golf seemed delighted to see us not just win, but very obviously enjoy our round. Five birdies (three for Masa, two for me) and that recurring Toyko theme—happiness for everyone.

After the round and before dinner came the aforementioned après-golf routine.

There was no conventional locker room with shower stalls. Instead the disrobed golfers squatted, hand towels slung over shoulders, on foot-high wooden stools scattered in a substantial room, washing themselves vigorously using handheld showers.

Nikesh and I joined the party, perching ourselves tentatively on adjacent stools. Naked and brown, self-conscious and bemused, we were reluctant participants in this alien ritual, silently observing the contradiction of people reserved in all respects yet so comfortable exposing themselves undertaking this most private of tasks.

Sato-san was in our neighborhood, smilingly doing his business. He had been speaking to Masa in Japanese—a conversation between two emperors without clothes—and now turned toward me.

"Do you know Jamie Dimon, Alok-san?" he inquired.

Evidently, playing as Masa's partner had conferred upon me

a halo that suggested I hung out with the king of Wall Street. Nikesh's calculated generosity had given me "face," more impressive than an elaborate epaulet, a fancy title, or my nudity.

I might have started off in the wrong seat, but even bare-assed on a wooden stool, I was in a good place.

6

FACETIME

I was in the office I shared with Nikesh, overlooking the increasingly familiar vista over Tokyo Bay. It was afternoon, I'd arrived that morning from London, and was nodding off when my iPhone and iPad convulsed simultaneously, jerking me out of postprandial somnolence.

An email from Suki-san, a calendar invite attached.

Masa would like to invite you to dinner at 6 P.M.

A few seconds later, Nikesh came by and asked if I was free that evening. For dinner with Mark Zuckerberg.

Every tech luminary visiting Tokyo made a pilgrimage to the twenty-sixth floor. If you were an artist visiting Giverny, this was your audience with Monet, if you were a fascist visiting Rome, this was like tea with Mussolini.

It was 1 A.M. in New Haven, not late by college standards. Some time ago, when Facebook was still considered cool, Samir had written a piece in the *Yale Daily News* exhorting Yalies to forsake social media. Oblivious to the irony, I had shared the article on Facebook. I don't know if any of my friends were persuaded, but I got many likes.

I initiated a WhatsApp chat with Samir.

Guess who I'm having dinner
with

?

Zuckerberg

Cool. Show him my article

Sure

And get a selfie

And put it on Facebook? Now
that would be douchey

Lol

My impression of Zuckerberg was based mostly on *The Social Network*. Which is to say I expected to meet an arrogant, brooding, and insecure autistic savant. For many troubled by the addictive scourge of social media, Zuck was Dr. Evil, just not as funny. For me, he was Dylan's "Jokerman"—manipulator of crowds, a dream twister.

■

Masa's dining room was as enchanting at night as it was at lunchtime. The illuminated interior Japanese garden on one side and the twinkling lights of ships on Tokyo Bay on the other provided surreal bookends for the dining space.

When Zuckerberg walked in, I had the impression of being in the presence of a Roman emperor. Was it his erect bearing, the stillness, or the patrician aura? Given his known man-crush on Augustus Caesar—he named his daughter August—this was likely not an accident. Zuckerberg, sporting his trademark gray Brunello Cucinelli fitted T-shirt and blue jeans, was another emperor with few clothes. Zuckerberg advocates a simplified wardrobe that "limits the time spent on making frivolous decisions." He is silent on how we should use those precious saved minutes—perhaps polishing our Facebook profile, maybe curating our Instagram feed? Had it been intentional, Cicero himself would have applauded this monumental irony.

Zuckerberg was accompanied by Dan Rose, then Facebook's head of corporate development, whom Nikesh seemed to know.

As we exchanged pleasantries, it became obvious that the Zuckerberg of *The Social Network* was an unfair caricature. Or maybe he'd come a long way since. Zuckerberg was anything but brooding. After introductions, he asked about my background. His black eyes bored directly into mine as he listened, exhibiting a politician's talent for making you feel, in the moment, as if you were the most important person in the world. It reminded me of my sole encounter with President Clinton at a Morgan Stanley event in Boca Raton in January 2001. As with Bill, you knew Zuck's love was an illusion, but you were seduced regardless. This was a man comfortable in his own skin, speaking with Masa as an equal despite being half his age. It was impressive. If Zuckerberg had an executive coach, I wanted their phone number.

Masa invited Zuckerberg to sit directly across from him, on this occasion Masa having his back to the open area facing the garden. *Fair enough, Dr. Evil has enemies.* Nikesh and I sat on either side of Masa.

Kato-san materialized. He was seated on his knees, at the head of the table, holding an iPad mini in both his hands. I blinked to make sure, but he was accompanied by a doppelgänger, iPad mini in his hands, the two of them like tenors holding songbooks, about to break into a duet. Upon closer examination, Kato-san's comrade sported a debonair pencil mustache and had a vaguely sinister air about him. If Kato-san read Spinoza, his apprentice looked like he favored Edgar Allan Poe.

"Kato-san," said Masa, "will read out the names of dishes. All the dishes are small bowls. If you want the dish, please raise your hand. Have as many as you want, but usually six or seven is enough."

And thus began an increasingly familiar and always entertaining predinner ritual. Kato-san read out the menu choices, his smile barely suppressed, aware he was putting on a performance. When you raised your hand, Kato-san's apprentice Akuga-san would make a note on his handheld device. There was never a mistake.

The food was Japanese and Chinese delicacies. The *toro* (fatty tuna) always sold well, but the one I craved—at times raising both hands piggishly—was the Hokkaido *uni* (sea urchin) served on a bed of sushi rice. Mild sweet- and saltiness, umami complexity, melt-in-your-mouth softness—I closed my eyes to savor every bite.

I had educated myself on Masa's Facebook history. In 2009, Masa wanted to invest but was outbid by Russian American entrepreneur Yuri Milner, an investment legend in his own right. Milner told Zuckerberg to name his price, eventually investing $200 million directly into the company at a valuation of $10 billion—rich for a business that was barely profitable.[1] He also bought another $100 million of shares from employees (a construct many VCs adopt to lower their average entry price) at a discounted valuation of $6.5 billion. In another twist, Milner assigned the voting rights in respect of his newly acquired shares to Zuckerberg, such that despite diluting his economic ownership, Zuckerberg increased his control of Facebook post-transaction.

As an icebreaker, Masa referenced this previous encounter with Zuckerberg.

"You know, Mark, I always regret how I never invested in Facebook. I was so stupid," said Masa. "You have built such a great business."

Masa's deferential tone to one so young was curious. A cynical view might be that Zuckerberg at age thirty was already richer than Masa. Maybe, but it wasn't just that. Masa Son revered entrepreneurs, and my cynicism about social media notwithstanding, Zuckerberg's role as the vanguard of an information revolution was undeniable.

"Thank you, Son-san. We were disappointed as well. We very much wanted you as a shareholder, it would have been our honor," said Zuckerberg, sounding equally formal.

"But as I recall, you thought the valuation was too rich?" he continued.

"Yes! I thought $10 billion was too much!" said Masa, shaking his head. "But Yuri was smart. He is such a great investor, so smart."

And then, alternatively turning to Nikesh and me, he added. "You guys should learn, we should never make the same mistake," he said, wagging his finger for emphasis.

Nikesh and I nodded, gravely.

For Masa, missing out on Facebook—the $10 billion would become $1 trillion in 2021—evidently made a profound impact. In tech investing, sometimes not being aggressive enough can be an expensive mistake. When ByteDance (the Chinese parent company of TikTok) came along, Masa's instructions were clear—invest the maximum amount available, at any price, even the seemingly outrageous $75 billion valuation.[2] (His instincts were on target, as TikTok would go on to exceed Facebook, Instagram, and Snap in engagement, and with Gen Z surpass Google in search.)

When I asked Yuri about the Facebook investment (two years later, over a poolside lunch at his home in Los Altos) he responded modestly. "Yes, that might seem brave. But I had an advantage over Masa, I was already operating a social network in Russia." Yuri had studied adoption and monetization in other countries, allowing him to project more accurately what Facebook could be worth. Yuri made another incisive observation in our conversation, one that reinforced his stature as the outsider who beats Valley insiders at their own game. When I raised Masa's AI fixation, the former physicist's prophetic response was that Microsoft and Google would capture much of the value created by AI. (In an astonishing dance of the elephants, the big tech "magnificent seven" would add over $4 trillion in market value in the months following the launch of ChatGPT in November 2022.)

■

Kato-san reappeared, this time holding a bottle. Romanée-Conti, the flagship wine from Domaine Romanée-Conti ("DRC"), a notch above La Tâche, a wine that occasionally comes up for auction at Sotheby's and trades for the price of a Tesla. My experience of wines is mostly about the company and the occasion, but sometimes the wine *is* the occasion. Amazingly, nobody noticed. I smiled appreciatively at Kato-san, who nodded serenely in acknowledgment.

You can tell a lot about people based on their beverage preferences when not constrained by budget. The Valley nouveau riche quaff alcoholic and opulent California cabernets like Screaming Eagle. Masa Son evidently favored Burgundian refinement. I liked that. It was also consistent with Masa's investment style. "Value investors" like Warren Buffett are bargain hunters, while "growth investors" like Masa care less about price. Appropriately, Buffett's tipple of choice is Cherry Coke.

Once the wine flowed and the food rolled, Zuckerberg launched into a story.

"Masa, this is a treat, thank you for hosting," he began. "Have any of you heard about my challenges—no?"

He looked around and saw blank expressions. I vaguely recalled reading stuff like wearing a tie every day or learning Mandarin.

"Well, every year I set myself a challenge. Last year it was to be a vegetarian, but only eat meat when I killed the animal myself."

Now that's fucking interesting, man.

"I killed a chicken once, in a restaurant, with my bare hands. That was quite an experience," he continued.

While Masa looked on in polite disbelief, Nikesh and I exchanged glances.

"Wow," said Masa. It was a prolonged exclamation, the "o" sound extended for what seemed like an eternity. "You—killed—the—chicken?" he asked, incredulous, pointing his finger at Zuckerberg.

"And then I shot a bison," Zuckerberg continued, his chest swelling proudly, enjoying the effect he was having on his host. "That was quite something. I'd never been hunting before. We pickled the meat, and I ate it for several months. But you know the best part? We had the head stuffed, and we put it in Sheryl's office. She wasn't very happy!" he said.

Everyone laughed, imagining a poised and unsuspecting Sheryl Sandberg walking into her office, an image evocative of the decapitated horse scene from *The Godfather*. Everyone except for Mark, whose painted-on smile remained painted on, and his colleague Dan, who had the bored air of one who's heard it all before.

I gazed outside, my senses elevated by the wine, fully expecting to see it raining fish on Tokyo Bay. Nikesh and I locked eyes and shook our heads, glad to have each other to share the moment.

But these anecdotes were as troubling as they were entertaining, suggestive of Facebook's frat house culture and its "move fast and break things" ethos. I have nothing against fraternities (or Zuck's Harvard final clubs) but did I really want John Belushi to be the world's self-appointed information tzar?

Zuck's enforced self-awareness seemed worthy. As he says, "I think many people forget that a living being has to die for you to eat meat, so my goal revolves around not letting myself forget." I recalled Samir, at age three, persuading me that "food chickens" were distinct from real chickens, an elegant piece of toddler rationalization that helped him defer the fundamental leap of faith required of carnivorous behavior—that animal suffering is less morally significant than human pain.

Fair enough, but did Zuckerberg need to resort to gory avian encounters or indulge America's peculiar fascination with guns? Strange behavior, but there's always the Elon Musk defense. "I reinvented electric cars and I'm sending people to Mars on a rocket ship. Did you think I was going to be a chill, normal dude?"[3] asks Elon. As the founder of a business with a value that would approach the GDP of Scandinavia, Zuckerberg might reasonably have the same query. But it's an oily slope when we readily accept, in our "idolatry of innovators,"[4] that erratic behavior is a necessary trait of outliers. Brian Chesky, founder of Airbnb, is a muscular counterexample. Later I would spend several hours one-on-one with Brian, and I found him chill and—other than intimidating biceps—refreshingly normal.

(In his quest to reclaim normality, Zuckerberg decided in 2020 to ditch annual challenges in favor of "long-term predictions." And the company's credo became, "Move fast with stable infrastructure." Which sounds terribly boring and grown-up. Probably a good thing.)

But what of the Romanée-Conti, you ask? Surely every sip had to be a Meg Ryan "I'll have what she's having" orgasmic event to justify that price tag? It is indeed a splendid wine, but beyond a certain price threshold it's mostly about collectability and projecting status. Masa, however, isn't a wine investor, nor was he making a statement. He had no need to impress me, yet offered a pour of DRC when we first met. And if the idea was to impress Zuckerberg, a recognizable California cult cabernet or a Bordeaux First Growth would have been more effective. No, Masa tried DRC, liked it, and for him the price was incidental. The one time he let price hold him back—Facebook at $10 billion—was a mistake that tormented him. A mistake not to be repeated.

7

CITY OF DJINNS

Hip cafés I find in New York, irony in London, but in Delhi I'm at home in my past, like all immigrants unable and in my case unwilling to jettison my history any more than I can lose my shadow.

On every trip, airborne nostalgia gives way to ground revulsion when confronted with the hideous red-yellow-brown patterned carpet, reeking faintly of disinfectant, at the airport terminal. (Regrettably, not all rugs tie rooms together.) This is followed by bemused soul-searching when asked at Immigration to identify myself as an Indian, a Foreigner, a PIO (Person of Indian Origin), or an OCI (Overseas Citizen of India). Because I am one or I've been one, all of them.

I had held on to my Indian passport until a traumatic visit to the concrete and featureless Czech consulate on Bayswater Road as a supplicant for a visa. Like a classical symphony, this involved four movements. Lining up in the drizzly gloom outside, a security check inside, waiting in a windowless sitting room, and then the finale—a trial conducted by a hirsute and humorless consulate officer who treated me like Kafka's dung beetle. All this for a weekend trip to Prague.

It was the last straw—or maybe the one that broke the camel's back, perhaps the type you clutch at? Regardless, I'd had enough. The trial on Bayswater Road followed by a visit to Kafka's house in Prague led to a self-inflicted metamorphosis. I traded my worn blue Indian travel document, sixth in a line of well-stamped antecedents, for a burgundy British passport, the gold Royal Crest on its cover a taunting symbol of oppression for my ancestors. Which made me feel like the Nawab of Bengal surrendering to Robert Clive at Plassey: I colonized myself.

So here I was, a Foreigner with an expired PIO card and a valid OCI card. But how can I accept being a "Foreigner" in Delhi? I still tear up when they play the national anthem before a World Cup cricket match, doesn't that count?

This time, as one does for everything in India, I had a *jugaad*—a hack—to create another option. Trips with Masa involved meetings with government ministers, so I talked myself into the VIP line. Except there was no line. Just a very lonely IO (immigration officer) who was trained to stamp first and not ask questions later.

■

I'd never met Adam Neumann, but I'd heard of him. My former colleague Derek, with typical banker hyperbole, had described him as a wunderkind transforming global real estate. "You have to meet this guy, Alok. This will be the hottest IPO since Google," he had gushed. When he explained the business, it seemed no different than Regus, the serviced office operator. But Derek was unrelenting. "Alok, this guy is something."

Masa and Adam were both keynote speakers at the Startup India Summit at Delhi's Vigyan Bhavan (Science Center), organized by Prime Minister Modi as part of his mission to promote Indian entrepreneurship.

At six-foot-five, Adam was like Delhi's Qutub Minar, towering over all in the neighborhood. With a dark mane of shoulder-length hair and chiseled features, he was an Adonis with minimal body fat, his confident strut evocative of a Tribeca ramp during Fashion Week, the sleeveless high-collar navy blue "Modi vest" worn over a flowing white *kurta* adding a dash of exoticism to his regal aura. There must have been a thousand people in the room, but the background chatter typical of large gatherings in India subsided when Adam took the stage.

Adam grandly declared that his WeWork venture would solve India's housing problems. My bullshit meter redlined. *How does this frat house formula of beer on tap and foosball tables solve housing India's middle class?*

Adam introduced himself to Masa during a coffee break.

"You are my hero, Son-san," said the consummate smooth operator, turning it on in this land of snake charmers, his tongue a weapon of mass seduction.

Masa's reactions to people were easy to read. He was always polite, but if you didn't make an impression, the smile was forced, the eye contact fleeting, the conversation stilted. Adam had Masa's enraptured attention.

Telecom entrepreneur Sunil Mittal had invited us for dinner that night. Sensing Masa's appetite to engage, Nikesh asked Adam to drop by after dinner. Adam accepted but forgot Sunil's address and didn't have Nikesh's phone number. All he had to work with was a Google search suggesting the Mittal home was on Amrita Shergill Marg. Undeterred, Adam instructed his driver to stop at every home on Amrita Shergill.

It was a chilly January night with dense seasonal fog. Adam's driver was a uniformed and turbaned Sikh who presumably knew the area but was trained to speak only when spoken to. Otherwise he might have told Adam there was no greater concentration of wealth and power in India than this leafy confine called Lutyens' Delhi, named after the architect Sir Edwin Lutyens, in the heart of the new imperial capital established by the British in 1911. I grew up a few miles away, on the campus of the All India Institute of Medical Sciences, a teaching hospital where my father was a professor. My earliest memory of Lutyens' Delhi is as a five-year-old, my nose pressed against the dusty window of my ramshackle school bus as it traversed these majestic tree-lined avenues, awestruck by the guards with their Kalashnikov automatic rifles patrolling the gates of the grand homes. The roads had different names then, redolent of India's colonial past. Amrita Shergill Marg was formerly Ratendone Road, named after the Viscount of Ratendone. Ministers and senior bureaucrats live here, in sprawling state-owned bungalows. Alongside them, in a triangular enclave bordering Lodhi Gardens, are the mansions of Delhi's billionaire class.

This was not, in other words, the kind of cheerful neighborhood whose tranquility is occasionally disrupted by a knock at the door. Outside most homes were armed guards, surly at being dragged away from warming their hands on glowing earthen *angeethis* by this tall apparition emerging from the fog out of a black Mercedes. But attitude is everything in India's hierarchical society, and it is a legacy of our colonial history that white foreigners always command respect. The man from the kibbutz arrived at Sunil's home just before 11 P.M., announcing his entrance with his customary greeting, his right arm raised in a dramatic salutation. "Shalom!"

Fortunately for Adam, 11 P.M. is relatively early for a Delhi social evening. Most guests were still clustered around the bar, nursing their tumblers of Johnnie Walker Blue Label. With one notable exception: Masa had departed for his hotel. If Adam was disappointed, he didn't show it. Sunil, who over the years has been a friend, confidante, and mentor, welcomed Adam graciously.

I don't recall if the tequila on offer was Adam's favored Don Julio 1942, but regardless he drained a shot, a catalyst to launch into his repertoire of jokes.

"How do you wink at an Arab?" asked the former Israeli naval officer.

Without waiting for a response, he closed his left eye, and lifted his hands as if cradling a rifle aimed directly at a guest.

Jokes let out forbidden thoughts, as Freud said. But then, as he fired comparable zingers at his own community, it became clear Adam was not a hater but an equal opportunity offender. For him, it was all about the attention.

■

Masa asked for Adam to be invited to an evening reception SoftBank was hosting the following evening at Le Cirque, the rooftop French restaurant at the Leela Palace Hotel, where we were all staying. The invitees were mainly founders of SoftBank's current and potential investee companies, along with select senior bureaucrats and industrialists.

Among them was a man who in a different era would have been the Maharaja of Gwalior—Jyotiraditya Scindia, then a member of Parliament and later a minister in the Modi government. In the days of the Raj, Gwalior was one of five "salute states": when the maharaja arrived, twenty-one gunshots announced his entrance. At Scindia's wedding to the Princess of Baroda (another former salute state) the erudite Prime Minister Manmohan Singh waited patiently *behind* me in the greeting line. The Harvard- and Stanford-educated Scindia (Jai, as we called him) had been an analyst and my junior-most apprentice at Morgan Stanley in India. He was always diligent and respectful with me, but no matter, in every meeting with Indian businessmen or bureaucrats, to my amusement and Jai's chagrin, I was relegated to the status of palanquin-bearer.

But Masa was unimpressed, barely acknowledging Jai's princely presence. That evening, Masa interacted meaningfully with only two individuals.

The first was Adam. The two migrated to a separate bar section of the restaurant, Adam gesticulating frequently with his hands, occasionally spreading his arms wide. Presumably referring to billions and billions of square feet of coworking space, like Carl Sagan describing stars in the universe. Masa leaned forward, enraptured, oblivious to the other guests staring enviously at this devilishly handsome *gora* who had cast the kind of spell on Masa they were here to themselves cast. What drew Masa to Adam? The "crazy" factor—the willingness to think not just big but on a cosmic scale.

Masa summoned me. *He wants my WeWork analysis?* I walked over and leaned forward, allowing him to whisper in my ear. Nikesh noticed and joined us, wondering what the boss wanted. We laughed when I told him: a glass of La Tâche.

There was a second lovefest at Le Cirque, involving Masa and my friend Timmy, whom he'd met when we played golf a few days earlier. Timmy was not a technologist or corporate chieftain, just a warm, straightforward guy. Masa invited him to the reception and sought him out. They sat together, Masa regularly throwing his head back, laughing, as relaxed as I'd ever seen him.

Timmy was filling a void in Masa's life neither knew existed. Masa had friendships in the business world, like Foxconn founder Terry Gou (who is Taiwanese, makes our iPhones in China, and calls Masa "boss") and Oracle founder Larry Ellison. But I've observed Masa with both. The Terry relationship was based on mutual admiration, with Larry it was a case of Larry's obsession with all things Japanese.

Masa was surrounded by people who either worked for him or had an agenda. Timmy was that rare exception who wasn't trying to sell Masa a plane or a Picasso, nor did he want a job, but for this reason featured at the top of Masa's "must see" list on visits to India.

Later, I asked Timmy what they chatted about.

"He is such a cool guy, we were negotiating strokes for our next game. He told me real men don't ask for shots!" said Timmy, laughing. "And then he talked about how much he loves his dog and all the designer stuff he buys for his poodle. He also said Alok is a highly intelligent person!"

I backslapped Timmy and gave him a pour from the bottle of La Tâche I'd guarded zealously all evening.

■

Among the guests at the reception that night were three young men who represented the best of an India that did not exist in the dysfunctional License Raj of my youth.

Kunal Bahl and Rohit Bansal were cofounders of Snapdeal, the e-commerce business taking on Amazon in India. Bhavish Aggarwal was the founder of Ola Cabs, the ridesharing business slugging it out with Uber. All three were about thirty when SoftBank first invested in their respective businesses in 2014.

This new breed of Indian tech entrepreneur was invariably an Indian Institute of Technology (IIT) graduate. The acceptance rate at IIT Mumbai hovers around 0.25 percent, making it twenty times tougher to get into than Harvard College or MIT. Moreover, entry is based on performance in a grueling entrance examination, no matter if daddy went there or the polo coach wanted you on the team. Unlike my encounters with America's educated elite, when I ran into IIT graduates I knew I could neither outsmart nor outwork them.

In a different era, Bhavish, Kunal, and Rohit would have followed in the footsteps of (Google CEO) Sundar Pichai and Satya Nadella, forsaking India for Silicon Valley. That they stayed in India, or in Kunal's case returned to India, is a function of opportunity. It started with the turn-of-the-century "world is flat" phenomenon, when outsourcing labor to India became the new new thing, but then came the internet and smartphones. In emerging markets the notion of leapfrogging, or bypassing legacy infrastructure, removed a major obstacle to the adoption of technology platforms like Amazon and Uber. Unlike the US, India had no organized retail sector, no Walmart or mall-centric shopping culture. Car ownership levels were low and public transportation abysmal. As a result, the transition to e-commerce and ridesharing would be faster: Masa's time machine could run rampant.

These young Indian entrepreneurs, bankrolled by SoftBank, understood this, as did Jeff Bezos and Travis Kalanick. SoftBank's backing of these local champions to confront American bad boys like Bezos and Kalanick gave Masa and Nikesh cult status in India, making headlines as Masa committed to investing at least $10 billion over ten years.

■

Ola Cabs and Snapdeal were both intriguing case studies in tech's profit-be-damned blitzscaling approach.

It is normal for an early-stage business to have negative income. But Ola was operating with negative *revenue,* a concept one associates with a charity rather than a business. The subsidies paid to a driver and/or promotions offered to a passenger were frequently greater than the fare collected. Uber was doing the same. Indian consumers weren't just free riders, they were paid to ride, frequently to eat, and sometimes to buy stuff. Ola and Uber were both bleeding cash (over time as much as $30 million per month) in this race to see who ran out of money last.

It was amusing to hear people vent about Uber exploiting drivers by not offering benefits, or "price gouging" by using artifices like surge pricing. Ironically, at the time ridesharing economics involved a massive transfer of wealth from investors to drivers and riders. For Uber's core business to be profitable, drivers needed to be eliminated altogether. Or for fares to rise substantially, but that would eliminate any price advantage relative to conventional taxi service. In the interim, Uber's viability depended on evolving beyond ridesharing into a "deliver anything" and/or a universal app, facilitating food delivery, payments, and other services. (Which, by 2023, it eventually did.)

With Snapdeal the competitive dynamic was distorted even

further by the presence of a second local competitor, Flipkart. Its backer was New York–based Tiger Global, perhaps the only technology investor to challenge SoftBank in scale and chutzpah. And then there was Amazon, determined not to cede the Indian market to a local player, as it had to Alibaba in China.

Consider a relatively high-ticket item like a Samsung Galaxy smartphone, available for sale on Flipkart's app or website for $500 (US dollar equivalent). Flipkart is a "marketplace," a virtual store where vendors can sell anything. Its business model is to charge the seller a commission, say 5 percent or $25 on the $500 Galaxy phone. The $500 is called gross merchandise value (GMV), while the $25 commission is Flipkart's actual revenue. After deducting its costs (technology, salaries, other) what's left would be profit, usually an approximation of cash flow. In good old-fashioned corporate finance, cash flow—"dollars you can buy beer with," as Professor Knutson at Wharton would say—is the *only* thing that matters when it comes to valuing a business.

Instead, private investors valued Flipkart and other online marketplaces, in India and elsewhere, as a multiple of not cash flows or profits, or even revenue, but GMV. This created a perverse incentive to pump up valuation by "buying" GMV. You could sell thousands of Galaxy smartphones for a discounted price of $400, not charge any commission and lose $100 on every transaction, hemorrhage cash in aggregate, and investors rewarded you with a higher valuation!

Of course, the idea behind these seemingly mindless giveaways was to encourage mass adoption before dialing up the profit engine. This is the Amazon playbook: when asked if he could spell "profit," Jeff Bezos once answered p-r-o-p-h-e-t.[1] (This seductive doctrine of inevitability and invincibility, of becoming so big the rules of the game no longer apply, has worked well for Amazon and Big Tech generally. Traditional antitrust law focuses primarily on consumer price impact, but it is difficult to argue with the Amazon consumer value proposition.

Amazon flexes in other ways—dictating terms to third-party sellers on its marketplace, for example.)

But how do you value a "business" with negative revenues? It's like putting a price tag on dreams, my finance training as useful as playing darts to prepare for the Tour de France.

SoftBank's investment in Ola Cabs was negotiated over a late-evening drink in the lobby bar of the Conrad Hotel. Bhavish argued for a $600 million valuation, citing last round valuation and what the business had accomplished since. I counteroffered $250 million, pointing out his argument relied on the greater fool theory, and took no account of the fact that the previous investors assumed Ola would grow as it had. Bhavish predictably reverted to "others are willing to pay more." We laughed, clicked glasses, shook hands, and settled on a number in the middle. About where Masa and Nikesh had instructed me to settle.

I'd seen financial markets depart from fundamentals with tragic consequences, valuing businesses based on phony metrics like "eyeballs" (a crude measure of traffic on a website) in 1999, rather than profits. But entry valuations are less consequential when it comes to early-stage technology investing. If ridesharing turned out to be as disruptive as Masa expected, whether Ola was valued at $250 million or $500 million would have limited relevance to long-term absolute returns. (Ola was valued at over $3.5 billion in 2023.[2]) While my starting point was the current size of the taxi market, Masa's thinking was higher order—he was imagining a future where people no longer owned cars. In every such negotiation, I would take a deep breath and remind myself about missing out on Facebook at $10 billion.

But then a funny thing happened, predictable in hindsight. When SoftBank invested in Ola Cabs, its rival TaxiForSure sold out to Ola. It didn't have a choice. Who would back TaxiForSure against an Ola bankrolled by the Crazy Guy? Masa's "who wins in a fight between a crazy guy and smart guy" question was not a gratuitous leitmotif, it was a canny competitive strategy. It was also a trick question: the Crazy Guy was in fact the smart guy.

■

The contrast between the understated Kunal, Rohit, and Bhavish and the showman Adam Neumann was stark. These fine young Indians were grounded and proud of their middle-class roots. When Nikesh and I accompanied Kunal and Rohit to Hangzhou for a meeting with the Alibaba management team, they shared a room at a three-star Holiday Inn. Unlike Adam, they evinced no interest in surfing or tequila, and while most were vegetarian, there was no vegan virtue signaling. No talk of unicorn dreams either, just an earnest desire to use technology to solve problems and a quiet determination to win against Bezos and Kalanick.

I was rooting for my "chill, normal dudes" in their battle against America's brashest exponents of capitalism.

■

A few weeks later Goldman Sachs approached us about investing in WeWork at an $8 billion valuation.[3]

Given Masa's obvious interest, I dug into the WeWork investment proposition. While the company was funded by Benchmark Capital, the pedigreed (eBay, Uber, Snap) venture firm, Adam was an unknown commodity in the Valley. His sole previous venture—baby clothes with sewn-in kneepads—had failed, but an early dose of humility is a desirable feature rather than a problematic bug in an entrepreneur's CV. But while this kneepad idea was cute (WeePad?), it wasn't exactly disruptive technology. As for the WeWork business model, the idea of communal working spaces played nicely into millennial preferences, allowing the company to extract higher rents per square foot than its more pedestrian competitors. But there was no way to justify the valuation pitched by Goldman Sachs. WeWork was a real estate business, not a technology platform with network effects or a scalable enterprise software business. The economics of commercial real estate are hyperlocal: every building is unique. To value this business as a multiple of revenue, as the bankers were advocating, seemed untenable.

There was another flaw in WeWork's business model. Asset-liability matching is a basic risk management concept, for a business or a household. If your job is temporary or you're a gig worker, it's not a good idea to lock yourself into a long-term mortgage—that's if a bank will lend you money at all. WeWork's assets were mostly short-term office rental agreements, many with early-stage companies and individuals. Its liabilities, however, were long-term, frequently ten-year-plus lease agreements with commercial landlords. In a recession (or a pandemic!), this mismatch could destroy a balance sheet. I'd seen more than my fair share of restructurings and bankruptcies (the US 1990–91 recession, the aftermath of the internet bubble) and felt strongly about this risk.

I assumed we'd seen the last of Adam Neumann, but we underestimated the ultimate salesman, the GOAT, a guy whose wife told him he was full of shit on their first date yet ended up marrying him within weeks.

■

I stayed for an extra day in Delhi to see my parents.

They lived, simply and comfortably, in a ground-floor flat of a South Delhi residential neighborhood. The British developed Lutyens' Delhi as their capital south of Old Delhi, the historic Mughal capital on the banks of the river Jamuna. New Delhi was the product of postindependence urbanization. In my youth, one of the nice things about New Delhi was that it was, well, new. The homes once shiny and bright now seemed dark and decrepit, the air once clean and fresh now noxious and stale, the streets once wide and pristine now congested and littered. But no matter, I spent the first twenty-one years of my life in this city of djinns, it will always be my first love, its history my history, its decline my sadness.

My mother always greeted me with a smile that radiated not merely affection but a wonderment that I was real and I was here. A smile that, more than any accolade or paycheck, made me feel special to be me. She was a medical student when she had me at age twenty-one. Three years later, when my younger brother Vivek was born, she took a break from her medical career to become a stay-at-home mother. She did everything for me. I couldn't even do my laundry, as Maya would discover to her dismay. Breast cancer and a titanium hip had slowed her down, but she continued to practice as an obstetrician-gynecologist.

My father could identify every variation of the hepatitis B virus, but he could not tell Citibank from SoftBank. He would have liked me to follow his path into medicine, but I was always too squeamish. We lived on the campus of a teaching hospital, and it didn't help that a couple of his misguided students decided that the cadaver lab might be an amusing outing for an impressionable ten-year-old Alok. I was proud of my father's achievements, which I knew were more substantive than mine. He was awarded the Padma Shri, one of India's highest civilian awards (the equivalent of a British knighthood) for services to the medical profession. He was eighty, frail after a series of heart attacks starting in his fifties, but still active as chairman of a charitable hospital he had led for over twenty years. Both of us carried a rogue gene that condemned us to early onset coronary artery disease, which for me meant waiting for the axe to fall.

Money was tight when my father was an academic. Eating animal protein—usually mutton; chicken was more expensive—was a luxury rarely enjoyed more than once a week. Things changed after he became a thriving private physician, but I still remember those early days. It affected my parents more than it did me, that devastating helplessness of denying your children, but their frustration made me determined to never put myself in that position.

We spoke in Hindi: other than casual interactions in India, these were now the only conversations I ever had in my first language. They didn't see their grandchildren often, so mostly we talked about Samir and Alya and their college lives.

Every time I saw my parents, I wondered if this might be the last. Like every other time, I saved the expressions of gratitude and love for another day.

I had breezed through Karl Ove Knausgaard's *My Struggle* wondering what kept me turning thirty-five hundred pages of a tome that made *Ulysses* seem racy by comparison. Knausgaard's prose is immersive, and in between frying onions and drinking beer he unleashes brilliant streams of literary consciousness—deciphering Celan's poetry, dissecting *Mein Kampf*, explaining Shakespeare's invention of humanity and the anticomedic mastery of *The Idiot*. But mostly I was fascinated by Knausgaard's continuous and searing self-excavation, including—paradoxically—interrogating publicly his desire for privacy, which I contrasted with my inability to express myself even in this most intimate of settings. My father rarely displayed emotion, at least not with me, and he was never a hugger. Did that have something to do with it? Or had three decades of living in a world where someone had to fall for you to rise made me uncomfortably numb—long on cash, short on empathy?

But maybe I was hiding behind tropes. Knausgaard, as he steals money from his grandmother and cheats on his girlfriend, reinforced for me that we are all flawed in ways that defy logic or explanation, condemned never to be quite good enough.

8

SHOW ME THE MONEY

It was 5 P.M. on a sunny Saturday in May 2016. Maya and I were motoring along SR 29 through Napa, our destination the French Laundry, Thomas Keller's three-Michelin-star tribute to California cuisine in Yountville.

A nine-course tasting menu (the only option at the French Laundry) seemed gluttonous. But unlike landmark birthdays, a thirtieth wedding anniversary is an actual achievement. One feels the pressure to mark the occasion, if only to deal with the "what are you doing to celebrate" question attached to every congratulatory message. Dinner at a destination restaurant and a night at the sleek Bardessono Hotel seemed like a reasonable, though predictable, response.

On a stunning day like this, we should have had the top down in my Porsche 911 Targa, perhaps sung along to Led Zeppelin's "Going to California" or the Eagles' "Take It Easy." Instead, the lid remained shut, and rather than Robert Plant's soaring exhortations or Glenn Frey's mellow notes, the deep voice that resonated in the vehicle's tiny cabin was that of Martin Lau, CEO of Chinese technology giant Tencent Holdings, live from Hong Kong on a Sunday morning.

This would lead to a most unusual bonding experience for

Maya and me, more meaningful than yet another overhyped and overpriced culinary experience.

■

Nikesh and I concluded SoftBank needed cash; we figured $20 billion. Our rationale was twofold.

First, in 2013 SoftBank took on $19 billion of debt to buy struggling US wireless carrier Sprint, which itself had over $30 billion in debt.[1] While not guaranteed by SoftBank, Sprint's debt was consolidated on SoftBank's balance sheet. Masa's vision of merging Sprint with T-Mobile had been faced down by antitrust opposition, leaving SoftBank stranded with an asset with the financial profile of a banana republic. SoftBank's own bonds were rated below investment grade by the US rating agencies. To execute Masa's ambitious investment program, a substantial capital cushion was required.

Despite his collapse in the 2001 market implosion, Masa's impulse was to push leverage to the limit. While private equity investors rely heavily on debt, their typical investee company generates stable cash flow, which they enhance by cutting costs. RJR Nabisco (the most celebrated leveraged buyout of the eighties) was sought after because of its nicotine-stained and sugary but very predictable cash generation.

Technology investing is more speculative; even a proven business is constantly threatened by disruption. BlackBerry once had an enviable 45 percent share of the smartphone market, but then came the iPhone. For this reason, venture investors like Sequoia Capital or even later-stage growth investors like Warburg Pincus eschew leverage, despite their multidecade track record of picking winners.

And all investors, public or private, worry about "tail risk." Returns on assets, like many natural phenomena, display a bell-shaped pattern every high school math student would recognize as a "normal distribution," except for one crucial difference—"fat tails," or a greater likelihood of extreme events. Like the 2008 financial crisis. Modest financial leverage is the key to survival, and after enlisting the emphatic support of CFO Goto-san, we persuaded Masa to limit leverage to no more than 25 percent of the value of SoftBank's underlying assets. Given that much of SoftBank's asset base included relatively mature and profitable businesses like SoftBank Mobile in Japan, this seemed a reasonable compromise.

Second, while Masa had an impressive track record investing ahead of technology megatrends, he frequently held on too long, as had been the case with Yahoo!. The message from investors was clear—enough about the three-hundred-year vision, show me the money. We needed to convince them that Masa's vision was supported by disciplined portfolio and risk management, leading to a narrowing of the substantial discount between the market value of SoftBank stock and its net worth.

To accomplish our goal of raising $20 billion, we zeroed in on two transactions—a sale of Supercell and concurrently a partial liquidation of SoftBank's Alibaba holdings, at the time approaching $100 billion.

Supercell was one of those B-side releases that became a sleeper hit. With increasingly ubiquitous smartphones and high-speed data networks, Masa identified an explosion in online gaming as a global megatrend. He called it right. Between 2010 and 2020, the gaming industry grew from $78 billion to $137 billion,[2] its growth surpassing every other entertainment sector, making it the second largest segment behind pay television and streaming.

In 2013, SoftBank invested $1.5 billion to acquire 50 percent of Supercell,[3] a Finnish developer of mobile games with *Clash of Clans* being its most celebrated success. I've never played *Clash of Clans,* or any other mobile game. Along with Cyberpunks and

Bored Apes, this is a phenomenon that passed me by, though my two millennials keep me in touch with these generational trends.

Nikesh and I understood the strategic value of Supercell to potential acquirers, among them Bobby Kotick's Activision Blizzard and Pony Ma's Tencent Holdings. Activision, owner of the *Call of Duty* and *Guitar Hero* franchises, needed to bulk up its mobile presence, while Tencent dominated mobile gaming in China but had global ambitions. We moved boldly to buy an additional 23 percent of Supercell from existing shareholders.[4] In doing so, unlike many of SoftBank's investments intended to play out over many years, we were being canny traders. Our intent was a quick flip as part of a deal to sell a substantial majority of the company, perhaps for as much as $10 billion.

After a controlled bidding process, we had the finalists down to the two Chinese archrivals, Tencent Holdings and Alibaba Group. However, despite SoftBank now owning 73 percent of Supercell, the company continued to operate independently, and any deal was complicated by employee and founder control. (Most US technology companies with founder CEOs have similarly warped governance. Meta, for example, has two classes of stock. Zuckerberg's Class B stock carries ten votes per share while the public owns Class A stock with one vote per share. A violation of shareholder democracy, until recently unacceptable in the UK.)

Further, Supercell had a unique inverted organizational structure. The CEO Ilkka Paananen was at the bottom, his role to be a facilitator for the "cells" or teams that developed and managed the games. It was decision-making by consensus, and to get this deal over the finish line, hand-holding with the founder team would be required, best done in person. In Helsinki.

■

I'd done one too many short-haul business trips from London to Europe's fine capital cities. I hated them almost as much as I did my weekly trips to Beijing while based in Hong Kong. Not the destinations—a weekend in Paris or Berlin was always a treat—but the experience. The crowded flights were invariably early morning or late night. If you stayed overnight, the day ended with room service dinner, frequently while on a conference call with lawyers nailing down a merger agreement, or with colleagues in New York or Asia. The "timeless elegance" of Europe's grand hotels did nothing to mitigate the disorientation that came from waking up in a strange bed, assuming the constant caffeination allowed you to sleep at all.

The website for Helsinki's 125-year-old Hotel Kämp therefore provoked a negative Pavlovian response, undeserved given Finland's dominance of the happiness league tables, challenged only by neighboring Denmark and Sweden. *What is it about these people, the blondness or the oily fish?* Sociologists say it's income equality, but is happiness then a relative state rather than a Freudian remission of individual pain? Was the icy Björn Borg "happy" merely because his rival McEnroe was sulky?

I wasn't looking forward to a week in the company of geeky though presumably happy Finnish millennial gamers. But being an empty nester has its positives. With salesmanship befitting Adam Neumann, I sold Maya on Sibelius and pickled herring. She saw through it but empathy and curiosity prevailed: she joined me.

Among the many fascinating stories in the Mahabharata is the tragic tale of the teenager Abhimanyu, son of the great warrior Arjuna. While in his mother Subhadra's womb, Abhimanyu hears Lord Krishna describe the secret of the impenetrable military formation Chakravyuha, a knowledge that proved pivotal on the battlefield of Kurukshetra. I never understood why Lord Krishna was discussing Chakravyuha with his very pregnant sister Subhadra; not surprisingly, Subhadra fell asleep midway through the discourse. As a result the fetal Abhimanyu, his sleep cycle presumably in sync with his mother's, learned how to penetrate Chakravyuha, but not how to escape once inside enemy ranks.

The resultant massacre of his sixteen-year-old son Abhimanyu enraged Arjuna, as Patroclus's death did Achilles, and provided a decisive tilt in this other mother of all battles.

There is so much to take away from this marvelous story—our layers of consciousness, what the subconscious mind absorbs, how all this plays into our destiny. That plus a reminder that all is fair in love and war, and that a little knowledge can be dangerous.

There were elements of the Abhimanyu tale in how Maya, with a mind trained in Schubert rather than spreadsheets, learned the Supercell deal from snippets of discussion over reindeer meat entrées in Helsinki and phone conversations thereafter. On that Saturday evening in Napa, in the final decisive stage of negotiation with Tencent, when Nikesh called with Martin Lau on the line, I could have said I was unavailable. But unlike warfare in ancient India, there are no rules in dealmaking regarding downing tools at sunset or observing the sabbath. We could have called the French Laundry to push back our reservation, but that would have prompted peals of hysterical laughter.

As always, Maya had a point of view.

"Why can't you talk to him while you're driving? This is not that complicated, try playing Rachmaninov. I heard your conversation last night, I'll help you out," she said.

I could have insisted that multitasking scrambles my brain, but this excuse no longer had currency. Besides, she had a point. We bankers thrive on making our roles seem complicated, it's what gets us paid.

Discussing deal details in the presence of even a family member was a potential violation of confidentiality protocols, which both SoftBank and I took seriously. But this situation required special dispensation. Nikesh was president of SoftBank and on the call. He told Martin it was my wedding anniversary and my wife was in the car, which drew a charming message of gratitude from Martin. With full disclosure all around, we kept our sleek chariot moving forward purposefully.

On her iPhone Notes app, Maya created and maintained a list of all open issues while Nikesh and I negotiated with Martin and his head of strategy, James Mitchell. She signaled several times, when I missed an issue or a detail, and by the time we reached Yountville, all items on the Sale & Purchase Agreement had been resolved. When I opened the Notes file she emailed me, I found a meticulously crafted list of all that had been agreed, which I forwarded to the team of lawyers standing by with minimal edits.

Thirty years on, she never ceases to amaze me. She had entered my life without knocking when we were teenagers, and suggested, over an evening stroll in Delhi's Lodhi Gardens, that we get married. I was twenty-three, but I agreed. She had that spark of life, and I wanted to be with her, always.

On our twenty-fifth wedding anniversary celebration, at the ballroom of the Mandarin Oriental Hyde Park in London on a fine summer evening, I was confronted with the daunting prospect of a speech where public professions of love seemed unavoidable. My first instinct was to plagiarize, preferably someone clever. John Nash was one of my idols, and his tribute to his wife as dramatized in *A Beautiful Mind* was a contender. But it seemed a tad dewy-eyed. I settled on the cynical yet lovable obsessive-compulsive novelist Melvin Udall, played masterfully by Jack Nicholson in *As Good as It Gets*. When asked by his sassy waitress girlfriend Carol to pay her a compliment, Melvin comes up with words that leave her stunned. "You make me want to be a better man," says Melvin.

It wasn't clever, not even original, but I meant it. Because the alternative version of me might have been someone Randle McMurphy finds in the *Cuckoo's Nest*. At least I can handle the truth.

■

Tencent edged out Alibaba as the eventual buyer in a deal that valued Supercell at $10.2 billion.[5] CEO Martin Lau was a former

Goldman Sachs banker and a "chill, normal dude"—a rare combination. But Martin had another attribute that proved decisive for the Supercell gamers. He was ranked in the top twenty of several hundred million *Clash of Clans* players globally. The happy Supercell gamers loved him, and for them Tencent as a winner was a foregone conclusion. The art of the deal was creating the illusion of competition, which we accomplished by making sure Martin saw me having breakfast with Joe Tsai, vice chairman and cofounder of Alibaba Group, at the Hotel Kämp in Helsinki. Whether this was worth an extra few hundred million dollars we will never know, but Tencent, the Supercell team, and SoftBank were all pleased with the outcome: a happy ending in a happy place.

As for the French Laundry, I'm sure the food was nice, but I don't remember a thing. Despite her impressive powers of recall, neither did Maya.

■

Finding the next $10 billion was deceptively complicated. This was a manageable 8 percent of the $120 billion public float of the New York Stock Exchange–listed Alibaba, but a signal to Wall Street that SoftBank was anything less than bullish would not be well received, and the prospect of SoftBank unloading or even dribbling its entire holding would depress Alibaba's share price. Operating with stealth was essential. Moreover, SoftBank was contractually reliant on cooperation with Alibaba management to comply with US securities law to sell and market Alibaba stock to investors.

As with Supercell, diplomacy was required, best done in person, in this case in Hong Kong.

Nikesh and I flew out to Hong Kong to meet with Alibaba's Joe Tsai. Flying with Nikesh wasn't quite the same as having my wife for a companion, but he was my closest friend, and we were fortunate to have each other as company. Moreover, the prospect of visiting Hong Kong, my home for much of the nineties, was always exciting.

During my first visits in the early 1990s, the adrenaline fired upon arrival at Kai Tak Airport in Kowloon, ranked by aviators as the most dangerous major airport in the world.[6] From the cockpit it must have felt like flying into a mountain, but once the distinctive red and white pattern on Checkerboard Hill was identified visually, the pilot had to make a perfectly timed sharp manual right turn to commence a low-altitude approach, threading the plane between Kowloon City's teeming vertical neighborhoods, close enough to wave at the children on the balconies, even smell the garlic and peanut oil aromas emanating from the woks in the tiny kitchens. The relief upon landing was temporary; the sensory assault as you navigated from Kowloon toward Hong Kong Island reminded you that this was the one city that made New York look sleepy.

We were there in 1997 when Prince Charles, with typically understated British pageantry, handed over the keys to President Jiang Zemin on a rainy evening, and nothing was ever the same. Ironically, Milton (Friedman)'s paradise found, his capitalist ideal, became a stifling extension of the Mandarin dragon's tail. Like New York, Hong Kong was never a friendly city, but now the taxi drivers seemed ruder, the salespeople less likely to smile. The new airport was indistinguishable from Heathrow's Terminal 5, a metaphor for the demise of Hong Kong's quirky Canto-colonial shabby chic.

We stayed at the slick Upper House Hotel in the glittering Pacific Place shopping mall, overlooking the harbor, and met Joe Tsai for dinner in the private room at the top-floor restaurant. Dinner for three at a round table that seated twelve wasn't exactly intimate, but unlike my breakfast with Joe in Helsinki, confidentiality was paramount. I booked the room in my name (first name only) with no mention of SoftBank or Alibaba.

Joe Tsai straddles two worlds with equal aplomb. While of

Taiwanese origin and his wealth created in mainland China, his résumé fits the profile of a *Mayflower* descendent—Lawrenceville, Yale College, Yale Law School, followed by tony New York law firm Sullivan & Cromwell. Along with Masa's old Gulfstream jet, Joe would later purchase the Brooklyn Nets while indulging his preppie passion for lacrosse via his ownership of teams in San Diego and Las Vegas. Joe is as passionate about promoting a better understanding of China as he is about lacrosse, and toward this end, he did what billionaires frequently do when they need a podium. He bought a newspaper. Joe brokered Alibaba's purchase of Hong Kong's *South China Morning Post* and became its chairman.

In person, Joe is thoughtful and soft-spoken, his casual wardrobe and demeanor suggestive of the tax lawyer that he was rather than the technology entrepreneur and media tycoon that he became. As we explained our motivation and objectives, his responses were thoughtful and analytical. Nikesh and I both liked Joe, and developed a relationship that evolved into a partnership as we later approached Yahoo! with a joint takeover proposal. SoftBank disposing of its Alibaba stake was a discussion Joe had anticipated, and he had an intriguing strategy to get the stock into friendly hands. Joe suggested Nikesh and I fly to Beijing, where he arranged for us to meet with potential quasi-sovereign buyers of Alibaba stock.

Despite my dealings there in the nineties, I had no nostalgic memories of Beijing, and unlike European cities, my aversion had everything to do with the place. Perhaps there was an Abhimanyu factor at work. Since China's treacherous attack on India in 1962 coincided with my time in utero, my mother must have heard some vile invective hurled at the Chinese. And unlike most European cities, English was not the lingua franca, which made every interaction tedious. It wasn't all bad. We hosted a memorable client event in Beijing—*Turandot* performed in the Forbidden City with Zubin Mehta conducting.

My business dealings in China left me with a cynical mistrust of China's unique brand of state capitalism. In 1999–2000, I worked with the Ministry of Communications to create China Unicom and to take the company public, raising almost $5 billion in its New York Stock Exchange debut. Creating China Unicom was a matter of multiple state decrees—licenses were awarded, pricing was mandated to guarantee profitability, executives were seconded from China Mobile. It seemed contrived, reversible on a whim.

Moreover, SoftBank, like other international investors, did not actually own shares in Alibaba. To circumvent restrictions on foreign ownership, investors owned shares in a Cayman Islands shell company known as a "variable interest entity," which had the legal rights to profits earned by Alibaba. But the enforceability of these claims was untested. Beijing could go full-on communist and denounce this VIE structure, or go laissez-faire Adam Smith and open up its tech sector to Google, Facebook, and Amazon. Either way, Alibaba shareholders were vulnerable.

This was always my concern when I thought about SoftBank's Alibaba stake, a fear that became reality in 2021–22 when Beijing decided that its tech giants, which had dominated in a market closed to Google and Facebook, needed to have their wings clipped. Outspoken Alibaba chairman Jack Ma "disappeared" for several months, and on October 24, 2022, on the first trading day immediately following the National Congress of the Chinese Communist Party, Alibaba stock plummeted by over 10 percent as markets adjusted to expectations of a "less economically liberal" future for China.

The Chinese team were friendly enough, but they were as return focused as any hedge fund manager. In Beijing as in New York, everyone wants a bargain. But the Chinese overplayed their hand, for we were not distressed sellers.

Our visit to Beijing was productive in a different way. Joe set us up to meet with Cheng Wei, founder and CEO of DiDi

Dache, the ridesharing app battling with Uber for the Chinese market. DiDi, backed by Alibaba, had already merged with Kuaidi Dache, backed by Tencent, to create a single Chinese rival to Uber. Over breakfast at the St. Regis, Nikesh shook hands with the youthfully earnest Cheng Wei on what would be the first of SoftBank's multitranche $11 billion investment in DiDi, a commitment that cemented SoftBank's status as the backer of the global anti-Uber coalition with investments in India, Southeast Asia, and now China.

The reverberations of the deal were felt in San Francisco. Travis Kalanick wisely decided not to mess with Masa's unpredictability—that "crazy guy" factor at work again. Uber threw in the towel and agreed to merge its Chinese business with DiDi, receiving a 17.7 percent stake in "new DiDi," which now had a monopoly on the ride-hailing business in China.[7]

This sequence of mergers (DiDi and Kuaidi and eventually Uber China) would be unthinkable from an antitrust perspective in most markets, and was an irresistible incentive for Masa in later years as he further increased SoftBank's stake in DiDi via the Vision Fund. But as DiDi and SoftBank would learn, all it took was for a whimsical bureaucrat in Beijing to whisper "Dracarys!" and your business would be engulfed in dragon fire. In August 2022, in another decisive attempt to curtail the power of Chinese big tech, the government banned the DiDi app for "collecting user data illegally."

As for disposition of our Alibaba stake, we worked with Joe and a team of bankers to come up with a practical solution—a combination of a $3.4 billion equity divestment and a $6.6 billion exchangeable bond issue.[8] The buyers of the equity were the Alibaba Partnership, led by Jack Ma and Joe Tsai, and the Government of Singapore Investment Corporation (GIC). The buyers of the exchangeable bond, organized by Morgan Stanley and Deutsche Bank, were public market investors who received an annual coupon of 5.75 percent for three years. At the end of three years, instead of (cash) repayment of principal (like a conventional bond), investors had the option to receive either a fixed number of Alibaba shares or equivalent value in cash, with the number of shares calculated at a price 17.5 percent higher than the price at the time of offering.

I enjoyed the geeky complexity of these transactions, and the neat elegance of matching investors who wanted both exposure to Alibaba stock and current income with SoftBank's desire to sell shares at a price higher than today's value. This was investment banking at its best, and that rarest of phenomena—a win-win rather than a zero-sum outcome. We preserved the element of surprise right through to the public announcement, and the deal went as well as I might have hoped.

Masa Son now had a war chest to play with; the games could begin in earnest. And he had an elephant deal in mind, a business he had coveted for many years.

These two seamlessly executed deals elevated me. James Gorman, the chairman and CEO of Morgan Stanley, sent a nice congratulatory note. Masa, always encouraged by Nikesh, now insisted on my inclusion in every discussion. Which felt great, but had an ugly downside. Unbeknownst to me, a cat and mouse game had begun. I was the mouse.

9

THIS AGGRESSION WILL NOT STAND, MAN

She was a sleek twin-engine beast, her exterior painted a muted white with gray trim, her tail number NG251GV. A beauty like this needed a name, something feline or reptilian. Like Cougar or Viper. But Cougar was redolent of middle-aged sexual frustration, so I settled on Viper. Soon "wheels-up at 10 A.M. on Viper" rolled off my tongue the way "I'm taking the Jubilee line to Canary Wharf" had in a prior incarnation.

Viper was SoftBank's Gulfstream G550, initially assigned exclusively to Nikesh, and my Homeric galley for much of this odyssey.

Viper's interiors, a soothing combination of light beige leather and honey bird's eye maple, were tastefully specified by Masa. The spacious cabin included a separate sleeping chamber with an en suite half bath, a dining or meeting area, another half bath, and four fully reclining seats, each supplied with a burgundy Loro Piana cashmere blanket. The stewardess Junko-san (soft-spoken, cultured, middle-aged) spoke five languages and could debate Bordeaux versus Burgundy and Tolstoy versus Dostoyevsky with equal fluency. She was my kind of traveling companion—she loved to fly because it gave her time to read.

Being dropped off and picked up at the aircraft was the highlight, typically by a shiny black long-wheelbase S-Class Mercedes, the chauffeur in secret service attire. I felt like Jagger bounding up the airstairs, waving at my adoring groupies gathered on the tarmac. Gone were all my early misgivings, now I was living the dream, a legend in my own mind.

Maya tormented me with visions of my carbon emissions choking off emperor penguins in Antarctica, but I assuaged my guilt by committing to a lifetime of electric vehicles. Besides, long-haul multidestination trips take a toll on aging bodies. Nikesh and I once started out in San Francisco and arrived in Tokyo five days later via New Delhi, Beijing, and Hong Kong, with packed schedules at each destination. Viper and Junko-San took much of the edge off: as far as flying goes, this was as good as it gets.

Or maybe not.

While Viper was what sweet dreams are made of, she was a hand-me-down from Masa. His new chariot was forty-eight inches longer, three inches taller, twelve inches wider, thirty knots faster. The Gulfstream G650ER. (The ER stands for Extended Range—seven hundred nautical miles farther.)

I have no clue about knots or nautical miles, but here's what I do know. There is always something or someone who is bigger, faster, flies farther, or lasts longer.

■

It was Thursday, January 21, 2016. Nikesh and I had flown in together from Delhi, arriving in Tokyo early in the morning on a bright and crisp winter day. Upon checking in at the Conrad, I realized our first meeting was a couple of hours away. Rather than an hour of gym torture, I decided to explore the scenic Hamarikyu Gardens across from the hotel.

I'd done some homework on Hamarikyu, and made my way to the centerpiece of this sanctuary—the recently rebuilt lakeside Matsu-no-Ochaya (Pine Tea House). The original structure, used by the Tokugawa shogun to entertain guests, was destroyed in the high-altitude carpet bombing of Tokyo in World War II.

If history is written by victors and soul-searching is a pastime for losers, there is no better example than Operation Meetinghouse—the firebombing of Tokyo on the night of March 9, 1945. Over one hundred thousand civilians died, more than at Hiroshima and Nagasaki, greater than the casualties at the Somme, D-Day, and Gettysburg, making it the deadliest night in wartime history.[1] Dresden at least had Kurt Vonnegut to cry out for its massacred children. I did not see a plaque here to commemorate the dead, but it was impossible to gaze upon this Zen serenity without the conjoint image of two thousand tons of incendiary bombs dropping on this and other Tokyo neighborhoods, the napalm devouring the wooden structures, the flames rising skyward, dancing madly on the trees and the water.

■

I arrived at Masa's office at 10 A.M., and after the usual exchange of pleasantries with Fumiko-san and Suki-san, entered the conference room expecting a relaxed catch-up discussion with Masa, Nikesh, and Ron. Instead I interrupted a meeting I had not been invited to. Ken Siegel was seated at the boardroom table, along with Masa, Nikesh, and Ron. The blinds were drawn, as always, the room dimly lit. Masa was at the head, facing his Ryōma portrait. Nikesh sat pensively to Masa's immediate right, his brow furrowed, with Ron in his customary position to Masa's left.

Masa nodded in welcome, while Ron smiled warmly and invited me to sit next to him. Unusually, Nikesh ignored me.

All seemed engrossed in the contents of a printed document. Except Masa, who played impatiently with his Apple Pencil—innocent and white, unaware of its future role in reshaping technology investing—scribbling on his leather-encased iPad.

"Maybe we should give Alok a chance to read the letter," suggested Ron.

I nodded gratefully, while Nikesh finally raised his head. "Yes, he should read it. There's a paragraph about you, Mr. Sama," he said, smiling unconvincingly.

It was a letter, dated January 20, 2016, addressed to the board of directors of SoftBank Group, on the letterhead of a New York law firm, Boies Schiller Flexner LLP. *Boies Schiller? Sounds familiar.*

"It's a serious firm, Alok," said Ken, reading my mind. "If it came from anyone else I'd be inclined to ignore, but David Boies is a player."

He explained that David Boies represented the federal government (successfully) in the historic antitrust case against Microsoft, and Al Gore (unsuccessfully) in the landmark Supreme Court *Bush v. Gore* case. (Later, Boies's public profile, bordering on notoriety, would increase as a result of his firm's controversial tactics representing Harvey Weinstein and Theranos.)

I sped through the letter. It was signed by Michael L. Schwartz, partner, and unusual in many respects. Boies Schiller was an American law firm writing to the board of a company organized under Japanese law. Moreover, there was no suggestion of legal transgression, so why was a law firm involved in the first place? Instead, much of the content was invective directed at Nikesh, organized into three broad categories.

First was conflict of interest, specifically Nikesh's legacy role as a senior advisor to Silver Lake, the well-regarded technology private equity firm. The letter also criticized Nikesh for poor investment performance and "questionable transactions," referring specifically to SoftBank's investment in an Indian start-up,

Housing .com. Finally, Nikesh's compensation was described as "alarming and intolerable."

The ask was an investigation within sixty days, failing which the anonymous shareholders whom Boies Schiller purportedly represented would resort to legal action.

I searched for my name, but trepidation turned to relief as it became obvious I wasn't the target. The brief paragraph about me seemed an afterthought, the main objection related to my compensation as a consultant prior to being engaged as a full-time SoftBank employee.

The tone of the letter was bombastic, the threats hollow and the contents complete and utter claptrap. Conflicts can be hairy, but the key to both sound corporate governance and ethical behavior is transparency. Nikesh's role as a senior advisor to Silver Lake was timely disclosed to SoftBank. Moreover, this was a case of "no harm, no foul," and if anyone should be concerned about conflict it was Silver Lake.

Challenging Nikesh's credentials seemed churlish. He had his detractors (arrogance was a recurring critique) but there was no denying his Google track record and status as one of the most sought-after technology executives. The Housing.com investment was indeed a write-off, but this is an occupational hazard in venture investing. For every ten investments, some will be duds, others middling successes; you invest hoping one might be a blockbuster. Moreover, it takes time for results to unfold, and after only eighteen months, it was too early to judge Nikesh's investment prowess. (Among his early deals, a $1 billion investment in Coupang, a South Korean e-commerce business, was a multiple bagger, the returns overwhelming the relatively modest $100 million write-off on Housing.com.)

My compensation as a consultant had been reviewed by two members of SoftBank's board, Ron and Nikesh, my engagement letter drafted by SoftBank's external counsel Morrison Foerster. Had SoftBank engaged an investment banking firm to perform identical services, it would have paid substantially more.

There was something troubling here, and it wasn't the issues raised. My engagement letter and compensation were a private matter. *How did these people get this information?*

Shareholders have the right to question the performance of executives, who act as their agents. But the conflicts inherent in this "agency problem" are minimized when managers are also owners. CEO Masayoshi Son was SoftBank's largest shareholder by far, his ownership increasing over time from 20 percent to over 30 percent based on the company's share buyback programs. Nikesh himself had made an impressive investment in SoftBank stock—$482 million,[2] likely the biggest purchase of employer stock by a professional manager. An independent research analyst would later note that "picking on Nikesh's performance seems entirely arbitrary. I'm inclined to trust Masa's judgment and Nikesh has already shown his commitment with the share purchase."[3]

Moreover, there was no mention of who these mysterious shareholders might be or how much stock they owned. Legitimate activist shareholders might engage law firms but do not hide behind them. Their proposals involve changes in strategy or capital structure, rarely personal attacks on executives.

Masa wanted to move on. He had complete confidence in Nikesh's integrity and would rather we spend our time discussing business. The only reason to take the letter seriously was the Boies Schiller imprimatur and David Boies's intimidating reputation. To protect SoftBank from future—frivolous—lawsuits, we agreed an internal investigation involving an independent law firm was required. Nikesh suggested going a step further and engaging not one but two independent law firms, an American and a Japanese, to look into the matter and report findings to a subcommittee of independent directors of SoftBank's board.

The findings would exonerate Nikesh, the investigation a matter of tidy housekeeping and proper hygiene. But there was a downside. Few understood media better than Nikesh. Like most public figures, his digital footprint was curated. The mere existence of an investigation, if it became public, would be damaging. We thought this risk could be managed by dealing with the matter confidentially. We were wrong.

■

When a man of Masa's refined sensibility tells you he has a favorite chef in Tokyo, it gets your attention. This honor belonged to Kasamoto Tatsuaki, and that night we headed to Tatsuaki-san's own newly opened tempura restaurant, Takiya.

I was skeptical at first. Wasn't tempura simply deep-fried shrimp and veggies? Then I sank my teeth into Tatsuaki-san's wagyu beef wrapped in shiso leaf, lightly tempura'd in a paper-thin crust, served with white truffle salt. The velvety Hokkaido sea urchin in nori leaf, also delicately batter fried, was equally divine. The most devout brahmin or committed rabbi would struggle in the face of such temptation. It helped that Tatsuaki-san was a showman. He described the aphrodisiacal power of the matsutake mushroom as he briefly dipped it in the batter, then thrust it into the sizzling safflower oil, which according to him lowers cholesterol. Better sex, longer life, what more could anyone want?

Nikesh was preoccupied. After dinner, he suggested a nightcap at the Conrad. We settled into the lobby bar, with its double height ceiling and glass windows overlooking the bright lights of Ginza. We ordered drinks—rum and coke for him, a Yamazaki whisky on the rocks for me. It was only 9 P.M., and the bar was still lively. The pianist (gloomy, middle-aged, receding hairline) was playing Keith Jarrett, his hands more expressive than the unsmiling visage. I'm a fan of Jarrett's improvised blend of jazz and classical, but it seemed a downbeat choice for the setting.

I noticed a woman seated at the bar, legs crossed, black sleeveless cocktail dress riding high on her thighs. She was tall, possibly South Indian, frizzy but stylized jet black hair cascading down to her shoulders, a pair of substantial gold hoop earrings guarding her slender neckline like sentinels. Her posture was upright, despite being perched on a stool, displaying chiseled features in profile. You would have noticed her anywhere, but at this glorified Hilton in a Japanese urban business complex, she stood out.

She smiled at us when we sat down, but Nikesh didn't notice. We did this drink-after-work routine often, frequently joined by other colleagues, but tonight was different. In this rare moment of vulnerability, Nikesh needed a friend. The gratuitous challenge to his integrity was hurtful, his formidable aura diminished. Both of us suffered from an unhealthy smartphone addiction, but now Nikesh's oversized Google Pixel was on the table in front of us.

I reassured him that an internal investigation, its findings a foregone conclusion, would put the matter to rest. Ken Siegel had already enlisted Shearman & Sterling and the Japanese firm Anderson Mōri to lead the probe, and a board subcommittee had been created to oversee the lawyers. But the investigation wasn't the issue. It was the hurtful realization that someone was out to damage him.

I saw Ayesha's photo flashing on the screen of his mobile device lying on the table. Presumably she had just woken up in Atherton and was responding to messages about the day's events. Nikesh picked up his phone and rose. After chatting briefly while standing in the lobby, he waved to me and started walking toward the elevator bank, evidently retiring for the evening.

The woman in black was headed in my direction. *She wants to talk to me?* This never happens, it's like I have a permanently illuminated off-duty sign on my head.

Up close, the combination of black mascara and crimson lipstick seemed overdone, her features more hardened than chiseled.

"Excuse me, was that Nikesh Arora with you?" she asked, her voice raspy. A smoker's voice.

The accent seemed American, but she pronounced Nikesh's name with perfect intonation. Not "Ni-kesh" but "Ni-kaish," not "A-raw-ra" but "A-row-ra." Had I been worthy of her attention, it would be "A-loke" rather than "A-lock." *Yes, definitely Indian.*

I answered affirmatively, bemused. I knew Nikesh had a following, but among tech bros in Bangalore, not women in Tokyo.

"Do you think he's coming back?" she asked, anxiously.

"I don't think so. Can I help? I'm happy to pass on a message if you want."

"No, no, never mind," she said, suddenly flustered. "Good night."

Just like that, she was gone.

I lingered awhile to finish my drink. The gloomy pianist was still playing Keith Jarrett, but this was the least strange thing about the day.

I didn't make anything of the encounter at the time. Three years later *The Wall Street Journal* described a botched "honey trap" targeting Nikesh. According to *The Journal*'s sources, Nikesh's hotel room had been "rigged with cameras in an attempt to obtain compromising images."

■

On April 21, 2016, Bloomberg News broke a story with the headline "SoftBank Investors Call for Internal Probe of No. 2 Arora." The Boies Schiller letter had been circulated to news outlets globally. Publications like *The Journal* or the *Financial Times* wouldn't touch the story; they were appropriately circumspect about the agenda. SoftBank and Masa issued strongly worded statements supporting Nikesh, but the damage was done. Multiple news wires, particularly in India where journalistic standards can be lax, lapped up the gossipy story of anonymous investors "lashing out" at a highflier. Never mind that Boies Schiller had already dropped "the case," presumably because there wasn't one. Never mind that the investor who stepped forward to accept responsibility was not a credible institution but an unknown forty-six-year-old Swiss national named Nicolas Giannakopoulos, who claimed—without proof—to own "a bit more" than $100,000 worth of shares of SoftBank and Sprint. *Who is this guy?* Partners at Boies Schiller, like supermodels, don't get out of bed for less than $1,000 an hour, and David Boies's billing rate was more than twice that. The legal tab could easily exceed the value of Giannakopoulos's investment, which made no economic sense—Giannakopoulos had to be a front.

In a different era, today's news became tomorrow's fish wrapping, but now the cyberstink persists, your reputation a matter (ironic in Nikesh's case) of what comes up in a Google search. People can, in Shakespearean fashion, filch from you your good name, robbing you and making themselves rich in the bargain. Obscure websites are willing to publish salacious headlines suggesting corporate scandal when none exist, frequently for a price. Having a reputable law firm burnish innuendo with flowery legal language provides enough of a patina of respectability to persuade even reputable wire services like Bloomberg News to get on the bandwagon. You want to trash someone's reputation? As my favorite Vietnam vet Walter Sobchak says, "There are ways, Dude. You don't wanna know about it, believe me."

If this Giannakopoulos guy is a hired gun, who sanctioned the hit? Was this a personal vendetta, a jilted lover? Could it be a bruised ego, someone—there were many—Nikesh chewed out in a meeting? Perhaps hell hath no fury like a banker scorned.

Or was it a business gripe? A few weeks ago Uber's chief business officer had dropped by to see Nikesh and me. I met him socially several years later and found him likable, but his Uber avatar was Darth Vader–inspired. SoftBank had invested in a string of Uber's global rivals, triggering bloody competition that left all hemorrhaging cash. Sitting on a couch in Nikesh's office on that sunny morning in San Carlos, his message was that SoftBank could invest alongside Uber in ridesharing globally, or else "we will destroy you." We assumed he meant a price war, but that just made us smile. These Uber guys might be smart, but they didn't get Masa's smart versus crazy thing. *Was something more sinister intended?*

Things were getting curiouser and curiouser.

10

CURVEBALL

We had a problem, similar to what an American suburban two-car family encounters occasionally, except that instead of a Chevy Suburban and Honda Accord, ours involved two Gulfstream jets. Viper had broken down, and its big sister, Masa's G650ER, was being serviced. Which left us with a vexing problem—the proletarian drudgery of short-haul commercial travel. Fortunately, the resourceful Tanaka-san made sure we had the use of the VIP private terminal at Haneda. A shiny black Toyota minivan drove us straight to the Japan Airlines aircraft just as the pilot was revving up the engines. Contact with the great unwashed was minimized, and the two-hour flight proceeded without incident.

Our destination was Masa's hometown, Fukuoka. In 2005, Masa did what some billionaires do when they wish to cock a snook at the athletic kid who mocked them or the cheerleader who spurned them in high school. He bought the local sports team. In this case the baseball franchise—Fukuoka Hawks. But Masa always had a unique angle. Not one involving adolescent complexes or Billy Beane–type data analytics, but a canny branding move that became a cornerstone of SoftBank's financing strategy. The team was renamed SoftBank Hawks, and SoftBank's locally issued yen bonds dubbed "SoftBank Hawks Bonds." In this, Masa embraced Nietzsche's observation that "what things are called is unspeakably more important than what they are." Targeting retail investors, SoftBank raised over $30 billion at rates below what a comparably rated issuer might pay and accounted for the majority of *all* issuance in the Japanese corporate bond market.[1] (It's as if Robert Kraft decided to borrow money by issuing "Patriot Bonds" to football fans. Because they love Tom Brady and America, investors accept a 6 percent rather than 10 percent yield.) Baseball fans loved these bonds, and SoftBank found an inexhaustible source of cheap capital. This was Masa at his irrepressible best—happiness for everyone!

It helped that the team's fortunes soared in sync with its mercurial owner, as the Hawks beat the Hanshin Tigers to win the Japan Series in 2014 and vanquished the Tokyo Yakult Swallows the following year for their second consecutive championship. Now, we were on our way to support the Hawks as they faced off against the Hokkaido Nippon-Ham Fighters in the third game of a tight playoff series.

We arrived in Fukuoka three hours before the main event, and Masa found himself in the awkwardly unfamiliar role of tour guide as we strolled around the medieval Hakata Old Town in Fukuoka's historic district.

It was a pleasant early-summer afternoon, and while Hakata had none of the mystical quality of Kyoto's Philosopher's Path, an accomplished guide might have made these shrines come alive, attached a story to every Buddha statue, perhaps arranged an "accidental" encounter with one of many aging peasants peddling flavored potato crackers. But our host was obsessively focused, as he had been on the flight and in the van, feverishly flipping through slides on his iPad. When a deal was in his sights, Masa went at it with a persistence that reminded me of my golden retriever Ellie chasing a squirrel in Hyde Park. This wasn't just any deal, this was Masa's obsession, his precious, codenamed "Adam" for the biblical association (the information revolution began with a computer chip?) or because the company's name started with an A, nobody really knew.

■

British chip designer Arm Holdings Plc used to be the most important company few had heard of.

At the heart of all computing is the microchip, a set of electronic circuits on a small piece of flat silicon. Intel and increasingly TSMC (Taiwan Semiconductor Manufacturing Company) are the two companies most closely associated with chip production. Arm's business, however, does not involve chip fabrication. Its employees are software engineers who design energy-efficient microprocessors essential for portable devices like iPhones. These patented designs are then used by the chip manufacturers, including Intel and TSMC, who typically pay Arm an upfront licensing fee and ongoing royalty payments based on sales of chips that use Arm's proprietary chip architecture.

In 2016, over 95 percent of smartphones contained multiple Arm-designed chips. Because of the energy and cost efficiency of Arm's design, technologists expected chips reliant on Arm's technology to dominate a future world of connected devices, called the "Internet of Things" (IoT).

Arm was headquartered in Cambridge (the one in Blighty), and listed on the London Stock Exchange. Despite its status as the crown jewel of British technology, Arm was global in every sense. Its customers included Intel and Texas Instruments in the US, Fujitsu and NEC in Japan, TSMC and MediaTek in Taiwan, Samsung in Korea. While the US was Arm's largest market and its CEO Simon Segars was based in San Jose, almost 20 percent of Arm's revenues came from China.

Arm's unique position in the global technology ecosystem depended not just on its intellectual property but also on its neutrality. Smartphones running on competing Apple iOS and Google Android operating systems relied on Arm designs, as did rival chip manufacturers in Shanghai or Silicon Valley.

A market position such as that enjoyed by Arm is usually competed away, but Arm straddled the Goldilocks zone of profitability masterfully—not high enough to compel customers to seek alternatives, not low enough to invite pushback from its public shareholders. Arm delivered the Holy Grail of predictable growth and consistent profitability, which also made it attractive to private equity buyers except that Arm shares were too expensive, the best form of defense against takeovers. Potential strategic interlopers like Google or Apple, who might have paid a premium, realized that a violation of Arm's neutrality would kill the golden goose. And then there was the geopolitical dimension. Arm was a national treasure, and persuading Her Majesty's government to allow a foreign takeover was as politically charged as giving up the Kohinoor diamond or the Elgin Marbles.

Like Switzerland, Arm seemed remote and impregnable. Except to this one guy on the north shore of Kyushu Island, now obsessively strolling the blackened cobblestone streets of his hometown. I watched him, bemused, as he brandished his Apple Pencil as if writing on an imaginary whiteboard, with the mad passion of Bernstein conducting a Mahler symphony.

A year earlier we had dissuaded Masa from making a move on Arm, on the grounds that a $30–35 billion acquisition was unaffordable. But with $20 billion of sale proceeds from Supercell and Alibaba, Masa was Arm'ed and dangerous.

Masa's central thesis was that markets underestimated how transformative the IoT revolution would be. While Arm might be expensive based on its fifteen billion chips shipped in 2015, he argued it was cheap based on over one trillion chips sold annually in a future world of ubiquitous robots and autonomous cars. He saw potential for raising prices, too, based on improvements in chip performance, and while smartphone growth might plateau, this would be offset by smarter smartphones using even more Arm chips.

As always, Masa had an original idea, a characteristic "crazy vision." Future Arm chips would have embedded narrowband connectivity, allowing Arm to partner with phone companies—including the two controlled by SoftBank in Japan and the US, and later an alliance with Vodafone to cover Europe—to provide revenue-generating services such as cybersecurity. Over time, Arm would become the centerpiece of SoftBank's strategy to reinvent itself around the IoT and AI, just as it had with the mobile internet almost ten years prior.

Through much of Masa's animated pitch, Nikesh remained aloof, his intermittent deep breaths and rolling eyes suggesting a disdain he could not suppress. This wasn't unusual. Like most married couples, Nikesh and Masa had their disagreements. Nikesh and I had discussed Arm privately. He liked the business, but for him, buying Arm was an expensive "bet the company" deal—a company he hoped to inherit in the immediate future.

▪

The Hawks versus Ham Fighters at Fukuoka was the first and only baseball game I've been to. It's not that I didn't care for American sport. When I arrived in the US, the colorful spectacle of brawny men in tights maneuvered strategically on a football field was irresistible. Soon I was as consumed with the fortunes of Joe Montana's 49ers as I had been with the exploits of the Indian cricket team. I've always favored traditional five-day test match cricket rather than the buzzy single-evening T20 variant, so the slow pace wasn't an issue. More a case of not investing time to appreciate the subtleties and history that make baseball as much a connoisseur's game as cricket. Regrettably, at some point it became too embarrassing to ask people to explain line drives and fly balls.

Fukuoka might have been an opportunity to change this, but my only memories of the evening are of events outside the stadium.

The evening started with a dramatic ritual in a chamber inside the home team's locker room. I stood next to Masa as we waited for the Hawks to emerge, en route to their dugout. They entered in single file. Instead of a casual high five, every player came to a standstill in front of Masa, towered above him, then bowed deeply. A loud "*hai*" exhalation was followed by a loud yet solemn proclamation in Japanese.

It sounded like a gladiator's final tribute—"Hail emperor, we who are about to die, salute you!" I asked Midori-san, an exemplary translator who worked for Goto-san, to explain.

"It is difficult to interpret, Alok-san," she responded. "Maybe you can say they are expressing their gratitude and commitment to Son-san?"

Gratitude and commitment. This is what was expected of all on the SoftBank payroll.

■

Upon entering the owner's suite, Masa's first act was to don a spiffy black SoftBank Hawks jacket, featuring a pair of sporty white stripes on each sleeve and his name, also in white, on the back. I half-jokingly asked if Nikesh and I could have one of these nifty jackets. We couldn't, but within minutes both of us had the next best thing—personalized white Hawks shirts, with NIKESH and ALOK on the back, along with Hawks baseball hats, black with bright yellow brims.

Tanaka-san took a photo capturing one of the last harmonious evenings of our three-way partnership—Masa, Nikesh, and me, in our Hawks gear, our backs turned to the camera.

Sadly, I will never be a baseball fan, but at least I got to look like one.

■

The highlight of the evening was a surprise visitor to the owner's suite—Masa's father. The senior Son-san was more Yoda-like than Yoda. If he had had a cane, he looked as if he might rest his chin on the grip end. Like Hemingway's Santiago, everything about him was old except for his eyes—black, sparkling, indomitable.

Masa's bow to the eighty-year-old Mitsunori Son was deeper and held longer than the custom, his eyes fixated humbly on the floor. No more talk of crazy visions, as Masa encouraged us to learn from his father.

While a capacity crowd of almost forty thousand watched the gladiators slugging it out on the diamond, we listened, enraptured, as the elder Son told us about a different kind of struggle. Those lively eyes crinkled and looked straight ahead at a forgotten land, beyond the ball field. He spoke no English. I hung on to every word of Midori-san's translation, knowing I was entering Masa's innermost sanctum.

Mitsunori-san came to Japan as an adolescent with his family, all of them refugees from the industrial town of Daegu in South Korea. Their nocturnal voyage traversing the Sea of Japan was fraught. Their boat almost sank, but they were rescued by a Japanese fisherman who delivered them to the coast near the seaside town of Fukuoka.

"My father changed businesses time and time again to support his family, going through mud and suffering each time," is how Masa described his father's entrepreneurial journey, but hearing this directly from Mitsunori-san was the clearest insight yet into Masa Son's extraordinary drive. It is also a sobering chime with Nvidia founder Jensen Huang's viral speech at Stanford encouraging students to experience "ample doses of pain and suffering" for their growth and success.[2]

The elder Son's first start-up was an alcohol business, manufacturing and selling *shōchū*, a distilled spirit popular with the Japanese masses. (Masa is not a drinking man—I never saw him drink more than half a glass of wine—but perhaps every sip of La Tâche reminded him of how far the Son clan had come?)

Mitsunori's face then lit up with the mischievous smile so typical of Masa when he has a new idea. The senior Son told us about his ingenious distribution strategy, which involved recruiting the chronically inebriated and offering them free booze as commission. In an initiative a McKinsey strategy consultant would describe as backward integration, Mitsunori began to raise pigs, feeding them the residue of his *shōchū* production. These fattened pigs, he explained, would be carted to the butchers in Tokyo most likely to pay top dollar.

His next move was an opportunistic diversification, from alcohol and pork to gambling. Following other Korean immigrants, he opened a pachinko parlor in Tokyo. (Pachinko is an arcade game, a cross between a pinball and slot machine, lying on the edge of legality in Japan, where gambling is outlawed.)

Eventually he added a coffee shop to his business interests, but struggled to attract customers, despite his conviction that the coffee was the best in the neighborhood. Until Masa came up with an ingenious solution.

I sometimes wondered about Masa's stories, which, if not apocryphal, were perhaps exaggerated? But Mitsunori repeated the story Masa had told us often, about how a ten-year-old Masa suggested his father give away free coffee to attract customers. It worked beyond expectations. People who came for free coffee were too polite not to buy full-priced pastries. And once they had sampled the excellent coffee, they would return as paying customers. Beyond his son's math grades, this convinced Mitsunori that his son was a genius. He laughed as he finished, affectionately and proudly wagging his finger at the beaming Masa.

Barack Obama says that "every man is trying to live up to his father's expectations or make up for their father's mistakes."[3]

Another trite aphorism that becomes a truth coming from an American president or a German philosopher, but regardless, Masa seemed decidedly in the former camp. Even at age fifty-nine, basking in the warm glow of parental approval meant more to Masa than a billion mobile subscribers or a trillion dollars under management. And observing him made me reflect on the relationship I had with my father, who never talked about mistakes he'd made or expectations he had of me. I never questioned his love, but we never had this level of engagement.

What seemed to matter as much as paternal approbation to Masa was introducing his chosen successor to his father. I caught the senior Son-san looking at Nikesh, as if sizing him up. The former pachinko wizard was like a poker player, his piercing black eyes giving nothing away as he gauged his opponent's hand.

Back in my Tokyo hotel room that night, I researched the history of Korean migration. I had heard sordid tales of "comfort women" forced into sexual slavery by the Imperial Japanese Army, but was unaware of the institutionalized nature of racism, akin to the Jim Crow laws of the American South. As a Zainichi ("living in Japan") Korean, Mitsunori Son had no voting rights, was required to be fingerprinted, and barred from all public and private sector employment. He never had a choice—fringe activities like illicit liquor and scrap recycling were his only options.

The burden of racism tends to lighten with generations, so I assumed Masa had it better. I never heard him talk about discrimination, but in a *Nikkei Asia* interview he shared childhood tales of verbal and physical abuse.[4] "I was in agony over my identity so much that I seriously contemplated taking my own life," he said.

Clichés become clichés for a reason. Poverty and racism had not broken Masa Son, just made him stronger, driving him to own the local baseball team, become the richest man in Japan, bring happiness to everyone. Hopefully, including himself.

On the return journey from Fukuoka (on the now-repaired Viper), Masa was subdued. I wondered if father and son had discussed Nikesh and the SoftBank succession. Perhaps the elder Son sensitized his brilliant son to the challenges associated with an Indian replacing a Korean as the steward of Japan's technology champion.

■

A few weeks later, in June 2016, Nikesh and I learned that the independent investigation had rendered an unequivocal and soon-to-be-announced verdict: the allegations in the Boies Schiller letter were "without merit."

That probe was like a colonoscopy, distasteful and invasive. Suited lawyers skulked around our San Carlos office, interviewing people in a glass-walled conference room. They smiled awkwardly when I passed by—they knew that I knew they were talking about me. It was nice to have this behind us. Well, maybe not behind, perhaps flung to the side.

Nikesh and I were expected in Tokyo the week of June 20 for the SoftBank annual shareholder meeting. We decided to spend a long weekend in Hawaii en route, where Nikesh arranged for us to stay at a friend's home in the Kuki'o development in Kona.

Kuki'o is where Silicon Valley hitters come to vacation. The mood here is Hawaiian chill rather than Hamptons chic, but while cocktail umbrellas and bright floral shirts rule, real estate prices are in the same nosebleed territory. Prime residential lots run into eight figures, and your neighbors might include Michael Dell.

Maya and Ayesha joined us, as did Alya and Nikesh and Ayesha's firstborn, a delightful toddler named Kiaan.

■

George Roberts hosted us for dinner on our first evening, starting with a sundowner in his ranch-style home on a promontory surrounded by the Pacific, followed by dinner on the beach at the nearby Four Seasons. George and his cousin Henry Kravis pioneered the leveraged buyout business on Wall Street in the eighties. I was a junior associate at Morgan Stanley at the time, watching in awe as they pulled off the $25 billion buyout of RJR Nabisco, the landmark deal that was the zenith of eighties leveraged excess and inspired *Barbarians at the Gate.*

George was soft-spoken, cerebral and in his seventies. He had no agenda in hosting us but gave us his undivided attention, spending more time talking to Maya than he did to me. A good call from someone with a knack for making the right bets. He served a delectable Château Cos d'Estournel with dinner, also an excellent choice. Like Masa, George favored French refinement, albeit Bordeaux rather than Burgundy. But while there were no limits on his Amex card, George picked a fine wine costing a tenth of La Tâche. Which made sense; George Roberts was a value investor.

George seemed more interested in discussing Indian spirituality than nostalgic reminiscences of a Wall Street warrior. We talked about the four stages of life prescribed by the Vedas, particularly the transition to *vanaprastha*, the forest hermit stage when a man has satisfied all his urges for *artha* (wealth) and *kama* (sex). *Vanaprastha* began at fifty for Vedic man, but is likely pushed back by at least a decade for millennium man.

It was a curious discussion to have with a Wall Street titan, for whom the power and money game never ends. The classy George was never a barbarian, but perhaps now he was at a different gate?

Jerry Yang invited us to his home (modernist, oceanfront, carved into volcanic rock) the following night. When Yahoo! was everyone's portal to the World Wide Web and valued at $125 billion, Jerry was as much of a titan in the Valley as Elon Musk became two decades later. In his choice of backronym—"Yet Another Hierarchical Officious Oracle," with an exclamation for emphasis—Jerry also led Elon in proving that Valley founders, if not actually funny, are indeed "different." In 1998, Yahoo! famously turned down an opportunity to buy what became one of the most powerful companies in history for the price of a studio apartment in Manhattan: Google for $1 *million.*[5] In the same grand tradition, in 2006 Yahoo! CEO Terry Semel fumbled a deal to buy Facebook for $1 billion and then YouTube for a bargain $1.65 billion.[6] Two years later, now installed as CEO, Jerry rejected Microsoft's offer to buy Yahoo! itself for $45 billion, only to see Yahoo!'s value plummet as the business imploded in the face of Google's onslaught. The fate of Yahoo!, its business eventually sold to bottom-fisher Apollo in 2023, is the ultimate case study in a truth universally unacknowledged in the Valley—savvy deal jocks create as much value as coder tech bros.

Yahoo!'s serendipitous $1 billion investment for 40 percent of Alibaba provided some redemption, but a lesser man might have allowed errors of this magnitude to destroy him. Jerry, however, is that rarest of breeds on Wall Street or in the Valley—a man at peace with himself, now living his admirable best life as a philanthropist, mentor to young entrepreneurs, and chairman of the Stanford University Board of Trustees.

In Jerry's eat-in kitchen, I was seated next to a wiry bespectacled guy in standard tech bro garb: black T-shirt, blue jeans, and sneakers. "Call me Max," he said.

In a typical Valley dinnertime conversation, Max started to discuss Elon Musk's theory that we are all living in a simulation. *Am I a nonplayer character in this simulation?* He then launched into a mathematical proof that there was a greater than 50 percent probability that this must be so. He was dead serious, and I couldn't question his logic. I let him finish, then stared at him and responded with my best Jeff Bridges impersonation.

"What the fuck you talking about, man?"

This could have gone either way, but fortunately Max was equally obsessed with that pot-smoking hippie from Venice Beach who calls himself the Dude. (Or His Dudeness, Duder, or, you know, El Duderino, if you're not into the whole brevity thing.) We moved on to discuss the symphonic structure of Pink Floyd's "Shine On You Crazy Diamond," and I knew I'd found a soulmate.

"Max" was Maksymilian Rafailovych Levchin, cofounder of PayPal, former chairman of Yelp, and founder of Affirm, and I am as much in awe of his splendid name as I am of his intellect. Those Russian names—Gogol's Akaky Akakievich Bashmachkin is a favorite—make my four-letter handle seem impoverished by comparison. And kudos to the Coen brothers for creating a masterpiece that connects a Ukrainian coder guy from Kyiv to an Indian finance dude from Delhi. You may disagree, in which case, "yeah, well, you know, that's just, like, your opinion, man . . ."

■

Nanea Golf Club, founded by George Roberts and Charles Schwab, is not merely private, it is a personal club: membership is by invitation only to friends and family of George and Chuck. Nanea's fairways and greens are manicured to perfection, as if Kylie Jenner's makeup team goes to work on the grass every morning, trimming and aligning every blade with surgical precision. Not that you spend any time admiring the grass; the ocean views from virtually every point are stunning, the water, even at a distance, as visually seductive as a David Hockney swimming pool. The understated clubhouse, designed to replicate the volcanic cones in the distance, blends into the landscape while providing the same panoramic vista.

Nikesh had been invited by George Roberts to become a member, and we were fortunate to be hosted by George himself for a round, with Jerry Yang completing our four-ball.

The signature hole at Nanea is the seventeenth, a long downhill par three with the tee box set at the highest point of the golf course. Tall fescue grass, evocative of course architect David McLay Kidd's native Scotland, runs most of the way down to the green, with jaw-dropping 360-degree views of Hawaii's Big Island and the ocean beyond.

George and Jerry were both single-digit handicap golfers, and our game had been competitive, with all to play for on the last two holes. Nikesh and I were partners, and as we stood on the tee, Nikesh came over and put his arm around my shoulder. Not to discuss club selection. He just looked at me and smiled.

We had learned to play golf at municipal driving ranges and public golf courses where you waited hours for a tee time. Private golf clubs in America are a funny business, usually the exclusive domain of the male WASP establishment, like Maidstone in East Hampton, or in response occasionally predominantly Jewish, like Atlantic in nearby Bridgehampton. There's always The Bridge next door, which embraces diversity for a $1 million-plus price tag, but most Indians remain on the outside looking in.

▪

When asked about memories of the Somme offensive, British infantrymen frequently came up with the same answer—the musical chirping of birds that preceded the aural assault of booming artillery. Golf at Nanea felt that way—a sweet moment of birdsong before the madness began.

Nikesh and I flew out to Tokyo that night, and arrived relaxed, upbeat, and unsuspecting.

We made our way to the twenty-sixth floor for a scheduled 9 A.M. meeting with Ron and Masa. Masa was waiting for us in his conference room, seated at the head of the table, bundled in his olive Uniqlo puffer jacket with the temperature set at the usual stifling 25 degrees. This much, at least, was normal.

Less normal, he was alone. The e-vite from Suki-san suggested the agenda was "Finance Strategy," but the finance team was absent, as was my omnipresent trumpeter friend Nakamura-san. And instead of his customary welcoming smile, Masa's features were frozen, his eyes fixated on the Ryōma portrait across from him.

"Nikesh, I need to speak to you alone," he said, his tone as stiff as his spine, his head barely turning toward us. It was more instruction than request. Normally polite to a fault, Masa did not apologize for ejecting Ron and me from the room.

Ron and I looked at each other and silently scurried out. I retreated to Nikesh's office and waited.

He walked in an hour later, nonchalant, smiling.

"It's over," he said.

"What's over, the meeting?"

"Let's take a walk, Mr. Sama," he said, still with that enigmatic half-smile.

I followed him out of the office, in the elevator down to the building lobby, then the escalator down to a Starbucks in the basement of the building. Nikesh stared silently and calmly at his shoes, his arms crossed. It wasn't until a perky barista in a green apron announced "Nik and Al" and we had our lukewarm cappuccinos in hand that he started to speak.

He had resigned his job, effective immediately.

"What the fuck?" felt like the right response.

Nikesh seemed relaxed, but he wasn't fooling me. I remembered the smile as he put his arm across my shoulder at Nanea. He hadn't seen this coming.

"We're making an announcement later today," he said.

A press statement went out at 3 P.M., in time for the Western media to pick up for their morning headlines.

Why would a man who earned over $50 million a year suddenly decide to quit? Why walk away from the trimmings of power: a Gulfstream jet, golf with George Roberts, an invite to Davos and the Allen Sun Valley Conference?

I asked the man.

"Well, he told me he's not ready to give up the CEO role anytime soon. It's not what we agreed, but so be it. He also wants to do the Arm deal, and he's all excited about that," he responded.

Masa had publicly anointed Nikesh as his successor and privately committed that he would hand him the reins after turning sixty. This somewhat arbitrary retirement age had always been part of Masa's well-telegraphed life plan.

Divorces can be sad, particularly when you've shared happy memories with both parties. The regret notwithstanding, I understood the logic for separation. Though Masa was fifty-nine, I'd seen him bounce around a ping-pong table like a child. This was a man in rude health, SoftBank his entire life. Besides, SoftBank without Masa was like a church without Jesus, even the idea of Masa as an éminence grise implausible.

At forty-eight, Nikesh was in his prime and impatient to prove himself as top dog. He had left Google because he did not see a clear path to the top, and to be CEO-in-waiting at SoftBank indefinitely was inconsistent with Nikesh's own life plan.

In his public statement, Masa would say, "I had hoped to hand over the reins of SoftBank to him on my 60th birthday—but I feel my work is not done. I want to cement SoftBank 2.0, develop Sprint to its true potential, and work on a few more crazy ideas. This will require me to be CEO for at least another five to ten years—this is not a time frame for me to keep Nikesh waiting for the top job."[7]

Was there more to the story? Too many things felt right about this marriage for it to end so abruptly. Was race a factor? Certainly not with Masa, but as a person of color you always wonder, though sometimes it becomes an excuse. For Nikesh and me, while assimilation in the West had been challenging, neither of us believed race held us back. On the contrary, we might even have benefited from the analytical and hard-working Indian immigrant stereotype. Was Japan that different? There's so much I loved about this culture, I didn't want to believe it.

"You should stay if you want. Masa likes you," Nikesh said as we made our way back to the office. "He asked, and I said you will make your own decision."

■

Once back in the office, I noticed a yellow Post-it note from Suki-san on my desk. Masa would like to see me.

I had no idea what to expect. Nikesh's comment notwithstanding, did Masa really want me to stay? Equally, I wasn't convinced I wanted to. The last couple of years had been exciting, but this pace was unsustainable. Moreover, with Nikesh gone I was an overmatched lion tamer. What about the dragons, lurking in the shadows? They had attacked Nikesh, would I become a target now? And despite Nikesh's seeming indifference, I felt disloyal to my friend if I stayed, particularly if he had been treated unfairly.

But affection and respect featured prominently in my feelings about Masa. Perversely, given the power dynamic, I'd developed a protective instinct toward him. I also felt a responsibility to the team Nikesh and I had built, many of whom I had mentoring relationships with. And while I knew this was a setback, his nine-figure settlement would tide Nikesh over nicely before his next gig.

It was all very confusing. I thought of my conversation with Max in Jerry Yang's kitchen and channeled my inner Dude. Everything flows, sometimes you just go with it. I breezed into Masa's conference room with no plan whatsoever.

Unlike our morning encounter, Masa smiled warmly when I entered, his posture relaxed. I made tracks to my customary position, to Masa's left, one seat removed from him, leaving room for an absent Ron. *I'm not making that mistake again.*

"You can sit here," Masa said. The tone was casual, the gesture less so. He pointed to Nikesh's usual chair with his right arm fully extended, the palm turned upward.

With hindsight, it wasn't right to sit in a chair that had been Nikesh's until a few hours earlier, and I never did in subsequent meetings. But in the moment, I did without pause, for Masa Son was never easily denied.

My first question was to inquire if the smear campaign had been a factor in Nikesh's departure.

"Absolutely not," he responded, shaking his head vigorously. "I have one hundred percent confidence in Nikesh's integrity."

He had agonized over the decision, not sleeping for many nights. He loved Nikesh like a younger brother, but he was such a great talent, it was not fair to hold him back. He talked about how much he would miss Nikesh, and how he hoped I would stay.

"Masa, I came here because of Nikesh and he will always be my friend. But I believe in your vision, and I love working with you," I responded.

"I am so happy to hear that," he said, taking a deep breath. He seemed vulnerable, his relief genuine. "And we have so much fun, we drink good wine, and sometimes we play golf and you lend me your driver! But I am so happy if you will stay."

"Maybe you can talk to Ron and the two of you decide how to organize," he said.

As I prepared to leave, he added.

"Together we will change the course of humanity."

Part II

11

THE CRYSTAL BALL

The morning sun framed Simon Robey's regal presence like an incandescent halo.

"If you do exactly as I say, you *will* win," he said softly, his buttery voice redolent of his choral scholar days at Oxford.

Robey occupied a substantial upholstered armchair placed in front of an east-facing window in the sparsely decorated living room of Masa's rental home, a French Revival–style stone manse on a flat acre in the exclusive Valley enclave of Atherton. An antique stone Buddha, about four feet tall, guarded Robey's throne, somehow preserving its dignity despite the tragic loss of its nose.

Robey's thumbs were hooked under his black silk suspenders, and he looked magisterial in his crisp white shirt and navy suit. He had asked me how he should dress, and this was his interpretation of "casual."

"But you *must* do as I say," Robey added sternly, like a schoolteacher lecturing a child on the existential significance of multiplication tables. Except he was addressing Masayoshi Son, perched cross-legged on a sofa across from him. I was lounging on a neighboring couch, marveling at the pliability of Masa's hip flexors.

It had been over ten years since I'd seen my former colleague in action, but Robey had lost none of the chutzpah that had made him Morgan Stanley's star M&A banker in Europe. He had launched his own boutique advisory firm, and he was now *Sir* Simon Robey, the title enhancing his patrician aura. He'd been knighted a few weeks earlier, I explained to Masa. But when I tried to draw a parallel with Ryōma, Masa seemed offended.

"No, that is not like Ryōma. Ryōma was a peasant, a man of the people."

Masa was looking at Robey quizzically, trying to decide if Sir Suspenders—as he playfully christened him—was smart, stupid, or just plain weird. But after navigating $2 trillion of cross-border merger deals over thirty years, Robey was a confident man with a lot to be confident about. M&A specialists are to investment banking what fighter pilots are to combat, and if there was a top gun school for dealmakers in Her Majesty's realm, Robey would be the dean.

"We need someone like him," I had explained to Masa, to pull off Project Adam. Acquiring Arm would always be challenging, but in the current environment it was the equivalent of Maverick's 4G inverted dive with a MiG-28. It was five days after England's fateful Brexit own goal, David Cameron had announced his resignation, a wounded London was struggling to rouse itself for the midsummer rites at Ascot, Henley, and Wimbledon. But there is opportunity in every calamity. The pound had taken a hit, making a deal cheaper in dollar or yen terms. And perhaps the new government could be persuaded to view a SoftBank investment as a vote of confidence? We needed an insider to work the quintessential old boy network of Oxbridge-educated civil servants who run the country while the feckless politicians come and go. We needed Robey.

He was reluctant. His franchise was based on advising British companies, frequently defending against unfriendly overtures from foreign intruders. Besides, Masa was known to be intractable. I assured Simon I had Masa's trust, and persuaded him to get in front of Masa and satisfy himself.

It was only two weeks after Nikesh's departure, and this would be my first major skirmish as the king's hand. By now, Ron Fisher and I had taken charge of the West Coast team, and Maya and I were spending even more of our time in our home in San Francisco's Presidio Heights.

Joining us for this meeting was Ron and Masa's trusted investment banking advisor Jeff Sine. Jeff was also a Morgan Stanley alum. We had worked together in New York in the eighties, and with Robey in the room, as a *New York Times* article noted,[1] the Arm deal was a Morgan Stanley reunion. Jeff was an old-school banker (straightforward, discreet, avuncular), his intellect and legal training providing an edge in the quality of his advice. Like Robey, he had his own boutique advisory firm, the New York–based Raine Group.

But the spotlight this morning was on Sir Suspenders, as he took us through the subtleties of the City of London's quintessentially British Takeover Code. Like cricket, the spirit of the code is sacrosanct, and all players in the M&A game, principals and agents, are expected to abide. I'm personally a fan of the Takeover Code, as I am of cricket. The code eliminates the games people play on Wall Street, frequently to the detriment of the average investor. It pushes a prospective buyer to make a straightforward cash offer—no "funny money" in the form of complex securities—and to clarify intent publicly with limited scope for clandestine negotiations.

Robey affirmed much of what Jeff and I had already shared with Masa: be prepared to pay a substantial premium over the current $22 billion market value of the company, have the cash lined up, and get ready to move confidentially and expeditiously. Any formal approach to the company would be directed to Arm's chairman, who would negotiate on behalf of its shareholders. Robey would work his network to make sure we had the support of key constituencies—the media, the investment community, the various government agencies.

By the time we were done, I could tell Masa was impressed. Robey was no samurai, but you don't bring a baseball player to a cricket match.

■

Dinner was set on the patio under a pergola, overlooking the pool and the immaculately landscaped gardens beyond. Kato-san, who traveled everywhere with Masa, was serving, as unobtrusive as ever. The wine was—well, what else?—La Tâche, an exceptional accompaniment to the thin-crusted truffle pizza that Kato-san was slicing with the concentration of a brain surgeon.

We were at Masa's rental home, where we had met Simon Robey that morning, and were now scheduled to dine with Simon Segars, CEO of Arm. There was no formal agenda , nor was it Masa's intention to discuss a strategic transaction.

Simon was accompanied by Tom Lantzsch, Arm's head of strategy. Ironically, despite England treating Arm like a national treasure, both Simon and Tom were based in Silicon Valley rather than Arm's Cambridgeshire headquarters.

Also joining us for dinner was Ron Fisher.

Simon was a tall and taciturn Brit, about fifty, balding, athletic in build and erect in posture. He was an engineer and among Arm's first employees, starting with the company in 1991. Tom was a languid and affable Texan and, like Simon, an engineer and Arm veteran.

Tom would later tell me that both Simon and he were mystified as to why they were there. But when Masa Son invites you to dinner, you show up.

Masa was irrepressible, his excitement mounting as he talked about trillions of connected cars and robots, and Arm's central role in Tomorrowland. As CEO of a public company, Simon would not be drawn into specific projections, let alone hyperbole, but as we chatted there was obvious alignment between Masa's and Simon's thinking on Arm's strategic direction. I'd looked at transcripts of Simon's investor presentations, so no surprise there.

Over dinner, Masa asked two pointed questions. The first was technical, regarding Arm's share in the market for thirty-two-bit MCUs. An MCU, or microcontroller unit, is effectively a computer on a tiny chip designed to perform a specific function. Thirty-two-bit MCUs, relative to sixteen- or eight-bit MCUs, are high-end processors. When he heard Simon's response—over 80 percent market share—Masa looked at me and smiled. This is what he had hoped for and what we had discussed in Fukuoka. If Arm could be as successful with MCUs in devices at the edge of the IoT (autonomous cars, for example) as it was with chips designed for smartphones, Masa's crazy vision could become reality.

The second question was loaded. What would Simon do differently if he was unshackled from the cycle of quarterly earnings and pressure to deliver the predictable profits investors insisted on? Simon smiled wistfully. Yes, he would invest more aggressively in the business, and accept the hit to short-term earnings. It was the right thing for the future, but his board would not unleash him, leery of an investment community that rarely looks beyond the next quarter.

Masa and I exchanged glances: we had our hook. Founder CEOs in the Valley frequently issue super voting shares to themselves, which gives them the freedom to make unpopular bets. (Zuckerberg's relentless—most said reckless—focus on the metaverse in 2022 was a prominent example.) Simon, despite his longevity at Arm, was treated like an employee rather than a founder by his board, none of whom were technologists. Being public was holding him back.

■

"Are you out of your mind?"

Maya had a point. I was leaving home at 1 A.M. on Sunday of the July 4 weekend, flying private at 2 A.M. from London's Luton airfield to Dalaman Airport in Turkey, three days after a terrorist attack in Istanbul had left forty-five people dead. From Dalaman, I would be driven one hundred kilometers to Marmaris, a fishing village in the Turkish Riviera. Masa would fly in from Tokyo on his G650 to meet me in Marmaris. Meanwhile, Viper had been dispatched to San Jose to pick up Arm CEO Simon Segars, and all three jets were scheduled to land in Dalaman at 8 A.M. We would all freshen up at the Elegance Hotel, then have a noon lunch at the waterfront Pineapple restaurant with Arm's chairman, Stuart Chambers, who was set to sail into Marmaris on his yacht. My plane would stand by, and I assured Maya I would be home in time to host her parents and sisters for dinner that same night.

"I don't think the food at the Pineapple is that bad," I said, laughing, "and it's not like I have a choice."

It was only five days after our Atherton meetings. Robey had provided Masa with direction, and the other Simon had answered his one diligence concern; there was no stopping Masa now. I drafted a letter from Masa addressed to Stuart Chambers outlining our all-cash bid at a healthy premium to the current share price, with no antitrust or regulatory contingencies. If, for example, the Chinese government objected to the change in control, SoftBank would be compelled to either shut down or divest Arm's Chinese business, almost 20 percent of Arm's total revenues.

In military parlance our strategy was "shock and awe"; in M&A lexicon it was a "bear hug." A parallel is making an unsolicited bid to buy an unlisted expensive home you had long coveted, but had never viewed from the inside, with no financing contingency. You might find the home termite-infested or be denied the use of the pool—that risk was all yours. And since the owners had expressed no intention of selling, you needed to offer a price well above market value to get their attention.

My keystrokes, as I drafted the offer letter, were concerningly tentative rather than fondly lingering: in over thirty years of dealmaking, this was as audacious as I'd seen. We were paying a hefty premium over an already inflated price. *Should I be restraining Masa?* But then again Arm was a terrific global business with a dominant market share and a protective moat in the form of patented technology, and Masa's crazy vision was no crazier than smartphones in 2005.

To maximize impact, we agreed the proposal needed to be delivered in person. But Stuart Chambers was on vacation, on a boat in the Mediterranean and unavailable for another two weeks. Masa would have none of it. If Stuart had been on a hiking trip to Tora Bora, Masa would have parachuted in, an armed Kato-san at his side, in full-on Rambo mode to ward off Taliban interference. He inquired if Stuart's boat was large enough to accommodate a helicopter landing. Mercifully, we never found out. Stuart agreed to meet us for lunch on dry land in Marmaris on Sunday, July 3, and Kato-san dispatched ahead of time to manage onsite logistics.

I wasn't expecting another terrorist attack, but I took some comfort in Kato-san's presence. He had the look of a man as proficient handling a Beretta 92 as he was uncorking fine Burgundy and slicing truffle pizza.

■

The interior of this VistaJet Bombardier was like the Hôtel Costes lobby—a Parisian den of euro chic opulence with deep house chill music playing softly in the background. The seats and walls were gray leather with dark walnut trim, the plush burgundy carpet really tied the room together. The comely stewardess, catwalk ready in her fitted gray jacket with red trim and a matching red scarf, assured me she was aware of my beverage preferences should I wish to imbibe.

On a different day, I might have kicked back and enjoyed an aperitif, but not tonight. Flying time was just over four hours, barely enough for a nap. I changed into the red candy-striped pajama suit—*what the fuck were they thinking?*—laid out for me and after takeoff slipped under the ribbed cashmere blanket. P. G. Wodehouse is my perfect antidote to stress, for there is nothing like an asinine yarn about a senile aristocrat who breeds prize pigs to divert from an equally convoluted reality. But tonight even the master could not deliver. Aside from the deal rush, I was nervous. *Turkey's on red alert. How will a jumpy Turkish Air Force pilot react to three radar blips converging purposefully on Dalaman at sunrise?* Perhaps I should uncork the Billecart-Salmon Rosé, play some tunes, maybe ask Ms. Red Scarf to join me for a drink? *Draped in cashmere, glass of pink bubbly in hand, jiving to the chorus of "Gimme Shelter," man, that's going out in style! Except that ridiculous prison-uniform outfit. . . .*

All I had by way of baggage was a black TUMI backpack, which contained a change of clothes, a laptop, and three printed copies of the unsigned offer letter. But for all Turkish border security seemed to care, I could have packed a pistol and a hand grenade. To be fair, terrorist expense accounts likely preclude private travel, certainly VistaJet, and it was early on a midsummer Sunday morning in a sleepy backwater of the Turkish Riviera.

■

After ninety minutes of driving through rugged Turkish countryside, I arrived at the Elegance Hotel, feeling like an F1 driver making a pit stop. The decorator's penchant for mauve notwithstanding, the room was adequate for my purpose, which was to shower and change. By 10 A.M., I was with Masa in his suite,

Kato-san serving me coffee and croissant on a dining table overlooking the azure waters of Marmaris Bay and the small island of Yildiz Adasi beyond. Despite his longer journey, Masa was animated, waxing on about Arm and its strategy. I was concerned he might come across as too keen, and said as much, though the irony that I was preaching to one of the most prolific dealmakers of all time was not lost on me.

"I understand. You are right," he said, with endearing honesty. "This is emotional for me. Maybe you should do all the talking, I will listen."

Masa says he felt warm tears streaming down his face when, as a teenager, he first saw a beautiful image on the cover of a magazine. For most men in his generation, this would have been a buxom *Playboy* Playmate. For Masayoshi Son it was a computer chip—the Intel 8080 microprocessor. For him, this deal was not just business, it was personal. Which meant that Arm shareholders might receive an offer they could not refuse.

It was a glorious morning, and we decided to go for a walk along the marina. Masa wore a half-sleeved shirt with a light-pink flowery print, and a white baseball cap to protect his scalp. I wore a bright blue linen shirt and white jeans and wondered how Robey might have dressed.

The boardwalk was missing the midsummer bustle, presumably because of the terrorist threat. As we strolled along the marina, Masa exhausted himself talking about Arm and wanted to talk about me. He asked about Maya and the kids, and listened attentively while repeatedly emphasizing how family was the most important thing. I told him I had been married over thirty years, and that this weekend was a family reunion in London, with Maya's father celebrating his eighty-fifth birthday.

We were walking past a detached faux-Spanish stucco structure, the exterior painted white, its entrance framed by palm trees, with a large sign on the façade—VOGUE DIAMOND. Not as grand as Tiffany or Mikimoto, but impressive—polished white marble floors with mosaic inlay, salesmen wearing smart white linen suits. Masa suggested we walk in.

Once inside, he asked me to choose a gift from him for Maya. I protested vigorously, but there was no denying him. Flustered, I sought the cheapest trinket available, but this was no Kmart. Impatient with my dallying, Masa took over. I left the store with a white Vogue Diamond bag, inside it a white box (red ribbon outside, blue velvet lining inside), the receptacle for a white gold necklace with a diamond pendant and a matching bracelet.

We would have our differences in the months to come, Masa and I, but no matter. We will always have Marmaris.

■

The building housing the Pineapple restaurant was similar in architectural style to Vogue Diamond except the exterior was painted bright yellow, the awning an even brighter orange. *Which came first, the restaurant name or the paint colors?* The stunning views from the first floor cleared the palm trees in front of the restaurant, showcasing Netsel Marina and the sea beyond.

We arrived just before noon to find Kato-san waiting. Given the setting, I would have expected the restaurant to be packed, yet we were the only ones here. *The terrorist scare?* No, Kato-san had booked the entire restaurant for as long as we wanted. He also held what looked like a twin wine cooler. Masa had instructed him to bring along two bottles of La Tâche, one a gift for Stuart Chambers, the other for lunchtime consumption.

Stuart and Simon arrived on schedule. Stuart greeted us with a broad smile, allaying my concerns about how he would react to this interruption to his vacation. About sixty, he looked relaxed, fit, and tanned, wearing a blue half-sleeved linen shirt, khaki shorts, and sandals. As if he'd just stepped off a boat, which he had. A career British corporate executive, Stuart was formerly chairman of glassmaker Pilkington Plc, and after the company was sold to Japanese rival Nippon Sheet Glass Ltd. he had taken over as chief executive of the Tokyo-listed parent. Which meant he was familiar with Masa's cult status in Japan, as he would tell me later, and excited to meet him.

Masa apologized profusely to Stuart for interrupting his vacation, and thanked him for accepting his "invitation." I spoke uninterrupted for fifteen minutes, walking Stuart and Simon through the key elements of our proposal. They listened attentively, nodding periodically. When I was done, I handed them two signed copies of the offer letter.

We proceeded with lunch, a preordered selection of pasta and grilled sea bass, the offer of wine declined by all. The conversation was stilted, lunch was hurried; nobody could ignore the elephant in the Pineapple. We knew Arm had retained Goldman Sachs and Lazard as their bankers. Stuart and Simon would have been instructed to listen politely, even coldly, and not engage.

After finishing their meal, Stuart suggested Simon and he excuse themselves, and that we meet again at 2 P.M., back at the Pineapple.

We called Robey, who was standing by. When we told him Stuart and Simon were seeing us again, he reacted as if encountering a crooked bow tie. "They're not supposed to do that," he mused. They were expected to retreat, reject our offer as "inadequate," and await our next move.

"I think Stuart is being respectful to Masa. Let's credit him with cultural sensitivity," I conjectured.

Sure enough, the meeting at 2 P.M. was perfunctory. Stuart confirmed they had read the letter, everything was clear and as I described. The company was not for sale, but as chairman, he had a fiduciary responsibility to consider our proposal seriously, and they would revert shortly.

Other suitors might have retreated, but not Masa. He asked Simon if he had time to join him for a walk along the nearby beach.

Engaging directly with the CEO of a company now formally a

takeover target was a breach of protocol. Simon turned to Stuart for guidance.

"We will only discuss technology," Masa explained, addressing Stuart, who was staring at him with raised eyebrows.

Stuart could have insisted it was inappropriate for Masa to interact with Simon. But that would have meant challenging Masa's integrity since the intent was to "only discuss technology." Any white lie would have been transparent; while Simon did have a plane to catch, Viper would not leave without him, and to suggest he had a conflict on a Sunday afternoon in Marmaris would be equally silly.

Stuart smiled graciously, nodded, picked up his La Tâche, and bade us farewell.

Masa called me an hour later, by which time I was halfway to Dalaman Airport. His conversation with Simon had been great, there was alignment on forward direction for Arm. A reluctant management team would have complicated any deal, so this was good.

Ms. Red Scarf was waiting for me at the bottom of the airstairs. This time I did allow myself that glass of champagne. My iPhone was connected to the sound system, and I chose Van Morrison's *Astral Weeks* to unwind. By the time the third track ("Sweet Thing") started playing, I was fast asleep, no pajamas or cashmere blankets required. Ms. Red Scarf gently nudged me awake when we landed at Luton, and I stumbled groggily toward the black limo waiting on the tarmac.

"You made it!" said Maya, her halogen smile lighting up the doorstep when I arrived home at 8 P.M. Her father had just arrived, and asked how I'd spent my Sunday.

"Nothing exciting," I responded, handing Maya the Vogue Diamond bag. "Just some shopping."

■

We received a written response from Stuart on Thursday, July 7: a predictable and categorical rejection. On Monday, July 11, we submitted a revised proposal, raising our bid by 10.7 percent, from the original 1,500 to 1,660 pence, now a 42 percent premium.

By this time, the bankers advising the Arm board would have provided three key inputs. First, they would have canvassed their global network to gauge the likelihood of an interloper willing to match the SoftBank bid. Second, they would have affirmed that the price offered was "fair," taking into account not only company prospects but also the fact that this was a change of control transaction; a buyer who seeks control is expected to pay a "control premium." Finally, they would have certified that the SoftBank proposal was airtight, particularly certainty of funds.

Goldman and Lazard were together paid over $50 million in fees for these services. This may seem absurd, but it was in line with precedent. M&A fees are based on transaction value, for when it comes to buying or selling companies with values in the tens of billions, no board takes a chance on a second-tier outfit that might perform identical services at a discounted price. For firms like Goldman Sachs and Morgan Stanley, the M&A business is an enormously lucrative franchise.

Robey wasn't exactly cut-price, but when it came to negotiating fees, his approach was as classy as I've seen from a banker. "I get to choose my clients, and you get to decide what to pay me," he said, sitting across from Masa and me, in the dining room of Masa's two-bedroom Opus Suite at the Berkeley Hotel in Knightsbridge. We paid his firm handsomely, well into eight figures.

While the bankers worked feverishly behind the scenes, the back channeling suggested we were within the kill zone. We agreed to meet in London on July 12, at 8 P.M., in Lazard's offices in Mayfair. At 7:30 that evening, our entourage, about twenty including bankers and lawyers, piled into a fleet of black limousines and rolled past Hyde Park Corner to Lazard's offices on Stratton Street across from the Ritz Hotel on Piccadilly.

The scheduled meeting was limited to the original Marmaris

couples (Masa and me, Stuart and Simon) while the broader team stood by in an adjacent boardroom.

Masa and I arrived first and settled ourselves into a wood-paneled corner meeting room, with side views of Piccadilly and Green Park beyond, the trees bathed in summertime sunlight despite the late hour. Stuart and Simon marched in five minutes late. Perhaps a tactical move to throw Masa off-balance, given the known Japanese obsession with punctuality?

Stuart was in power garb—dark gray pinstripe suit, white shirt, navy club tie. He sat directly across from Masa and looked at him expectantly, no longer the genial sailor we had encountered only nine days earlier, the Mediterranean warmth replaced with British froideur. Marmaris seemed as far away as my childhood.

Masa was taken aback; even the suggestion of rudeness disturbed his aura.

I launched into a meticulously crafted and rehearsed pitch, marshaling the arguments as to why our offer of 1,660 pence per share was generous for Arm shareholders, how the recovery of the pound since our last proposal had made the deal more expensive, and why this must be our best and final offer.

Stuart listened, nodding occasionally, but with the distracted air of a preoccupied parent. I could have described the mating habits of newts and his response would have been the same: our offer was "inadequate" and undervalued the company. There was no reference to competing interest or arguments to suggest the company was worth more.

I leaned across to whisper in Masa's ear, but he had played this game more often than I ever will. He thanked Stuart for his time, told him we had made our best offer, and stood up to leave.

Stuart and Simon looked at us, dumbfounded. I sprang to my feet, made a show of aligning the dimple in my tie knot while avoiding eye contact, nodded curtly to Stuart and Simon, and followed Masa out the door.

It was theatrical, but I applauded Masa's discipline when so tantalizingly close to his mesmerizing prize. We rode together in silence, in the car and the elevators, and within ten minutes we were back in his hotel suite. Once there, he sat by himself, silent and expressionless. *Is he second-guessing his move*?

What happens next? Nobody knew, so we ordered pepperoni pizza and drank beer. Except Masa, who remained *in situ.* Jeff Sine suggested Robey chat with his counterparts at Goldman and Lazard, but Robey was gone. The Royal Opera House (ROH), where he had served as chairman since 2008, was honoring him that night at a dinner.

Robey soon resurfaced, resplendent in black tie, but not even the sight of his black silk suspenders made Masa smile. The ROH had commissioned a bust of Robey for the lobby of the Opera House in Covent Garden and further honored him with a rare gift—a concert at the Opera House with Robey singing accompanied by the ROH orchestra.

Robey was beaming, as happy as his Englishness would allow him to be. I always liked Robey; it made me smile to see him like this. I suggested he sing something upbeat to lift Masa, perhaps Verdi's "Libiamo?"

But then Masa's phone rang, its shrill urgency reverberating. It was a brief conversation; all Masa said was, "OK." He hung up and asked where the Lanesborough Hotel was. He needed to meet Stuart there right away.

The Lanesborough was only a hundred yards away, at Hyde Park Corner. Robey offered to escort Masa.

Thirty minutes later, Masa was back. He sat down calmly, evidently resolved to resume his former catatonic state. But then his lips parted, his face broke into a gradually widening smile, until he could no longer control himself.

"Seventeen hundred pence," he said, now tossing his head back and laughing.[2]

A lesser Briton might have leaped out of his chair, arms

raised, as if England had just scored in a World Cup final against Germany. Maybe even belt out "Nessun Dorma." Perhaps Robey evaluated both alternatives, remembered queen and country, and settled on a stately and satisfied smile instead. And since neither he nor Masa were huggers, they channeled their excitement into the palms of their hands in a vigorous and emotional handshake.

"Thank you so much. You are my lucky charm," Masa told the smiling Sir Suspenders.

■

Where is Masa? It was late on Sunday evening a couple of weeks later, and Masa had a packed day on Monday, including his meeting with the new prime minister, Theresa May.

All had gone well after Masa's handshake agreement with Stuart. The following day, Masa and I were hosted by Stuart and Simon for an amicable lunch—the Marmaris warmth was back—at the Langham in Portland Place, where we discussed our execution plan. Masa left that night for Tokyo while I remained in London, leading a team of lawyers and bankers for a two-day due-diligence session at Lazard's offices. Robey connected me to Roland Rudd, whose firm Finsbury helped SoftBank orchestrate media strategy. Even before the deal announcement, Robey had briefed the late Sir Jeremy Heywood, the cabinet secretary and the highest ranking official in Her Majesty's Civil Service. Heywood was another former Morgan Stanley colleague, and played a crucial role in navigating 10 Downing and beyond.

Old boy networks are great when deployed in your favor, and the trinity of Robey, Rudd, and Heywood, all contemporaries at Oxford, served us well. The narrative that this was a vote of confidence in post-Brexit Britain was well received, and any concerns that Arm might be damaged under foreign ownership were preemptively addressed by SoftBank pledging to double

Arm's UK headcount within five years. (A commitment SoftBank would exceed.)

But this week was important, and I had no idea if Masa had even arrived. I called him. Yes, he was in London. He didn't have a place to stay, but it was okay now, a suite at the Shangri-La Hotel had been arranged.

The Shangri-La? I'd been there once for dinner. It was a new hotel, occupying the higher floors of the futuristic and phallic Shard building—but on the wrong side of the Thames.

"Masa, you can't stay there, all our meetings are in Central London," I said.

He suggested I speak with Theresa, Ron Fisher's assistant, who managed Masa's schedule when he traveled overseas. I messaged Theresa, who told me she would have someone call me right away. My phone rang a few minutes later, a US number with an unfamiliar area code.

"Is this Alok?" barked a very American male voice. He pronounced my name *A-Lock,* with that harsh emphasis on the second syllable I always found execrable.

"Yes . . . and you're helping Masa plan his London trip?" I said, equally impatient.

"I am Bob. And we never use real names, please. For this project, his code name is Kurobe."

Bob? Kurobe?

"Look, whatever your name is, I'm supposed to meet Mr. Son at 8 A.M. tomorrow, and he is meeting with the prime minister of this country. So stop fucking around, and tell me what the *fuck* is going on."

Sometimes a couple of authoritative F-bombs can be effective.

"Yes, yes, sorry sir," said "Bob," suddenly respectful. "We had a nice fully staffed town house booked for him in Belgravia, but when he arrived he said the stairs were too steep for his dog. We booked him a suite at Claridge's, but he said last time Japanese tourists took photographs. He prefers modern, so we booked him at Shangri-La. Now you say he can't stay there so we have no idea what to do."

I imagined a retinue of liveried servants in Eaton Square looking on mournfully as Masa walked out on them.

"Don't worry, Bob, I'll take it from here," I said, laughing. Maya and I would have done the same for Ellie.

Theresa—not the PM, the other Theresa—explained that "Bob" was likely an overzealous ex-military type employed by an elite concierge service she used for Masa.

I called my assistant Connie (Cantonese, hyperactive, efficient) and she procured a two-bedroom suite at the Bulgari Hotel in Knightsbridge.

I called Masa later. The hotel was nice and he liked being across the street from Hyde Park. Happiness for everyone.

■

The Arm deal was approved by its shareholders on August 31 and closed immediately thereafter, a scarcely believable two months following our first approach to the company. The execution straddled the sleepy holiday period in Europe and the turmoil around Brexit. For an acquisition of this size and complexity, we had broken so many records I felt like Michael Phelps. Perhaps our timing had been opportune, and like Napoleon's generals, I had been lucky rather than good. We did not surface any diligence concerns—no termites—nor were there regulatory challenges or competing bids. Masa's bold approach was vindicated.

Masa and I visited Cambridge, where he addressed Arm employees at a town hall meeting. His presentation included one of his stock slides showing IQ as a normal distribution, with tiny color portraits of Einstein and da Vinci at the tangential right tail. With his own idea of relativity, Masa placed Leonardo to the right of Albert. In Masa's mind Leonardo, like Steve Jobs, was that rare combination of intellect and aesthete that made him more of an outlier. His punchline was a red arrow labeled "singularity" pointed downward past both Einstein and da Vinci, indicating machine intelligence surpassing human intelligence.

If the going rate for pictures was a thousand words, this one rated a bid for ten. But no matter, Masa liked images even for trite observations. On this occasion, there were a few puzzled expressions in the crowd. I had asked Tanaka-san to substitute smiling selfies of the two of us for Einstein and da Vinci, with Tanaka-san's photo taking da Vinci's place and mine replacing Einstein's. Tanaka-san was terrified, but I assured him I would take responsibility. We sat together and enjoyed our little secret; I smiled and he giggled.

When we told Masa later, he laughed longer than I'd ever seen him laugh, throwing his head back, wagging his right index finger at the two of us in mock accusation.

It remains my happiest memory of Masayoshi Son.

■

The stock market's reaction to the Arm deal was less joyful. SoftBank's share price took an immediate hit, and the company's market value declined by almost $10 billion, equal to the premium paid above Arm's preannouncement market value. There were no synergies, nor did we provide other arguments to justify this premium. Sometimes markets really are efficient.

Masa didn't care. The congratulations poured in. Many, Jack Ma among them, hailed the deal as a masterstroke. Not only did Masa have his own vision for Arm, he also persuaded himself that owning Arm would give him unique insights into global technology trends. Arm's revenue streams would provide clues as to what types of processors were gaining traction, and therefore which technologies to back. Arm would give Masa an edge in placing his future investment bets: it was his private crystal ball.

Project Adam thus became the progenitor for Project Crystal Ball—the creation of the most unusual and consequential $100 billion SoftBank Vision Fund.

12

THAT'S FAR OUT, MAN

Calvin Cottar was a big game hunter, the fourth generation of renowned stalkers of Africa's Big Five. Calvin's great-grandfather, inspired by Teddy Roosevelt's *Africa Game Trails,* immigrated to Kenya from Oklahoma in 1919. The highlight of the book, which I read in preparation for our safari holiday, is a meticulous record of the 512 animals shot by Teddy and his son Kermit on their trip to East Africa. Teddy shot nine lions to Kermit's eight, but drew a blank on leopards and cheetahs, of which Kermit bagged seven and three, respectively. (In case you're wondering, Kermit did not shoot any frogs.) Elephants, hippos, and monkeys also feature on the kill list of this great American president, celebrated for his credentials as a conservationist. *Like Churchill and his colonial racism, does every moon have a dark side? Or are some moons all dark but occasionally and brilliantly illuminated by starlight?*

It was late August, only a few weeks after the closure of the Arm acquisition, and I was at Cottar's 1920s Camp in the Masai Mara for a family holiday. Calvin's glory days with a rifle are behind him; he is now a passionate environmentalist, hosting tourists in his safari camp of white canvas tents decorated with antique furniture collected by his family over the last hundred years. Calvin (tall, bald, fiftysomething) was the type of person whose Zen company raises your own life expectancy.

Calvin himself was our dedicated guide as we set out for daily 5 A.M. game drives, expecting only to see the stark beauty of Africa but always surprised by what the bush threw at us. Samir and I would take turns riding out front with Calvin, with Maya and Alya in the back seat and our vigilant Masai "spotter" bringing up the rear of the safari vehicle.

On this (our fourth) morning, the highlight was a rare cheetah sighting. They hunt at dawn or dusk, Calvin explained, and he could tell this one was hungry from the stomach curvature. The prospect of watching this aerodynamic beast run twice as fast as Usain Bolt was irresistible. We resolved to stick with the cheetah for as long as it took, following at a discreet distance, soon crossing over from Kenya's Mara into Tanzania's Serengeti. Calvin seemed as unbothered as the fast cat at this unceremonious border crossing. "Nobody will give us any trouble," he explained, "they all know me."

The sun climbed higher and with it the temperature. Soon, the cheetah seemed as ready for a siesta as I was. But Samir and Alya were resolute—we had to stay. Calvin looked to me for guidance. I nodded.

"A glass of chilled Chardonnay and some lunch would hit the spot though," I said, smiling wistfully.

A quick set of radio instructions and within thirty minutes we had a picnic set up under the wide canopy of an umbrella thorn tree, the cheetah settled in the pale yellow tall grass a hundred yards away.

In this idyllic moment, as I settled into a canvas folding chair, it is a measure of sorry addiction that my first impulse was to reach for my iPhone. I hadn't checked emails all day, and while coverage was sporadic, whenever we passed by a tower my phone exploded with a burst of messages. I ignored all except one, with the subject "Project Crystal Ball" from Tanaka-san.

Masa knows you are on holiday, but he wants you to review the attached presentation. Apparently Masa was making some type of investor pitch the following day.

My associations with important events tend to be musical, my Spotify playlists remembrances of things past, each track a madeleine. Project Crystal Ball, however, is tagged with the image of a hungry cheetah in the Serengeti and an American president who shot small black-and-white monkeys with a Winchester Model 1895 lever-action rifle he fondly called his Big Stick.

■

The investment case for the Vision Fund (at the time codenamed "Project Crystal Ball") opened with Masa's familiar vision of a trillion connected devices, with the IoT as the next big thing in the evolution of SoftBank, just as the mobile internet had driven its reincarnation. Critical to his thesis was Arm and its role as the predictive crystal ball to guide future investments.

It then highlighted SoftBank's investment record, delivering an annualized 44 percent return over the past eighteen years. Over the same time frame, Buffett's Berkshire Hathaway had returned 20 percent and Blackstone only 15 percent. These numbers were startling: Masa Son was suggesting he was more than twice as good as the Oracle of Omaha, perhaps the most revered investor of all time.

I requested the raw data, and the figures seemed accurate. Berkshire avoided leverage while Masa embraced it, and this along with currency effects distorted the comparison. The Sprint acquisition, for example, was financed in yen, which had depreciated, thereby boosting the value of an otherwise challenged investment. (If you buy a $1 million home with $200,000 down and an $800,000 equivalent yen-denominated mortgage, and the yen depreciates by 12.5 percent, your mortgage becomes $700,000 in dollar terms and your home equity $300,000—a 50 percent increase with no change in the value of the home. If your home appreciates by a modest 20 percent, your equity is now worth $500,000—an extravagant 2.5 times return on invested capital. Such is the seductive, addictive, and occasionally destructive power of financial engineering.)

No matter, Masa's record identifying and—more impressively—manufacturing winners was undeniable. Many unfairly dismiss him as a one-hit wonder, but there is so much more to the SoftBank story than Alibaba. Yahoo! was a great early-stage investment; Vodafone was a remarkable turnaround story; Yahoo! Japan was created from scratch; Supercell was a savvy trade with profits fully realized.

A critical differentiating factor of the Vision Fund was its embedded leverage in the form of "preferred equity." In this the Vision Fund represented the convergence of two worlds that were hitherto a continent apart—Wall Street–structured finance and Bay Area technology. Over a private dinner a few months later, Goldman Sachs CEO David Solomon described this financial engineering as "pure genius." (Doubtless instruments like CDO-Squareds seemed ingenious to David's peers in 2007, and that stuff blew up the financial world).

■

Investing in technology is not for the fainthearted. Had W. G. Sebald embarked on a walking tour of Silicon Valley instead of East Anglia, he might have written a different type of masterpiece, and enjoyed nicer weather besides. But the essence of *Rings of Saturn* would be the same. That haunting and recurring theme, "On every new thing there lies already the shadow of annihilation." Just as video killed the radio star, Google killed Yahoo!, iPhone killed BlackBerry, Spotify killed compact discs, Netflix killed DVDs, Facebook killed MySpace, and TikTok is killing Facebook, Instagram, and everything else, while software is eating the world.

Harry Markowitz won a Nobel Prize for the insight that diversification is the only free lunch in the investment business. However, if all investments are in tech, much of the benefit of diversification is lost since tech valuations are correlated. For early-stage companies, profits are in the distant future, and therefore valuations are sensitive to interest rates. Shifting sentiment plays a role, and frequently both market psychology and monetary policy are factors, creating boom/bust cycles such as the internet bubble of 1999–2000 and the more recent recalibration of tech in 2022.

There is a frequently overlooked temporal dimension to diversification. Other things being equal, a fund that invests $100 million a year over ten years is less risky than a fund that invests $500 million a year over two years. The former fund will likely invest across market cycles, which should lead to a lower volatility of outcomes, even if both funds make an identical number of investments with a similar risk profile. Masa's track record was based on investing over eighteen years, while the Vision Fund intended to commit its corpus over a two-to-three-year period—a much riskier proposition.

The Vision Fund introduced leverage—frequently two layers—into this combustible mix of volatility and correlation. (Yes, it's complicated—a lotta ins, a lotta outs, a lotta strands to keep in my head, man.)

Every time an investment was made, over 50 percent of the purchase price was capital drawn from SoftBank and the investors. The balance was "mezzanine" (alternatively referred to as "preferred equity") financing provided solely by the investors. This mezzanine capital was like debt, but while it paid annual cash interest at 7 percent, it had no fixed repayment date. Investors would be repaid when investments were sold.

In the initial years, when it was investing rather than divesting, the only way the Vision Fund could meet its annual interest obligations was to draw down capital from fund investors, who could thus be required to contribute cash to the fund to pay themselves interest—the ingenious circularity that had so impressed financial engineers like David Solomon.

Crucially, this mezzanine financing was not secured by the underlying investments, the way a home mortgage is secured by property. Which opened up the possibility of a second layer of debt. Brokerage firms routinely allow purchase of shares in listed companies "on margin," lending up to 50 percent of the value of a listed stock, secured by the underlying shares, or using derivatives. If it chose to deal in public stocks, the Vision Fund's firepower could theoretically be over twice its already massive size.

Double leverage is like chasing espresso martinis with Red Bull shots—you could fly to the icy peak of Mount Everest and crash to the dark bottom of Mariana Trench faster than a cheetah chasing a gazelle. Which I found scary. Son-san, however, was made of sterner stuff. Not because he was an inveterate gambler but because he was a devout believer. In Masa's Einsteinian universe, Heisenberg's uncertainty principle was worryingly irrelevant, and his god did not play dice.

I had a brief chat with him on the phone from Africa, suggesting the leverage was too much for anyone to swallow. Why not solicit investment in Sprint instead, where we desperately needed capital? He listened politely but his mind was made up. "Let me try," he said.

Our African cheetah never did make a kill. When we departed our picnic spot at dusk, I assumed Masa wouldn't close his deal either.

■

Rajeev Misra was an alchemist with an uncanny knack for survival. At Deutsche Bank, he oversaw a global credit business unmatched in size and complexity. Remarkably, unlike most of his brethren, he emerged unscathed through the 2008 financial crisis thanks to a well-timed bet against subprime mortgages.

In 2006, while at Deutsche Bank, Rajeev had engineered a creative $10 billion structured financing package that allowed Masa to consummate his audacious Vodafone Japan takeover. That was Masa's comeback deal, and he never forgot Rajeev's role. When Masa hired Rajeev at SoftBank in a nebulous "head of strategic finance" role, perhaps he expected a similar coup, though not even he could have foreseen the magnitude of what unfolded.

Rajeev walked barefoot around the office, usually vaping, a cappuccino in a Starbucks paper cup always within reach. His hair was slicked back, on his wrist a platinum Rolex watch with an ice blue dial along with an Indian bead bracelet, a combination as quirky as the man. He laughed loudly, but you never knew what idea was tickling his fancy except that it was big and bold.

I knew Rajeev socially and respected his credit-trading skills. At one point we had agreed to jointly teach a course in investments at the London Business School. Nikesh and Rajeev were friends too, but Nikesh was ex-Google and wary of leveraged finance. (Big Tech avoids debt the way DiCaprio shuns women over twenty-five.) Which meant that while Nikesh was around, Rajeev and I seldom crossed paths, though on one comical occasion we sat together in the Concorde Room at Heathrow's Terminal 5, both assuming the other was keeping track of time. We missed our flight to Tokyo. (The Concorde Room—a notch above the First Class lounge—is a sanctuary where British Airways' most valued clients commiserate with each other about the tyranny of flying commercial.)

Rajeev's main achievement at SoftBank was a structured deal that allowed Sprint to raise capital secured by its spectrum assets, relieving some of the pressure of its balance sheet. However, absent a meaningful executive role, by the summer of 2016, Rajeev was considering joining a group of former Deutsche Bank colleagues who had created their own firm, FAB Partners, named after the founders Faissola the Italian, Ariburnu the Turk and Al-Bassam the Saudi. Had Rajeev joined, they could have been the Fab Four, but instead renamed themselves Centricus.

Michele Faissola had connections with the Qataris and Nizar Al-Bassam with the Saudis. While Nizar struggled to make the Saudi connection, Faissola arranged for Masa to meet with the Qataris in late August. According to the FAB team, Masa started with the idea of a $20 billion fund, but then unilaterally decided on a $100 billion corpus, altering the presentation on his flight to Qatar.

I joined Masa for a follow-up discussion with a Gulf investor contingent at Arm's office in San Jose a few weeks later. They stroked their beards pensively but didn't reach for their wallets. No matter, their participation was irrelevant.

■

Mohammed bin Salman's passion was video games, his favorite the history-themed *Age of Empires*. MBS's reality was also a game—a frequently bloody game of thrones. By 2016, the thirty-one-year-old MBS (bearded, substantial, red-and-white checked *keffiyeh*) was deputy crown prince. But he would soon outmaneuver his last remaining rival, his older cousin the Crown Prince Mohammed bin Nayef, and claim the keys to the Kingdom of Saudi Arabia.

But being a Saudi prince is risky business. In 2009, the elder Mohammed survived a suicide bomber with plastic explosives in his anal canal.[1] (The strategy backfired, so to speak: the would-be assassin, an Al-Qaeda operative named Abdullah al-Asiri, died instantaneously.) As MBS advanced, lurking in the shadows and waiting for him to falter were the Wahhabi fundamentalist clerics and the sons of former king Abdullah. Presumably, a man in his position scoffed at the quotidian volatility associated with leveraged investments in technology.

The prize in MBS's game of thrones was a kingdom under siege. It was not just the religious schism with Iran and the battle for regional hegemony that endangered the kingdom, but an economic threat loomed as well. When MBS assumed power in

2016, 42 percent of gross domestic product and 84 percent of exports were oil related,[2] a precarious position given the global shift away from fossil fuels and the success of fracking in the Permian Basin. Crude oil prices had plummeted in the last two years, and the Saudi budget deficit stood at a record 13.5 percent.[3]

In April 2016 MBS responded with Saudi Vision 2030, a grand strategic plan to restructure the economy and wean the kingdom off its oil addiction. Creating a vibrant technology sector in Saudi was a key piece of the puzzle, and toward this end MBS abandoned his traditional headgear and favored mustard-colored robes for a trip to Silicon Valley. At a dinner at the Fairmont Hotel in San Francisco, MBS addressed a dream team of venture capitalists, including Marc Andreessen, Peter Thiel, Michael Moritz, and John Doerr. "I need a bridge between Saudi and Silicon Valley. I need you to help our reforms," he asked them.[4] Nobody cared. For these Valley princelings, their modestly sized funds were exclusive clubs, with new investors routinely denied access. The Saudi prince had little to offer them, and nobody seemed interested in his oily and moribund economy.

In a remarkable alignment of stars, MBS made an official visit in September 2016 to Tokyo, home to the one person in the world who could match him in grand illusions. After weeks of persistent effort, on MBS's last day in Tokyo, Nizar Al-Bassam arranged an audience for Masa at the Geihinkan state guest house, where MBS was being hosted as a visiting royal.

In advance of the meeting, Tanaka-san sent me an email with "Presentation to Saudi Prince" in the subject line. I loved Tanaka-san's lack of guile. No clever tags, no self-important and alarmist "private and confidential" labels, just a simple descriptive title that left no doubt as to the contents. (In this Tanaka-san was like great artists of a different era: if Renoir labeled a work *Melon et Tomates,* one could, with certainty, expect an impressionist rendition of a fruit and some vegetables.)

Masa's pitch, informed by Nizar, was presumably delivered

with typical fervor. With admirable panache, this is how Masa Son sold his proposition to MBS:

"You come to Tokyo as a first time. I want to give you a gift. I want to give you a Masa gift. A trillion-dollar gift. You invest $100 billion to my fund, I give you a trillion dollars."[5]

The meeting lasted forty-five minutes, and Masa came away with $45 billion, to be invested in what he now called "The Vision Fund," the title a clever nod to MBS's Saudi Vision 2030.

"One billion per minute," is how Masa famously summarized the MBS meeting. Which may seem hyperbolic, since negotiations to finalize the investment dragged on several months, but the headline is fair. Once MBS shook hands, the deal was done. No asset allocator, in Saudi or elsewhere, could contemplate a commitment of this magnitude.

The Masa-MBS summit was on Saturday, September 3. I was in London, and Masa called me in the evening, late night for him. It was an unusual call, but not because of the hour. Masa never called just to chat, he always had an agenda. On this occasion he was too excited to sleep and wanted to talk about his meeting. He seemed wowed by MBS's youth, intensity, and entourage of thirteen planes and five hundred people. According to Masa, when he made his pitch, MBS had said, "Where have you been all this time?"

Masa knew little about the Saudi monarchy, but for him MBS being hosted by the Japanese royal family was validation enough. Besides, we were in the pre-Khashoggi era, when MBS was positively viewed as an agent for change in Saudi Arabia. (I welcomed change in Saudi. On my sole visit to Riyadh many years ago, the immigration officer inquired about my religion, then asked why my company hadn't sent a Muslim employee instead.)

Absent their bromantic and serendipitous rendezvous in Tokyo, there would have been no Vision Fund. MBS was Dr. Livingstone to Masa's Stanley, or vice versa, the two together like Butch and Sundance, Rosencrantz and Guildenstern, burger and fries.

■

Ten days later, speaking on Kara Swisher's *Recode Decode* podcast, the influential venture capitalist Bill Gurley voiced concern about a bubble.[6] Gurley had attended an investor conference in Las Vegas where he heard five of eight unicorns talk about "trillions" in their presentations. "We have done something in the ecosystem to encourage this type of outlandish promotion, where you need to use words like 'trillion,'" Gurley said. "And I think it's dangerous. When we act like we have the right to disrupt everything or eat every industry, we look like entitled brats," he continued.

Gurley acknowledged that capital allocators like him are complicit in start-ups' exploding valuations and irrational competition. "I think everybody has to play the game," he said. "With interest rates so low, money sloshes around."

Eerily, Gurley was echoing Citigroup CEO Chuck Prince on the eve of the 2008 financial crisis. "As long as the music is playing, you've got to get up and dance," Prince had said.[7]

Gurley's words struck me as rare interiority from someone who had been around long enough to realize a unicorn is a mythical beast. But here's the irony. The latest Benchmark Capital (Gurley's firm) fund was a paltry $550 million, and his warning about "too much money" came just as Masa Son was persuading the sovereigns of Saudi Arabia and the United Arab Emirates to part with $60 *billion*.

Even Rajeev, the architect of the fund structure alongside Masa, had no conviction this Vision Fund would become reality. The size was wildly ambitious. It was the largest pool of capital in the history of the investment business, exceeding the dollar volume of *all* technology venture investments in the United States in 2016. *Where will all this money go?*

As with Wittgenstein's rabbit-duck illusion, why do people reach such different conclusions when confronted with identical data? Should I take a stand, the way Nikesh might have? Then I remembered the Fukuoka gladiators—"gratitude and commitment." Besides, rabbit-duck type debates with your boss have conclusions as predictable as the denouement of an *Oedipus Rex* performance.

■

It is never a pleasant feeling when your boss, even if he happens to be the Prince of Arabia, wants an outsider to help you with your job. This is perhaps how Yasir Al-Rumayyan felt when tasked with finalizing MBS's handshake commitment to Masa.

Yasir, the suave ex-banker who headed the Saudi Public Investment Fund (PIF), was building his own investment team. In June 2016, PIF had committed $3.5 billion to what was then the most celebrated Silicon Valley start-up—Travis Kalanick's Uber. This deal was PIF's coming-out party, with Yasir joining Uber's board and a commitment by Uber to invest in Saudi as part of Vision 2030.

Along with his team, Yasir arrived in Tokyo following MBS's tryst with Masa, and found himself in SoftBank's boardroom confronted with Masa's standard fare of crystal balls and connected robots and singularity.

I sat across from Yasir, watching carefully for reaction. Placed in his position, I might have felt like a man in a doctor's office waiting for a hemorrhoidectomy, but Yasir seemed to take it in his stride.

Masa's presentation featured his favorite slide—a goose on one half of the page, five golden eggs on the other, the headline a head-scratcher for the ages: "Which is more important?" This particular deck featured a variation. The title was "SoftBank = Producer of Golden Eggs," with the goose labeled "AI Revolution," and in its wake a trail of freshly laid golden eggs.

Alone among his colleagues, Yasir Al-Rumayyan was clean shaven. He now stroked his naked chin in the international gesture for deep contemplation, coming to terms with the baffling originality of Masayoshi Son.

Rajeev and I went out with Yasir that night to a bar lounge in Ginza. While most around us drank fine XO cognac and smoked Cuban cigars, Yasir proudly shared photos of the site for the futuristic "smart city" Neom, with its own robo-dino Jurassic Park, all part of MBS's Vision 2030. Yasir and I had a common passion for golf, and we had an animated conversation about golfing greats. I made a case for the talented, swashbuckling, and occasionally tragic Greg Norman. I recalled that conversation years later when Yasir shook professional golf by creating LIV Golf to challenge the PGA Tour. His choice of CEO for LIV Golf—the Great White Shark, Greg Norman.

Someone—*who?*—told Masa that Yasir was offended when I suggested PIF's role in the Vision Fund was that of a passive investor. Perhaps I had underestimated the importance of optics. SoftBank was supposed to be a partner and catalyze the creation of a vibrant Saudi technology industry—exactly what MBS had asked of the Silicon Valley crowd. Masa hosted Yasir for golf the following day and eventually invited him to join SoftBank's board. After extracting a few concessions, including veto rights for deals over $3 billion, Yasir was along for the ride.[8]

■

Mohammed bin Zayed Al Nahyan ("MBZ") was then the Crown Prince of the UAE, and followed the lead of his Saudi younger big brother, MBS, in committing to the Vision Fund. The entity he charged with managing the investment was the state-owned Mubadala Investment Company. Mubadala's management team had a more pragmatic approach to the SoftBank relationship, perhaps because it was already an established global investment organization and a credible technology investor. Mubadala's team cut MBZ's preliminary commitment in half, to $15 billion. They also negotiated an investment commitment going in the opposite direction—SoftBank agreed to invest in a newly created Mubadala venture fund.

On Tuesday, November 8, I had dinner with Ibrahim Ajami, the point person at Mubadala for the SoftBank investment and the head of Mubadala Ventures. The dinner venue was RN74 in downtown San Francisco, a wine-themed restaurant named after the Route Nationale 74 that traverses Burgundy's wine country. Joining us was Ervin Tu, a bright and earnest M&A banker I had recruited from Goldman Sachs and tasked with leading the execution process for the Vision Fund. The dinner kicked off Ibrahim's due diligence in advance of formalizing Mubadala's commitment.

Lean, with hair trimmed close to his scalp, the US-educated Ibrahim was calmly accepting of the inevitability of the Vision Fund. "So, your boss has convinced the crown princes of Saudi and UAE to invest $60 billion in a leveraged technology investment fund," said Ibrahim, shaking his head incredulously, to start our conversation.

It was a big day in America. Through dinner, Ervin was checking his iPhone regularly, as were all around us. Before we got to our main course and our second glass of Burgundy, the results of the contest Ervin was tracking became inevitable. America was about to elect its first orange president. People looked as if they wanted to swap their delicate pours of Louis Jadot for a double shot of Jack Daniel's.

My politics skew right on economic issues and left on social matters. Growing up in India created a visceral mistrust of big government. But being right wing in America (guns, evangelicals, the right to life) has its own baggage. With Trump, however, I never got past his gilded aesthetic. But as a businessman I saw the opportunity, as I knew my boss would. A Republican administration meant a new head of the Federal Communications Commission (FCC) and a fresh approach to antitrust. *The Sprint/T-Mobile merger is back on the table.*

■

The SoftBank Vision Fund eventually closed in 2017 with a size of just under $100 billion, including the embedded leverage.[9] The Saudis provided $45 billion via PIF, of which $30 billion was in the form of mezzanine capital at an annual cash cost of 7 percent. A further $15 billion came from the United Arab Emirates via Mubadala, with equity and mezzanine in the same ratio. The balance was "friends and family," including Apple (SoftBank was one of the biggest buyers of iPhones globally), Foxconn (founder Terry Gou was Masa's friend), Sharp, and, according to media reports, the Japanophile Larry Ellison.[10]

The Crazy Guy, as Masa called himself, was no longer just a Crazy Guy. Henceforth, he was a Crazy Guy with $100 billion.

■

If you can get a private audience with the Crown Prince of Saudi Arabia, the prime minister of India, and the president-elect of the United States, you know you're a player. If you can meet all three, in Riyadh, New Delhi, and New York, respectively, within the space of five days, you've probably set a world record.

Masa met with MBS in Riyadh on December 1, 2016, to push forward the Vision Fund, following which Masa and I met with Narendra Modi on December 3.

In my days running Morgan Stanley's investment banking business in India in the nineties, even when CEO John Mack visited we never got beyond the finance minister. To be granted an audience with the prime minister was a measure of Masa's growing stature and the world's obsession with technology.

We saw Modi in the sprawling twelve-acre compound on Lok Kalyan Marg that serves as residence and office of the PM, in the heart of Lutyens' Delhi, the stately enclave that is the seat of power in India.

Our meeting with Modi was at 5 P.M., and despite the choking smog we could still appreciate the immaculate tree-lined lawns, the early-evening tranquility broken by the occasional scream of a peacock.

The compound was a collection of white single-story colonial-era bungalows. One was dedicated to security screening, the second served as a comfortable waiting room, and the third was our destination—the PM's office.

Modi greeted Masa with a vigorous two-handed politician's handshake. I instinctively folded my hands in the traditional Indian *namaste* greeting, but Modi countered with a firm Western handshake. That moment, captured on national television, remains implanted in my hippocampus. Evidently my fitted Isaia suit and Hermès tie—you can always count on an ex-banker for a fancy dress style—left Modi in no doubt regarding my cultural identity. The way I dress, the way I speak, I can fool everyone except myself. I might have a British passport and divide my time between London and New York, but I am homeless if New Delhi is not my home.

Modi wore the standard Indian politician's garb of a loose white *kurta,* over it a navy high-collar garment now known as a "Modi vest," which is a sleeveless version of the Nehru jacket made fashionable by Armani. Except that Nehru never actually wore a Nehru jacket, he wore a longer version called an *achkan.*

It is all very confusing, like so many things in India.

Masa did all the talking. At their last meeting in 2014, Masa had committed to investing $10 billion in India over ten years. (As always with Masa, a neat mathematical construction—a billion a minute with MBS, a billion a year with Modi.) This time, Masa committed to 20 gigawatts of solar power and one million electric vehicles—an astonishing proposition in a country that had only 3.7 gigawatts of installed solar power capacity and produced a paltry 22,000 electric vehicles. This would lead to five million skilled jobs, the entire proposition cleverly acknowledging Modi's "Make in India" campaign to promote indigenous manufacturing.[11]

Masa also proudly described the venture that now dominated his mind space—his Vision Fund.

Modi listened and nodded. A half smile teased the edges of his white beard, but beyond acknowledging the alignment with his strategic goals, he barely said a word. A silver-tongued demagogue, a Mozart to Trump's Salieri, was rendered speechless by Masayoshi Son's fantastical story of singularity and robots and the internet of things and hundreds of billions of dollars.

■

Masa and I had another encounter in Delhi, for me more meaningful than our meeting with Modi.

Masa was invited to speak at a leadership summit organized by the *Hindustan Times.* His allegorical anecdotes, always delivered with a light touch, went down well in these settings. On this occasion, Masa talked about how he was the richest man in the world in the year 2000, and worried constantly about what to do with his money. But then the market crashed and solved his problem.

"All gone, no more stress!" he said.

And then he laughed. Boisterous infectious laughter, reverberating through the auditorium. A man cracking himself up about losing $60 billion dollars. They laughed with him, over a thousand people, then applauded as if he'd just won an Oscar.

I spotted a chuckling and familiar face in the audience, seated in the front row next to Shobhana Bhartia, the chairperson of the media group hosting the summit.

As a teenager I had marched into the Silhouette barber shop at Delhi's Oberoi Hotel, armed with a copy of *Filmfare* magazine featuring him on the cover, and demanded my hair be styled exactly like his. Like *Don,* the Indian Godfather, a younger Brando or taller Pacino but with thick, black, and coiffed hair.

It was the Big B, it was Amitabh Bachchan, the biggest superstar in the history of Indian cinema. (Regrettably, known to Western audiences only for his portrayal of the reprobate Meyer Wolfsheim in the regrettable Baz Luhrmann version of *Gatsby*.)

I scurried up to Masa as he stepped off the stage and escorted him toward Ms. Bhartia, who introduced us to Amitabh. I was too self-conscious to do the selfie thing, but a photo of Masa and Amitabh shaking hands remains a prized digital keepsake. Masa smiled politely while I explained who this was. Amitabh put his arm across my shoulder, then turned to Masa.

"You are the real star, Mr. Son, that was quite a performance," he said, in that rich Morgan Freeman baritone that delivered brooding dialogue with dramatic and frequently ironic flair. He wore black-rimmed glasses, his hair now gray and thinning, an elegantly trimmed white goatee elevating his gravitas. But that voice, it hadn't changed.

By 2017, Masa was soaring so high that a memorable one-liner from *Don* came to mind. *Don ko pakadna mushkil hi nahi. Namumkin hai.* To catch Don was not only difficult. It was impossible.

■

Masa left Delhi later that night to meet with President-elect Donald Trump at Trump Tower on Fifth Avenue. I might have gone with him, except I'd been in New York the previous week. Besides, Trump was no Amitabh Bachchan, not even a Modi, and Ron Fisher was available to accompany Masa.

In his meeting, Masa promised to invest $50 billion and create fifty thousand jobs in the United States.[12] (Again, that numerical symmetry.) This commitment was clever positioning on his part. As a technology fund, the Vision Fund would automatically target the US as a primary destination.

The two posed for a photo in the gilded lobby, following which Trump tweeted that "Masa said he would never do this had we not won the election."[13] Never mind that the Vision Fund had been announced in October, why let the facts get in the way of a great story?

After Trump introduced him to the gaggle of reporters as "one of the great men of business," a journalist asked Masa to spell his name. This would not happen again.

I talked to Masa after his meeting. He couldn't remember a thing Trump said, or if he did, I don't remember his response.

I asked if anyone had joined Trump for the meeting.

"Yes, yes," he said. "Ivanka! She is so charming and so intelligent and so beautiful."

■

Julius Caesar was my introduction to Shakespeare, and as a teenager I memorized every line. Upon Caesar's triumphant return to Rome, the envious Cassius observes that Caesar "doth bestride the narrow world like a Colossus, and we petty men walk under his huge legs and peep about." The metaphor captures Masa Son's ascension wonderfully, but here's the strange thing. Those petty men who loved Caesar but loved Rome more, they were supposed to slay Caesar. Instead, they came after me.

13

FIRST BLOOD

THIS WILL NOT STOP, it said.

The message was anonymous and handwritten, the caps reinforced the vague threat. Scribbled on the same scrap of yellow notepaper was a name, Olivier Leflaive, along with a series of digits, likely a mobile phone number, with an international prefix I recognized as Switzerland.

It was morning in Tokyo, and I was in a meeting in Masa's conference room. My phone blinked with dual notifications. A missed call and a WhatsApp from Nikesh. A picture of the note, with a terse message. Call me right away.

Ron Fisher was staring at me from across the table. He looked at his phone, then the door and nodded. We excused ourselves and ducked into what was formerly Nikesh's office, now shared by Ron and me.

Nikesh did not start the conversation with our normal exchange of pleasantries, sometimes involving Hindi swear words we would never repeat in front of our parents. Someone had knocked on the front door of his home in Atherton and delivered the sinister note to his housekeeper. Nikesh and his wife were away, but his two infant children were home.

Nikesh assumed "THIS" meant the smear campaign, and was

calling to let us know. Since Giannakopoulos was based in Geneva, the connection seemed plausible. It was strange they would send Nikesh this message, perhaps an extortion attempt?

When I called later, Nikesh seemed less agitated. He had already arranged twenty-four-hour protection at his home and informed the local police. From that day on, every time I visit him, someone pops out of the bushes and verifies my identity as I make my way past the gates, a legacy of our shared nightmare.

We speculated what "THIS" meant. More letters, personal intimidation?

Someone was shooting arrows into the air, as Longfellow wrote. They would soon fall to earth, we knew not where.

■

The first arrows were fired on July 14, 2016, but instead of Switzerland, the launchpad was midtown Manhattan. Some were directed eastward to Tokyo, others westward to Kansas City.

The projectiles took the form of three progressively strident letters, sent a few weeks apart, on the letterhead of a New York law firm, Mintz & Gold. All were addressed to the board of directors of SoftBank Group in Tokyo and Sprint Corp in Kansas City.

The signatory was Ira Lee Sorkin, partner at Mintz & Gold. I'd never heard of Sorkin, but a search suggested his clients included two of the most notorious scamsters of our times—Bernie Madoff, who needs no introduction, and Jordan Belfort, who inspired Scorsese's *The Wolf of Wall Street*. For variety, Sorkin also represented Monzer al-Kassar, a Syrian arms dealer who played a central role in the Iran-Contra scandal.

The target of these letters seemed unworthy of a man with such fine bedfellows. It was me.

Has anyone ever written nasty letters about you? I should have been tougher, the business I was in. But I wasn't. A friend pointed out that when people start writing letters to boards about you, it means you have finally arrived. I know what he meant. Like great Caesar, I had become a target. Except I never wanted a crown.

The three Mintz & Gold letters were followed by an even more brazen submission from the same mystery man from Geneva, Nicolas Giannakopoulos, who claimed to be behind the campaign directed at Nikesh. Now, he described me as "potentially dangerous."

"Apparently" and "possibly" featured in these letters with the frequency of F-bombs in *Lebowski.* These were not legal documents or legitimate shareholder complaints. SoftBank's lawyers at Morrison & Foerster described the "ludicrous allegations and innuendo" in the letters as "unremarkable and uninformed," not warranting investigation or even a response. No matter, since there was no telling how this saga might unfold, I wanted a probe on the record, including engaging an Indian law firm to examine the most "substantive" allegation—my "apparent active role" in an Indian real estate developer, Vatika Group.

In a prior incarnation, I had arranged a $150 million investment in Vatika alongside Goldman Sachs and served as a non-executive director representing the investor group. The Sorkin letters portrayed Vatika as a controversial organization involved in ninety ongoing legal proceedings, which they interpreted as "signals of potential illegality."

The findings were risible. Many of these legal proceedings had nothing to do with the company I was associated with. "Vatika" in Hindi means "garden" and features frequently in Indian entity names. Moreover, in many of the legal disputes involving the actual Vatika Group, the company was an aggrieved petitioner rather than a defendant, while others were minor civil disputes (cracked marble floors, leaky roof) not material enough to warrant the attention of a board member.

There was no evidence of impropriety at Vatika, nor did I have any executive responsibility, but real estate developers in emerging markets are assumed to operate on the fringe of the law. As a speculative sabotage tactic, it was clever to throw out an association with an Indian real estate firm as potentially controversial.

The threatening tone of the letters was sufficient to persuade Morrison & Foerster to write a dismissive note to Mintz & Gold characterizing their clients' allegations as "nothing more than a cynical attempt to leverage unfounded claims into a shakedown."

We never heard from Mintz & Gold and/or Giannakopoulos again. But this much was evident. Whoever had wanted Nikesh out of the way now had me firmly in their sights. When Nikesh was the sole target, there was a possibility that this was a personal vendetta. But when the same frontman—Giannakopoulos—started to nip at my heels, the agenda had to be SoftBank related.

Even more disturbing was the detailed personal financial information Giannakopoulos and his cronies had access to, including granular details of my compensation and personal investments. The unavoidable conclusion was that my personal email account had been hacked—a criminal offense.

I've been called many things, but to be labeled "dangerous" by people who associate with Madoff and Belfort was ironic. Part of me wished I was dangerous, maybe devastatingly cool and dangerous—like Clint Eastwood in *Dirty Harry.* But I wasn't. I was scared. Powerful people were out to hurt me. I needed help.

■

As had been the case with Nikesh, SoftBank supported me in the face of these troubling attacks. Now vice-chairman and still my good friend Ron Fisher acknowledged the need for a lawyer to represent me, and agreed that SoftBank would pay my expenses to not only defend myself, but also investigate who might be behind this scheme. Guided by Ron and my other old friend Jeff Sine, I soon had the right person in my corner.

Mark MacDougall was a senior partner at Akin Gump, an adjunct professor at Georgetown, and a former federal prosecutor.

"Reputational recovery" was one of his specialties. He explained what this means in an article about him in *The American Lawyer*. "It is our job to kill the false story. Not the bad story, which is what a PR guy does."[1] Mark had served on the board of IMG, the global media and entertainment company, which suggested familiarity with the world of dealmaking. According to Akin Gump's website, aside from "senior political figures and prominent executives," his clients included "an occasional spy."

He was exactly what I needed.

Mark was based in Washington, DC, and we met over a video call. In his sixties, he looked like a warmly intelligent academic. He wore a suit, but the style was button-down Brooks Brothers rather than point-collar Brioni. Even his virtual presence was comforting—it felt like a fireside chat. In his spare time, Mark provides pro bono defense to death row inmates. My case seemed embarrassingly trivial by comparison, and I half expected him to be cynical. Instead, Mark was empathetic; he understood how torturous it is to be at the receiving end of a reputational attack.

Mark was sure an investigative firm was involved, and I agreed with his recommendation to retain Kroll to do our detective work. I knew Kroll from my banking days; we frequently used them for background checks on prospective clients.

Meanwhile, a friend (the CEO of a European bank) introduced me to an Israeli intelligence officer named Avram Ben-Gurion, who had helped him identify a social media stalker. Avram provided contact details of an Israeli Air Force general as a reference. Ron was well connected in Tel Aviv and was able to verify Avram was kosher.

Avram reached out on WhatsApp, and asked me to download the Telegram app so we might communicate securely. I thought WhatsApp was "end-to-end encrypted," but I assumed Israeli spies knew better. Once we connected on Telegram, Avram asked me to download the Signal app, and to change my settings to "Disappearing Messages" and mask my IP address.

Signal and Telegram would become mainstream, but at the time it felt like a *Black Mirror* episode. It also felt ridiculous—Israeli spies, a crack DC lawyer, and Kroll facing off against an unknown saboteur with hotshot New York lawyers and shady Swiss operators on his payroll. *All this to chase me out of a job I never sought?*

■

A message arrived from Thomas "Tommy" Helsby, who headed Kroll's London office. Not on Signal or Telegram, but plain old email. He had something he wanted to share and needed to see me urgently. I thought he might propose an evening rendezvous at a smoky London pub where we would swap secrets over tumblers of peaty Islay malt whisky. Instead, he proposed dropping by my office in Mayfair at noon for a cup of tea.

What does a real spy look like? I ran through the list of usual subjects and settled on John le Carré's cuckolded spymaster George Smiley. "Small, podgy and at best middle-aged, he was by appearance one of London's meek who do not inherit the earth."[2] *Yes, definitely Smiley. Real people to solve real problems.*

I was behind my sleek, dark walnut David Linley desk when Connie escorted Tommy into my office. I invited him to sit on the creamy mohair velvet couch, across from the Georgian marble fireplace, above it Matthieu Ricard's *Tibetan Monk in Meditation* self-portrait, next to it an upholstered gray bouclé armchair, perfect for that afternoon siesta bankers of a different era might have enjoyed after a leisurely claret lunch.

Tommy was tall and angular, in his sixties, with thinning gray hair. He seemed frail, his clothes a size too large, his handshake the brush of sandpaper against my fingers. Like the professorial Smiley, he was the antithesis of the debonair spy who might love you or shag you.

When I asked Tommy about his background, he smilingly described himself as a "failed philosopher," an enigmatic icebreaker that had presumably served him well. I wanted to ask how a philosopher defines success, but now was not the time for a philosophical discussion or to congratulate Tommy on his stoicism in the face of failure. I was focused on the contents of the white envelope he had placed on the coffee table.

Kroll's agents had obtained from a journalist a stack of emails and documents, including the results of the ultimate body cavity search—my application to purchase shares in a Manhattan co-op. My bank and brokerage statements, compensation details, assets held in a trust created for my family, it was all in there. The package also included email correspondence between Nikesh's wife, Ayesha, and her accountants, and press clippings about Nikesh, but nothing emanating from Nikesh's own email account. Apropos for a man who went on to run a global cybersecurity business, Nikesh was an early adopter of the two-factor authentication technology now embedded in most email platforms.

These documents had been circulated widely to the London press, along with the suggestions of irregularity alluded to in the Sorkin letters. Fortunately, everyone saw through this insidious scheme.

Kroll had also determined that K2 Intelligence, set up by Tommy's former boss Jules Kroll, had been engaged to investigate me. Kroll had even connected with the K2 agents involved in my project, who suggested their firm had resigned when pushed to do something they considered "over the line." *Like hacking my email?* As for K2's client, all Kroll knew was that he was a "dangerous guy."

That word again. Dangerous? The type who cheats at golf, or the kind who eats your liver with fava beans and a nice Chianti?

I was impressed, and told him as much. Tommy had been with Kroll since 1981 and had crossed paths with most in the apparently incestuous community of private investigators. Much of the information he passed on was acquired in quid pro quo exchanges between agents. Like a trailer for a thriller, they teased but stopped short of the spoiler—who was behind this?

We chatted more, over tea and biscuits, the early afternoon sun now streaming in through the towering floor-to-ceiling windows overlooking majestic Grosvenor Street. Like me, Tommy had studied mathematics in college. He talked about his abandoned Cambridge dissertation on "the metaphysical basis for formal logic." I wasn't sure what that meant. I told him as a teenager I was obsessed with cracking Fermat's last theorem. He knew exactly what that meant.

Tommy's former clients included a US presidential campaign looking to discredit opponents and the Russian Federation trying to trace offshore KGB assets following the collapse of the Berlin Wall. His views on Russian oligarchs, frequently his subjects, occasionally his clients, were intriguing. Contrary to their roguish image, most were scientists or academics, cultured and philanthropic, who happened to be in the right place at the right time. I suggested he write a book. *The Philosopher's Guide to the Oligarchy* has bestseller written all over it.

We agreed to meet again, perhaps for a drink at the Black Cross in Notting Hill? Sadly, I never saw Tommy again. At Mark's insistence, all his communications thereafter were through Mark so that any revelations would be protected by attorney-client privilege.

Tommy had another secret, one I discovered a few months later when Mark came to London for a funeral service. When we met, the failed philosopher with sandpaper hands was in the final stage of a losing battle with cancer. With him died some of the greatest stories never told.

■

The UK Data Protection Act requires you to divulge, upon request, any information you possess about a UK national. If Mary hires Sherlock to tail her husband Dick whom she suspects of having an affair, Dick can demand that Sherlock disgorge any personal data he possesses about Dick, including photos of Dick with his pants down. Sherlock, however, is not required to reveal the identity of his client.

I authorized Mark to submit the required "Subject Access Request" on my behalf, following which K2 delivered what promised to be a fascinating read. We are all heroes in our own story, but third-party narratives can be more discerning. *What do these guys have on me?*

The forty-nine-page document was innocuous, uninspiring, even flattering. I was described as "a great team leader, with a proven track record in managing multiple teams across geographies and continents. Sama is also a great number cruncher and known in his circles as a financial engineer. He is a hard negotiator and a glib talker, which makes him a successful banker and investor."

The prose wasn't exactly Nabokovian, but at least I wasn't accused of pedophilia. I smiled, but one man's amusement can be another's chagrin. I imagined the perpetrator of this sinister scheme reading those lines, his eager anticipation turning to befuddlement, then anger, followed by an agitated phone call demanding a refund.

I gulped down the contents, but not without a reflective pause at a choice of adjective in the last sentence of that introductory paragraph. Being described as "potentially dangerous," as the Sorkin letters had, was amusing, even aspirational. But to be labeled "glib" was irksome, perhaps because it had an element of truth? Bankers are supposed to be smooth, but I always went for thoughtful and trustworthy. "Glib" suggested a lack of substance, even disingenuity. *Am I reading too much into the wordsmithing skills of the ex-cop who might have written this report?*

The report concluded that "most of his career of nearly three decades was uneventful, minus the large transactions and advisory fees." It was stated drily, with no intended irony, but as a summary of my career it was undeniably true and devastatingly boring. Had my life been on trial, I would be vaguely troubled by the tremulous case for the defense. *I see stories everywhere, I am living one myself. Is it finally time, in the second half of life, to break on through to the other side, into the realm of thought and fascination?*

Desperately seeking inspiration, K2 engaged subcontractors to conduct interviews with former colleagues and clients described only as "sources." An unnamed client said I was "a fine man and a wonderful guy," an anonymous colleague described me as a "role model for young professionals." I was touched. Not even bankers say nice things about bankers. Except for Lloyd Blankfein, who once said Goldman Sachs does god's work, which some believe is a nice thing.

There was reference to a speculative news article mentioning the Vatika Group and dodgy dealings with politicians—presumably the impetus for the fiction presented in the accusatory letters—but more interesting was a section of the report entitled "The Missing Years." The investigators were stumped, unable to chronicle my movements following my departure from Morgan Stanley and setting up my new business, Baer Capital Partners.

I could have told them I enrolled in French- and Italian-language programs but didn't quite learn either. I could have told them I tried reading Proust but never made it beyond *Swann's Way*. I could have told them about carding two consecutive sub-80 rounds to win the President's Putter at my golf club. I could have told them about long summer days watching my son play cricket in fields of dreams all over England. I might have told them "The Missing Years" was my life before and after.

But mostly I wanted to tell them to fuck off and leave me alone.

■

Amanpuri, ironically the "place of peace," is where things started to fall apart.

While the top 1 percent rejoice in the *White Lotus* exclusivity of a Four Seasons resort, the top 0.1 percent luxuriate in the exquisite serenity of an Aman. Most "Aman junkies," among them the oligarchs favored by my erstwhile philosopher friend, agree that founder Adrian Zecha and architect Ed Tuttle achieved perfection with their first venture—Amanpuri on the island of Phuket. The property overlooks the turquoise Andaman Sea, and the "rooms" are detached wooden Thai-style pavilions, built on stilts with steeply pitched roofs, scattered across the hillside like grains of rice flung seemingly randomly but actually located strategically to allow blissful immersion in the rainforest while enjoying panoramic ocean vistas. A dramatic stone staircase the width of a sprint track runs from the reception area down to the crescent-shaped white sandy beach, where the expensively Botoxed patrons recline under blue-and-white-striped sun umbrellas sipping chilled Provençal rosé.

Over the New Year holiday period, all rooms are set aside for the sybaritic haves and have-mores at rates in excess of $5,000 a night. Many are hosted at private villas, among the owners a Dutch diamond heiress, a Hong Kong taipan, and Swiss watchmaker Franck Muller, who guarantees a good time for all at his annual soirée.

Upon landing on Christmas Eve, I noticed a series of missed calls from Masa, and I called him before I got to the immigration counter. We were about to make the first investment from the Vision Fund, a multibillion-dollar stake in the NASDAQ-listed Nvidia Corp, whose chips were becoming the de facto industry standard for machine learning. But Masa was not calling to discuss the transaction. He was calling to tell me he wanted me to stand down from the Vision Fund. Only temporarily, he hastened to add. He had been told by a "reliable source" that I was going to be investigated by an Indian law enforcement agency because I had an influential enemy, and he could not risk jeopardizing the fund while the Saudis and the Emiratis were conducting due diligence.

I was stunned. Law enforcement agencies? My idea of breaking bad was moving my ball in the rough, my brushes with the long arm of the law all courtesy of a vindictively Orwellian speed camera on the Hammersmith flyover in West London. *Who is this "reliable source," pouring pestilence into Masa's ear?*

Masa and I had discussed the smear campaign, most recently when we were together in India. He never questioned my integrity, always acknowledging that I was being stalked by a pack of wild dogs for reasons neither of us understood. Now, for the first time, a missile launched by the reprobates behind this scheme had hit a target. This was no longer amusing.

I called Masa a couple of hours later to explain why his approach might backfire. I had featured prominently in interactions with investors and was on the board of the Vision Fund and related entities in the US and the UK. If I resigned, my exit would be newsworthy, creating a public controversy.

Masa countered that there was much to do at SoftBank outside the Vision Fund, including the revived prospects of a Sprint and T-Mobile merger, and that recusing me from the Vision Fund was plausible independent of any phantom threats.

Perhaps there was some justice in my ejection since I was at best ambivalent about this Vision Fund. While Masa insisted I was family and he wanted me by his side, the conclusion was inescapable. The Vision Fund was the sacred cow, I was expendable. It wasn't personal, except that it was. In my pantheon of relationships not involving blood or romance, Masa Son featured prominently. On the day after Christmas, I had to yank lawyers away from their families to arrange what felt like an amputation with aspirin as anesthetic.

Nikesh was with me in Phuket, as were our respective families. On December 30, we were invited for dinner to private equity investor Anil Thadani's villa. Anil was Adrian Zecha's financial partner when Amanpuri was conceived, and by dint had secured for himself a spectacular waterfront lot on a promontory. It was a surreal setting—moon above, ocean below—but rather than mingling with friends and family, Nikesh and I were in Anil's glasshouse study on a call with our man in Tel Aviv, Avram Ben-Gurion. His unnamed sources, presumably his network of ex-Israeli intelligence officers, were telling him this was an inside job involving SoftBank's Japanese employees, possibly racially motivated.

I thought of the trumpeter Nakamura-san, the genial Goto-san, and my favorite, the bouncy Tanaka-san, who once refused to cut his birthday cake in the office until I arrived. *No, Avram, you're wrong.* My Japanese friends were, well, my friends. They were *not* racist, and none of them devious or cosmopolitan enough to pull off an insidious global scheme such as this. Moreover, the perpetrator had spent over a million dollars recruiting prominent New York lawyers, expensive intelligence agencies in London, and shady operators in Geneva. No, Avram was wrong, deeper pockets were behind this.

But what if it wasn't employees but other reprehensible elements of Japanese society—Samir made the somewhat absurdist suggestion that it might be the *yakuza*—threatened by brown gaijin in senior leadership roles, pushing racial tolerance beyond acceptable limits? Particularly now, with the explosive power of the Vision Fund to reshape global technology.

There were others with plausible motives. Nikesh and I had backed DiDi in China, Ola Cabs in India, and Grab in Southeast Asia, effectively creating an Asian anti-Uber coalition that was costing Uber tens of millions monthly. Stories about Uber's dysfunctional culture were making the rounds, including the sinister "God View" customer tracking tool. I once again recalled our meeting when the man from Uber threatened to "destroy" us.

But this was all speculation: we needed proof.

■

New Year's Eve promised relief, but 2016 presented a challenge for Amanpuri management. King Bhumibol Adulyadej had died peacefully in October. He was eighty-eight, and one might have celebrated his life, but instead his successor announced a full year of mourning. But while the ocean was lovely, dark, and deep, Amanpuri had its books to keep. Which meant that as captive patrons we paid over $1,000 per head for a nonalcoholic dining experience featuring funereal music performed by beautiful Thai boys in black wraparound skirts while morose waiters served Japanese wagyu beef and Tasmanian king crab to the splendidly attired and immaculately coiffed guests. For the first time in Amanpuri's storied history, the servers and the served found common cause in a collective, peaceful misery. *Happy Fucking New Year.*

14

LET ME ROLL IT

When does a technology company stop being a technology company? Light bulbs and General Electric were high-tech once upon a time. By 2017, one might legitimately ask if Google or Facebook deserved that label. Google's search technology was over a decade old and its "moonshots" viewed as distractions from its core advertising business. Social networks were novel in 2012, and even then the utility was questionable. (In January 2018 both Google and Facebook were reclassified in the S&P 500 index under "Communications.") Nvidia, on the other hand, provoked no such doubts. The Latin root of the name (*invidere*) means "to look enviously," appropriate for a company that joined the trillion-dollar club in May 2023, supplanting Tesla as the new darling of hedge fund managers and retail online traders.

Nvidia was birthed by Taiwanese American entrepreneur Jensen Huang in 1993. While too intense to be called chill, Jensen seemed normal, his only apparent idiosyncrasy being that trademark black leather biker jacket.

Nvidia's first successful product was its graphics processing unit (GPU). Early GPU applications were primarily in gaming. The Nvidia GPU chip gave us the immersive explosions in *Call of Duty* and experiential crashes in *Grand Theft Auto.*

The GPU evolved into the GPGPU, or general-purpose GPU, which exponentially accelerated processing power for computers of all types and became a key enabler for machine learning applications crunching massive amounts of data, frequently in the form of images. (Early versions of ChatGPT, for example, were powered by over ten thousand Nvidia graphics processors, while later iterations required progressively more.) Hyperscalers (massive data centers that enable cloud computing) like Amazon Web Services, Microsoft Azure, and Google Cloud became increasingly reliant on Nvidia-designed $10,000 Ampere A100 (later H100) chips.

Even in early 2017, Nvidia promised to power the AI arms race in much the same way Intel enabled the PC revolution and Cisco provided the plumbing for the internet. Crucially, like Intel and Cisco and the makers of picks and shovels used in the California gold rush, Nvidia's business model was agnostic. Its success did not depend on OpenAI's ChatGPT outperforming Google's Gemini or Anthropic's Claude; Nvidia made money every which way.

As with Arm, the investment community understood this, and valued Nvidia stock accordingly. As with Arm, Masa believed—and this was five years before the hype cycle around ChatGPT—that markets underestimated and undervalued the AI opportunity. He wanted to go all in and acquire the company. Despite the hefty price tag (approaching $80 billion including a control premium—for a business that would be worth $2 trillion seven years later) I was enthusiastic, even more than I had been about Arm. Unlike Arm, no transformation was required, for Nvidia was riding what promised to be the transformative technology of the next decade. This was Masa at his vintage and irrepressible best, the visionary action figure I so admired.

Masa invited Jensen Huang to dinner at his home in Woodside. Unfortunately, Jensen preemptively killed any prospect of a merger. Leadership in AI was strategic to the United States, which made Nvidia one of the most important American companies of this century. The interagency CFIUS (Committee on Foreign Investment in the United States) would never allow a foreign takeover.

Thwarted in his grand design, Masa did the next best thing. His Vision Fund accumulated a small (under the 5 percent public disclosure threshold) stake in Nvidia in early 2017. The shares were purchased on margin, and within a few months the stock started to "pop," generating a relatively quick $3.3 billion return.[1]

Had he held on through to 2023, as one might expect of a technologist betting on a multidecade trend, the Vision Fund's profit would have been transformative—over 20 times—atoning for much of what came next. This was the paradox of a leveraged fund structure—the pressure to recycle capital to investors forces short(er)-term thinking. But in those early months, there was nothing but self-affirmation, a dream start to what Bloomberg described as an "eccentric relentless dealmaking spree."

After draining yet another three-pointer, Steph Curry remarked, "I might be delusional, but every time I shoot, I feel like it's going in."[2] Tiger Woods would nod in agreement, the way Nicklaus refused to acknowledge ever missing a three-foot putt that mattered. Great athletes create their own reality; self-deception allows them to bend outcomes.

It is a technique that works less well for investors.

■

Why is his name Herman Narula? According to his Wikipedia page, his father's proud Punjabi handle was Harpinder Singh Narula. As a child, I was in awe of all my friends with Singh in their name. It means "lion" and is evocative of turbaned warriors on horseback wielding shiny swords called *kirpans.* Was Herman perhaps born Harminder Singh Narula? If so, why tinker with such a splendid, kingly exoticism? *I wish I had a big-cocked name like that . . .*

I had no clue what this young man was saying, hence this random stream of consciousness.

It was a Friday afternoon in April of 2017, and I was in the ground-floor conference room of the Georgian townhouse on Grosvenor Street that served as SoftBank's London office. For the last few months I had been a three-state version of Schrödinger's cat—officially dead as far as the Vision Fund was concerned, unofficially alive when asked to volunteer an opinion regarding Vision Fund deals, and officially alive overseeing non–Vision Fund assets.

Herman (piercing black eyes, black hair, stubble beard) was seated across from me. Unusual for a millennial start-up founder, he was wearing a black suit and white shirt, perhaps for my benefit?

He was self-assured, the type of annoyingly impressive person who speaks as fast as he thinks. Herman had a computer science degree from Cambridge University and his venture funding came from Andreessen Horowitz, a redoubtable pedigree that underwrote his brilliance. He was describing his business, something about simulation software that "enabled virtual worlds for video games, defense organizations, and metaverse environments." His company's product was called SpatialOS, a distributed, cloud-based platform. I vaguely knew what that meant, but when I asked Herman about the company's revenue model, he shot me that patronizing look typical of millennial founders confronting clueless boomers. Perhaps he asked himself the same question I was struggling with: *What the fuck you talking about, man?*

Herman's start-up, appropriately enough, was called Improbable.

Rajeev Misra was supposed to join us for the meeting, but he was late. He now barged into the conference room, barefoot, then froze at the edge of the table, studying Herman with intense concentration. He rotated his head to look at me, went back and forth a few more times, as if watching a ping-pong match, until his face lit up in a eureka moment.

"Alok, this guy looks like your son!" he pronounced, with the dramatic flair of a referee announcing the winner of a boxing match.

Rajeev wasn't trying to disparage the guy, and it's conceivable he thought this was Samir. With Rajeev I could never tell. But I made it worse by laughing. Herman looked on, bewildered.

My behavior was inexcusable, particularly since Herman was indeed my son's age and a handsome young man besides. I apologized, but the damage was done. He now directed his pitch to Rajeev, who listened patiently while vaping, and then proceeded to ask the same questions I had. After each response, he registered a loud exhalation on his JUUL device, accompanied by a deep *hmmm*.

Later that evening, Maya and I had dinner at the Arts Club with Max Levchin and his wife, Nellie, who were visiting from San Francisco. Max is the smartest guy I know in the Valley; could he explain why "distributed simulation software that enabled virtual worlds" was a winning idea? Or at least what it meant?

We were still discussing Herman and his SpatialOS while walking out of the club. On the doorstep, as we waited for the doorman to hail us a cab, Max concluded that he didn't get it. "You should really get someone to diligence the tech," he said. At which point a young South Asian man who had been standing directly in front of us turned around and faced me directly.

"Hi, Alok," he said.

It was Herman.

Being in Max's company turned out to be my redemption. I once visited a fintech start-up in Bangalore that had a conference room named after Max; he had that kind of following among millennial coders. While Herman stared adoringly at Max, I looked on wondering if this was reality or yet another simulation, with me in an increasingly familiar role of NPC.

My skepticism was irrelevant, for being unofficially alive was meaningless. Herman came to SoftBank looking for $75 million. Masa Son gave him $500 million, valuing Improbable Worlds Limited at $1 billion,[3] making it one of many fortunate unicorns as Icarus began to fly again—this time with bigger Arabian wings.

■

Since our strange encounter in New Delhi, Adam Neumann had raised $690 million in a Series F funding round led by Chinese private equity investor Hony Capital and its parent Legend Holdings. The valuation was a startling $16.2 billion, almost twice what we had rejected earlier that year.[4] WeWork investors now included Goldman Sachs, J. P. Morgan, Fidelity Investments, Wellington Management, and T. Rowe Price. The last three were public market investors, playing WeWork in anticipation of an imminent IPO. For them this was guaranteed participation in a "hot" deal, where the price jumps when shares are free to trade.

Adam was reconnected to Masa through Mark Schwartz, who served on SoftBank's board. Mark (intense, bespectacled, uncommonly thick beard) had formed a close relationship with Masa while chairman of Goldman Sachs Asia.

At Masa's request, Ron Fisher and I visited Adam Neumann in November 2016, at WeWork's headquarters, a stately prewar low-rise in Chelsea at the corner of Sixth Avenue and Eighteenth Street.

Each expansive floor plate in the building was renovated in the style of an industrial chic SoHo loft with exposed pipes, airy twelve-foot ceilings, and two-toned columns. The focal point of the central common area was an elongated kitchen/bar counter. From the gentle splash of bubbly kombucha poured into glass tumblers to the animated exchanges among groups seated on the colorful couches, WeWork's urban capitalist kibbutz ethos was on full display. Everyone seemed skinny and happy in WeWorld, as if the receptionist checked your body fat percentage and clocked you on a smile meter before allowing entry. Ron and I looked at each other and smiled, feeling like parents visiting a college dorm.

Michael Gross—the warm-up act—showed us around the property. Michael's title was COO or CFO or maybe both. With his boyish good looks and blond charm, he seemed as hip as his environment. He was the former CEO of the Morgans Hotel Group, their flagship property the Art Deco Delano in Miami's South Beach. I had stayed at the Delano. With its risqué lobby scene and absurdly tiny rooms, the Delano was a triumph of style over substance. But I loved the Delano look, as I did the WeWork patina.

Michael demoed the clunky in-house social network. He was trying to legitimize WeWork's tech credentials, but I didn't get it. *Everyone is on Facebook, WhatsApp, or Slack. Who needs a separate walled garden?* When Masa visited a few weeks later, an employee was tasked with making waffles in the main kitchen so the bakery odor would waft through the space.[5] Ron and I didn't merit the waffle treatment, but I caught a whiff of snake oil.

Adam rose from his desk to greet us. He seemed even taller than I remembered, his jet-black hair glossier, his mane increasingly like an ethereal halo—a lofty valuation makes any entrepreneur seem messianic.

Adam introduced himself.

"We met before," I said. "You remember, Adam? In Delhi?"

"Of course, of course! You're the LinkedIn guy, right?" he exclaimed.

Ron and I did the eye-roll thing.

Adam was confusing me with another Indian in the SoftBank ranks—Deep Nishar, the former chief technology officer of LinkedIn. Deep has a debonair Clark Gable mustache and is smarter than me, but no matter. In Adam's eyes, Deep and I had something in common beyond our ethnicity. We weren't Masa.

I could have been offended, at least corrected Adam, but frankly, I didn't give a damn.

According to Adam, WeWork was increasingly signing up established and conventional businesses. Banks, for example, looking for a contemporary community-oriented spatial makeover so their staid number-crunching analysts could feel like hip tech bros. I liked this. Sales cycles with large corporations were cumbersome, but they signed long-term leases that matched the duration of WeWork's lease commitments. But beyond highlighting the presence of pedigreed venture firm Benchmark Capital on his cap table, Adam said nothing to address what was always my central concern—why should WeWork be valued like a tech business?

Adam suggested we make a trip downtown to 110 Wall Street, where he was showcasing a new concept he called WeLive. As with WeWork, staged or not, WeLive offered a compelling proposition to a millennial—seamless transition from college dorm to urban residential life. As with most WeWork facilities, each floor had a substantial common area with large inviting couches, the mandatory big-screen TV, and kitchenette with coffee machine and snack bar. The apartments, like the office cubicles, were cramped, but tastefully renovated with an exposed brick downtown vibe.

The key selling point for a tenant, according to Adam or Michael (I forget which) was that at WeLive you were guaranteed to get laid every night. It sounded exhausting.

To be fair to Adam, the WeLive business case was at least as compelling as that for WeWork, and the beer and sex on tap had something to do with it. WeWork and WeLive could do for commercial and residential real estate what Starbucks had done for coffee shops. The clever combination of branding and space planning would allow Adam to extract premium rents for space, just as Starbucks commands premium prices for mediocre coffee. As with Starbucks, tenants were paying for what wasn't on the menu—the experience. This insight, combined with creating a machinery to replicate this "We" experience globally and on demand, was Adam's main achievement, for which he deserves credit.

But offering free Wi-Fi didn't make Starbucks a technology company, nor was it ever positioned as such. In the public markets, Starbucks never traded at the double-digit revenue multiples accorded to software businesses, which promise infinite scalability with minimal variable cost. (Once you develop a product like Microsoft Office, you can sell subscriptions with no incremental production cost.) With WeWork, as with Starbucks, you pay to procure and fit out each additional site.

Ron and I relayed our thoughts to Masa. As always, he listened politely, but Mark Schwartz had already scheduled for him to meet Adam in New York on December 6, 2016.

Masa's visit to WeWork lasted twelve minutes.[6] Adam gave him a whirlwind tour, following which Masa asked Adam to join him in the black SUV driving Masa uptown from Chelsea to Trump Tower, where he was scheduled to meet with the president-elect.

I'm not sure what the WeWork waffles were infused with, but Masa emerged dangerously decisive. As the black Cadillac Escalade maneuvered through Manhattan traffic, he sketched out the strawman for a deal on his trusty iPad, which was signed by both Masa and Adam using Masa's Apple Pencil—which had now acquired a majestic aura, coming to terms with its destiny as a weapon of mass financial seduction. SoftBank agreed to invest $4.4 billion in WeWork at a valuation of $19.5 billion.[7] Of the $4.4 billion, $3.1 billion would go into primary and secondary WeWork shares, while the balance of $1.3 billion, in a deal structure redolent of Masa's good old "time machine management" strategy, would be invested in three joint ventures—WeWork China, WeWork Japan, and WeWork Pacific.[8] Ron Fisher and Mark Schwartz would join the WeWork board, both representing SoftBank. An entity controlled by Adam cashed out $360 million, while Benchmark was canny enough to take $128 million off the table, a nice return on its investment of $15 million.[9]

The deal was labeled the largest growth investment in technology. Except that, again, WeWork isn't a technology company.

So why did one of the most astute technologists of all time not recognize this disconnect? There was Adam's salesmanship, but perhaps less obviously, Adam solved a fundamental problem for Masa. As with the internet and with smartphones, Masa was early and right in identifying AI as a technology megatrend. But he could not spend $100 billion on AI start-ups. He was probably five years too early, but even in 2023, arguably at the peak of the AI hype cycle, he would have struggled to deploy capital on that scale. (Total venture investment in generative AI in 2023 was just over $26 billion—much of it by the tech titans rather than venture investors.[10]) Similarly, the convergence of biology and machine learning was transforming medicine, but Masa could not spend $100 billion on biotech start-ups.

There's something else about Adam Neumann that Masa didn't get. Like Monty Python's Brian, Adam Neumann may have looked like Jesus, but he wasn't the Messiah. He was a very naughty boy.

■

"Where's Ritesh?" asked Masa, walking briskly up to me.

We were in Delhi, and as on prior visits we hosted a cocktail party at the Le Cirque rooftop restaurant at the Leela Palace Hotel. Earlier in the day, over a cup of tea at the Taj Hotel, that inexhaustibly charming Apple Pencil, full of money, had signed a $1.4 billion investment in Vijay Shekhar Sharma's payments business Paytm—the same start-up Nikesh had rejected three years earlier—at a nosebleed valuation of $7 billion.[11]

In attendance at the Leela reception was the growing cadre of SoftBank portfolio company founders, plus an assortment of local industrialists and senior bureaucrats. But Masa had eyes for one person only—the unassuming and unshaven twenty-three-year old founder of OYO Rooms, Ritesh Agarwal. Ritesh had started the company at age seventeen, dropping out of college at twenty after receiving a $100,000 Thiel Fellowship, created by venture capitalist Peter Thiel to encourage student entrepreneurs.

The Indian hotel market is notoriously fragmented, dominated by single-unit owners instead of chains like Holiday Inn. OYO was like Uber but for budget hotel rooms. Hotels on the OYO platform were co-branded, and with the OYO name came the promise of a minimum standard of hygiene and sanitation, along with amenities like freshly cooked breakfast and Wi-Fi. What venture capitalists call "product market fit" was perfect in the Indian context: OYO solved an occupancy problem for property owners while budget travelers had greater choice. SoftBank had already invested $100 million in OYO in 2015, and the company's performance had been in line with its business plan.

I pointed Masa in the direction of Ritesh, who was in a corner speaking with Ola Cabs founder Bhavish Aggarwal. Normally in attire that bordered on scruffy, Ritesh was wearing a solid gray suit and a white shirt. He stiffened as Masa approached, bowed deferentially, then stood to attention, both hands clasped together behind him, like an earnest student facing an intimidating headmaster, leaning forward so he could hang on every word. Masa was animated, gesticulating with his hands while Ritesh listened respectfully, nodding occasionally. I continued to mingle while keeping an eye on Masa and Ritesh. Soon the latter began to shift uncomfortably and shake his head, his body language like mine at Vogue Diamond when confronted with Masa's unsolicited generosity.

Masa summoned me, and while Ritesh hung his head in embarrassment, Masa placed his hand on my shoulder and gave me the outline of the deal he had offered—SoftBank to invest $500 million, voting rights in respect of the new shares assigned to Ritesh, and dilution (reduction of percentage ownership) for Ritesh neutralized by issuing warrants. No further diligence required and the deal would be closed within four weeks.

Ritesh had not come here looking for money, but in what became a recurring theme, Masa made him an offer he could not refuse, anticipating and addressing every possible objection—dilution, loss of control, management distraction.

I suggested we at least discuss this with the SoftBank team that managed the OYO investment, but he dismissed my objections. "He is the one person who reminds me of me when I was young," he explained, looking proudly at Ritesh.

A few weeks later the deal was executed, though the size was cut in half and the valuation adjusted downward after strenuous objection from the other shareholders.[12] The Vision Fund later led another funding round of $1 billion, pushing the valuation to $5 billion.[13] This was unusual in another respect. Venture investors avoid leading a follow-on fundraising for an investee company, seeking independent validation instead. Otherwise, as Marc Andreessen so sensorially describes, "you can be thinking your shit smells like ice-cream."[14]

OYO is the quintessential case study in how too much capital can distort a business. Ritesh is the real deal—a passionate entrepreneur with an innovative idea, using technology to solve problems for suppliers and customers on his platform. The network effects within India were strong; with each additional hotel owner and hotel guest, the platform became more valuable for all. But when you give people too much money, they tend to spend it. With the promise of theoretically unlimited capital, Ritesh steered OYO in two different directions, both antithetical to its roots. International expansion, including developed markets like the US and Western Europe, became a priority. But unlike India, these markets were well served by hotel chains, and Airbnb was expanding at breakneck speed to offer a viable alternative. OYO also began to invest in renovating and owning properties, deviating from the capital-light model that is a defining characteristic of technology platforms.

The company would become a bloated chimera—a confused mix of technology platform, property manager, and real estate developer.

■

Other Vision Fund investee companies had business models that seemed more comprehensible than Improbable, but challenged regardless.

Wag was an "Uber for dogs" start-up; its mobile app connected dog owners to independent dog walkers. The Los Angeles–based Wag persuaded the Vision Fund to part with $300 million using a brilliant piece of salesmanship—their deck started with a photograph of Masa's beloved poodle.[15] But while driving is a regulated and licensed activity, "dog walking" is a nebulous skill, and the emotional stakes associated with losing your dog not quite the same as your Uber driver showing up late. And consider the case of the dog walker who lets himself into your apartment to pick up Snoopy but then lounges on your sofa drinking your beer while enjoying your Netflix subscription with Snoopy cuddled in his lap.

The Vision Fund directed $375 million of its largesse at Zume, Inc. (formerly Zume Pizza),[16] valuing the company at $2.25 billion. Zume's business model: pizza made by robots and cooked during delivery. Aside from the risibility, here's the fundamental question. Domino's has a mobile app for orders and might use an AI algorithm to improve the accuracy of its delivery times, but does that make it a technology company?

In the same vein, Compass described itself as a "real estate technology company," but its business was residential real estate brokerage. Its brokers might use a nifty smartphone app, but they weren't robots. It attracted $450 million from the SoftBank Vision Fund.[17] Katerra, a "technology-driven" construction company, received $865 million. Vivek Ramaswamy's Roivant received $1.1 billion, its stated mission to "apply technology" to drug development.[18] Smooth-talking Aussie Lex Greensill seduced the Vision Fund into investing a chunky $1.5 billion in his supply chain financing business, Greensill Capital.[19] In this case, not even a pretense of being a technology company—Greensill was a provider of working capital, some of it to technology businesses. Satellite entrepreneur Greg Wyler's OneWeb promised to deliver ubiquitous broadband connectivity via eight hundred satellites in low (under one thousand kilometers) earth orbit. Flawed execution resulted in over $1 billion of SoftBank's capital wiped out.[20] (Elon Musk, who at one point was collaborating with Wyler, eventually delivered on this "internet in space" promise; in typical Elon style, his Starlink mega constellation will eventually have forty-two thousand birds, each with a thirty-six-foot wingspan.[21])

Ride-hailing would come to be the single largest component of the Vision Fund. The aggregate commitment to DiDi in China was a staggering $11 billion, likely an enduring world record for the largest investment in a private company. Singapore-based Grab grabbed an additional $1.5 billion.[22] And then there's the strange case of Uber. As a rule, conventional private equity investors steer clear of the conflicts created when investing in competing businesses. But "conventional" was as cruel an insult as "normal" for Masa. After a simultaneous negotiation with Uber and Lyft, and despite backing Uber's competitors like Ola, the Vision Fund invested $7.3 billion in Uber,[23] prompting CEO Dara Khosrowshahi to make a comment that encapsulates how many founders felt about the Vision Fund: "I'd rather have their capital cannon behind me, all right?"[24]

The Vision Fund dealt in size, with many of its individual investments bigger than an average technology venture fund. But equally notable was the speed. Capital was deployed with the frequency of politicians making promises, creating a self-fulfillingly euphoric environment.

No cracks were evident in the early days. On the contrary, with successes like Nvidia, Masa enthused about performance exceeding his 44 percent historical record. At this point, Warren Buffett's delightful metaphor was irresistible: you can never tell who's swimming naked until the tide goes out. (It's a worn-out line but if you can do better, please do so here_____________.)

Fortunately, a lot of what went into the Vision Fund was unimpeachable. Apart from Nvidia, this included a 25 percent stake in Arm transferred at cost from SoftBank. (Eventually sold to SoftBank pre-IPO for a 2X return.) A $2 billion investment in ByteDance, the Chinese parent of TikTok, was vintage Masa. He identified ByteDance's AI technology as differentiated far in advance of TikTok emerging as a global social media titan, and by 2023 ByteDance would be worth at least 3X SoftBank's entry valuation.[25] A $1 billion investment in Coupang—a Nikesh deal transferred to the Vision Fund—and $680 million invested in DoorDash would turn out to be collateral beneficiaries of the pandemic.[26] A $1 billion commitment to Michael Rubin's Fanatics,[27] the online retailer of licensed sports merchandise, was a stellar performer, likely to return a multiple of capital invested. A $900 million investment in General Motors' autonomous driving affiliate Cruise was later sold to General Motors for $2.1 billion.[28] Many of Deep Nishar's investments, among them 10x Genomics and Relay Therapeutics, performed spectacularly well.

But Deep's commitments were in tens of millions, not enough to generate the elusive "alpha" of outperformance in the context of a $100 billion fund. Others, like Arm, Ola, and Grab, would also be successful, but none were blockbusters as Nvidia might have been had the fund held on.

■

In his classic *Only the Paranoid Survive*, Intel founder Andy Grove describes the moment every leader dreads, when massive change occurs and a company must either transform or fall by the wayside. For Zuckerberg, this "strategic inflection point" came when TikTok overtook Facebook and Instagram in user engagement, forcing him to rename his company and leap into the metaverse.

Staying a step ahead of this innovation cycle is the key to venture investing, and nobody plays it better than Sequoia Capital. Its investee companies include Apple, Google, Instagram, Airbnb, YouTube, Zoom, PayPal, WhatsApp, and ByteDance.

As Sequoia's global managing partner, Doug Leone was Silicon Valley royalty. In 2017, for the first time in his investing career, Doug might have wondered if his own business was at a strategic inflection point. Sequoia's first fund, launched in 1974, was a paltry $11 million. In 2016, the largest venture funds in the Valley rarely exceeded $1 billion; anything larger was considered unwieldy. (A handful of larger funds—Silver Lake, for example—focused more on buyouts and less on venture and growth investing.) SoftBank's Vision Fund was an unimaginable $100 billion.

Masa invited me to join him for the meeting with Doug at One Circle Star Way, SoftBank's US headquarters in San Carlos. The low-rise concrete-and-glass building was no more than fifty yards away from Highway 101. From my office on the north side of the building you could read the number plates on the fleet of Teslas trapped in the unrelenting freeway jam. San Carlos itself was in nowhere land, too far south of San Francisco but not close enough to upmarket Sand Hill Road, where Sequoia was located. It was a strange choice for someone of Masa's refined aesthete, but one his team made based on potential need for space for a merged Sprint/T-Mobile.

Masa's office suite, where we met Doug, occupied the entire south side of the fourth floor and included a dining room, a sitting room, a study with a capacious private bathroom, and a meeting room that could seat fifty people. It overlooked the sprawling parking lot, but then more pleasingly Redwoods State Park in the distance.

Doug was dressed casually, in blue jeans and a full-sleeved red-and-blue check shirt. He was balding, middle-aged, a barrel-chested self-made man whose first job was collecting golf balls by hand at a municipal driving range. Masa invited Doug to join us at a small conference table at one end of the room.

Like most CEOs, Doug was not given to a prolonged exchange of pleasantries. He immediately launched into a tirade. The source of his agitation was SoftBank's recent decision to increase its investment in OYO, a Sequoia portfolio company.

"You can't do deals like that," said Doug. "OYO doesn't need the money. We think international expansion is a bad idea, they need to be profitable in India first. And giving Ritesh your voting rights is terrible. It marginalizes us."

"You're doing this everywhere. It won't work," he continued. "We need to work together to build these companies."

Masa would never allow himself the indulgence of being rude. He nodded politely, his smile forced. He took time to respond, speaking softly, knowing he carried the bigger stick.

"I respect your opinion, thank you so much. But I believe Ritesh is a talented entrepreneur. I think OYO can be bigger than Airbnb, and I want to support him and make him a global champion. We will give him so much money, nobody can stand in his way."

This was the essence of Masa's investment style—unleashing Jedi knights like Ritesh with whom "he felt the Force" and challenging them to be ambitious enough while flooding them with capital. It's what worked with Jack Ma and Alibaba. Masa looked at founders the way founders want to be looked at by an investor. The antithesis of the dispassionate venture capitalist who keeps founders on a tight leash, drip-feeding capital in tens rather than hundreds of millions.

It was a short meeting, and Leone left with a puzzled look on his face. When Jack Nicklaus arrived at the 1965 Masters, the legendary Bobby Jones said, "He plays a game with which I'm not familiar." I suspect Doug had a similar reaction to Masa.

Leone's predecessor, the wiry, literary, and philanthropic Welshman Sir Michael Moritz, had crossed paths with Masa twenty years earlier. Moritz now had this advice to offer his Sequoia partners. "There is at least one difference between Kim Jong-Un and Masayoshi Son. The former has ICBMs that he lobs in the air while the latter doesn't hesitate to use his new arsenal to obliterate the hard-earned returns of venture and growth-equity firms. As Mike Tyson once said, 'Everyone has a plan until they get punched in the face.' It's time to bite some ear."[29]

It was a strange comment coming from a revered Valley elder—sanctimonious, confrontational, Neanderthal. And ironic. Sequoia's entire investment portfolio was marked higher because SoftBank pumped up tech valuations. And thanks to the Vision Fund, Sequoia's next flagship Global Growth Fund would be $8.2 billion,[30] more than four times the size of its predecessor. Which meant a minimum additional $120 million in annual management fees, regardless of performance. *Instead of biting Son-san's ear, why not send him a thank-you note?*

For the Valley establishment, the creation of the Vision Fund was like that alien, menacing, and transformative *Space Odyssey* monolith materializing on the divide in Sand Hill Road. From 2013 to 2023, the market value of all unicorns would skyrocket from $100 billion to $5 trillion.[31] To remain a player in this ocean of liquidity, Sequoia, like everyone else, needed a bigger boat. This would be Masa Son's enduring legacy. A billion dollars wasn't cool anymore. You know what was cool? A hundred billion dollars.

15

GAME OF PHONES

Paris Hilton reappeared. Like a comet. The last time I saw her was the night of that pill in Ibiza, and here she was again, regally blonde and perfumed, the glitter on her fluttering eyelids as dazzling as her smile, a butterfly floating up the aisle of the shuttle bus. *Is this a harbinger of more upheaval in my life?*

It was August 2017. Maya and I, along with a group of friends, were in Ibiza for a long weekend, and the bus was taking us to a house party. I was on the phone with Masa Son, as had been the case much of the day, discussing the kind of explosive deal that might have provoked Ms. Hilton's signature reaction—"That's Hot!"

Preoccupied as I was, I wondered about the Paris Hilton phenomenon. I'm certain she is no dumb blonde, just very good at pretending to be one. For most, "follow your passion" turns out to be clichéd and hopeless career advice. If I followed it, I'd be sitting on a beach in Barbados smoking weed while reading Zadie Smith and listening to Steely Dan. ("Follow your talent" has been offered as an alternative. If I followed it, I'd be sitting on a beach in Barbados smoking weed while reading Zadie Smith and listening to Steely Dan). I applaud Ms. Hilton for turning a fantastical lifestyle she evidently loves into a lucrative business, and reserve my judgment for her twenty-five million Instagram followers (including, curiously enough, your narrator).

Financial markets have influencers, too. Investors track every move icons like Warren Buffett make. Their endorsement, ideally accompanied by cash and always obtained at a price, elevates any deal. As would be the case in the transaction Masa and I were discussing.

Later that night, we were back at Pacha, this time for Flower Power Night. Like Mossad agents at Claridge's, Creedence Clearwater Revival in the home of electronic dance music was disorienting. I wore a red paisley bandana inspired by David Foster Wallace and a necklace with a chunky peace pendant. But instead of rollin' to "Proud Mary" inside, I was in the parking lot, a bottle of Pellegrino in my hand, on a marathon conference call with Masa and Jeff Sine's team at Raine.

Our meeting lasted through to 5 A.M., at which point it was wheels-up on VistaJet, initially to New York and then onward to Denver to meet with the ultimate influencer in the world of media deals—John Malone. At stake was what might be a mammoth and byzantine coda to Masa Son's extraordinary career: the takeover of cable giant Charter Communications and a concurrent merger with wireless carrier Sprint, leaving SoftBank in control of the largest communications business in the United States.

■

SoftBank's US game of phones began in 2014, when wireless service in the United States was demonstrably crap. Relative to Japan, a YouTube video or PowerPoint presentation took four times longer to download. In geek speak, SoftBank Mobile consistently delivered a robust 50 Mbps download speed in downtown Tokyo compared with a meager 10–15 Mbps in Manhattan. Suburban areas were worse, and San Francisco no better.

The US market was theoretically more competitive, which

usually means lower prices and better service. It featured four major nationwide operators (Verizon, AT&T, T-Mobile, and Sprint) compared to three in Japan. However, over 70 percent of industry profits flowed to Verizon and AT&T while T-Mobile and Sprint were debt-laden and struggling to survive. This wasn't a competitive market, it was a cozy duopoly with no incentive to upgrade service. Why serve filet when you can get away with selling chuck?

In 2011, T-Mobile's controlling shareholder Deutsche Telekom had agreed to sell T-Mobile to AT&T for $39 billion, but the FCC and Justice Department scuttled the deal. Fortunately for T-Mobile, its advisors negotiated a punitive prenuptial agreement (a "breakup fee" in deal parlance) requiring AT&T to pay $3 billion in cash, contribute wireless spectrum worth $1 billion, and commit to a "roaming agreement" that allowed T-Mobile to buy capacity on AT&T's network on favorable terms.[1] A rejuvenated T-Mobile, led by the magenta-clad smooth operator John Legere, shook up the industry with a price war, its newfound mojo vindicating the regulator's decision to block the AT&T deal.

Meanwhile, while Sprint was hemorrhaging cash and customers, it had the largest spectrum holdings (the licensed airwaves that transmit data) of any operator. Crucially, Sprint's "mid-band" spectrum was the communications equivalent of beachfront property, ideal for the deployment of Fifth Generation (5G) networks that would deliver TikTok videos with the same speed as text messages.

Masa Son understood telecom the way Julius Caesar understood combat. He observed the competitive field, saw the opportunity, made his move.

The first leg of his strategy was acquiring Sprint, a deal SoftBank consummated in 2013 after a takeover battle with Charlie Ergen's Dish Network. The price tag was $21.5 billion, of which $5 billion went into Sprint and $16.5 billion went to its shareholders.[2]

The next stratagem in this game was a merger between Sprint and T-Mobile. John Legere's flamboyant aggression combined with Sprint's spectrum holdings would create a potent third player, pushing all to invest and upgrade their networks. Just like Japan almost ten years previously.

Unfortunately, the Democrat appointees at the helm of the FCC and Justice Department disagreed, their objection based on potentially higher consumer prices and lost jobs. But a Sprint and T-Mobile combination was different from an AT&T and T-Mobile merger. The plummeting value of Sprint's debt and equity suggested financial distress, and a failed Sprint would mean even greater job losses and obviously reduced competition. Even T-Mobile, for all John Legere's bluster, could not keep pace with AT&T and Verizon given the capital required to upgrade nationwide networks to 5G technology standards.

A stymied Masayoshi Son went public with his arguments.

In 2001, he had allegedly threatened to set himself on fire while in the offices of the Japanese Ministry of Posts and Telecommunications over a regulatory dispute. (When I asked him about the story, Masa said it was true—except he had no petrol or matches.) There was no self-immolation threat in Washington, DC, but Masa was irrepressibly vocal in his indictment of the FCC's misplaced stance.

"At my home in Silicon Valley I say, oh my god. How can America live like this?" he said at a technology conference,[3] reinforcing his commitment to transform US telecommunications, just as he had in Japan.

It was a lost cause.

In August 2014, a frustrated SoftBank announced it had aborted plans for an American blitzkrieg. Instead, we hunkered down in a bunker, tangibly Masa's new home in the verdant Kansas City suburb of Mission Hills, with easy access to Sprint's headquarters in Overland Park.

Confronted with over $10 billion in debt maturities over

three years, we received some unsolicited advice from (for me) a weirdly thrilling source. Masa, Nikesh, and I gathered around a speakerphone placed on a casual dining table in Masa's Woodside home to listen to the master of debt—Michael Milken, now a rehabilitated and professorial philanthropist. Milken proposed an opportunistic Sprint debt-exchange offer to alleviate the pain of this overdose victim of financial MDMA. But Sprint was past the point of such Band-Aid fixes.

Masa replaced incumbent CEO Dan Hesse with Marcelo Claure, a Bolivian entrepreneur whose handset distribution business SoftBank had purchased in 2013. An imposing six-foot-six, always attired in solemn black, the hulking soccer-mad Marcelo was what Masa proudly described as his "street fighter." (Like every other ten-figure moneybags I seem to meet, the genial and driven Marcelo owned a sports team, in his case La Paz–based Club Bolivar, and later Inter Miami CF in partnership with David Beckham.) One of Marcelo's first major decisions was not something you associate with a street-fighting man. Instead, he did what many American CEOs do when faced with a crisis—he hired McKinsey. Separately, the alchemist Rajeev Misra engineered a financial lifeline, raising capital by securitizing Sprint's spectrum assets and handset leases.

Meanwhile, Masa focused relentlessly on Sprint's network. For this, he enlisted SoftBank's in-house mop-headed and bespectacled "mad scientist" Takashi Tsutsui. Tsutsui-san's English was incomprehensible; Tanaka-san suggested his Japanese posed a similar challenge.

Masa believed Sprint's network could be reengineered without reliance on traditional towers. A telecom tower is a vertical rental property, typically owned by an independent company that leases space on the tower to a phone company to house the antennas and radios at the core of every wireless network. If Sprint could eliminate tower leases altogether, the impact on profitability would be profound.

It didn't work. Sometimes even mad scientists get their numbers wrong.

Meanwhile the nimble Legere took dead aim at his lumbering rival Marcelo, his taunting tweets—"@marcelo go back to the kiddie pool"[4]—reminiscent of Ali taking on Frazier. But this was no Fight of the Century, the result a foregone conclusion with no possibility of a rematch. McKinsey's restructuring advice and Misra's financial legerdemain merely postponed the inevitable. Masa couldn't throw in the towel despite seeing his man totter. To do so would destroy his credibility with the Japanese lenders who backed his extraordinary adventures.

In November 2016, relief came from an unexpected quarter—Donald Trump's surprising victory meant a Republican administration with a less dogmatic view of regulation in the communications industry.

Two years on, the arguments in favor of a merger were even stronger. Broadband infrastructure was a national priority. Not so kids in America could watch TikTok videos, but as an essential business tool. While American consumers had lower monthly bills than their Japanese counterparts, they paid more per unit of data. And while horizontal mergers involving firms in the same industry invariably result in job losses, in this case the marginal fourth player would potentially fold, resulting in even greater dislocation in employment.

With newly appointed Republican heads at the FCC and Justice Department willing to give Masa a fair hearing, the time had come for the Japanese to engage with the Germans for their progeny to unite on American soil: "Project Nations" was reborn.

In a nomenclature bereft of creativity, some investment banking analyst coded Sprint as Spain, T-Mobile as Thailand, and Deutsche Telekom as Denmark. Confusingly, Masa and I made our way to Germany to meet with Denmark.

■

The calendar invite was for 0930 on Tuesday, May 23, at Deutsche Telekom's headquarters in Bonn. It happened to be my thirty-first wedding anniversary, but more concerning was the meeting location. This merger involved four prominent listed companies, and discretion was therefore essential. I was assured the meeting would be at an "appropriate venue," to be confirmed an hour prior to the meeting. Very secret service, but those days this clandestine stuff seemed quotidian.

I flew overnight from New York on Viper, the sleepless airtime neatly synchronized with Dylan's *Bootleg Series* repeated once, landing at Cologne Bonn Airport early on a fine spring morning. After the usual cleanup routine at a local Marriott, I arrived at our meeting venue—Schloss Marienfels, a mid-nineteenth-century castle, surrounded by forty acres of forest and built on a hillside overlooking the Rhine. The schloss was privately owned by Frank Asbeck, celebrity founder of photovoltaic manufacturer SolarWorld, and known in his fatherland as the Sun King. The architecture was Gothic, the walls painted pale yellow, the slate roof blue-gray, on a single turret fluttered a German flag. Like the castle in *Snow White,* it managed to be simultaneously pretty and intimidating.

We met on the—appropriately—sunny terrace overlooking the river, our princely and charming host the tall, bald, and jovial Tim Höttges, CEO of Deutsche Telekom. Joining him were Thomas Dannenfeldt, CFO, and Thorsten Langheim, chief dealmaker and T-Mobile board member.

Tim admired Masa and made it clear he was looking for an alliance with SoftBank as part of any deal. This resonated with Masa, but Tim's colleagues came on too strong. The state of Sprint's finances notwithstanding, you did not treat Masayoshi Son as if you were the International Monetary Fund dictating terms to an emerging nation, for this was a man soaring where only eagles dare. We left behind a trio of stunned Germans after Masa pointed out they weren't knights in shining armor, nor was

Sprint a damsel in distress. Rather, SoftBank was a conqueror with its eye set on the US communications market, T-Mobile one of its many potential targets.

Within an hour, Masa and I were wheels-up in our respective vehicles—Viper and Viper's big sister, Masa's G650ER.

Just like that, the eagles had landed and the eagles had flown.

■

That flight to Luton would be my last on Viper. A single aircraft shared by Ron Fisher, Rajeev Misra, and myself meant frequent and wasteful repositioning. I negotiated a deal to sell Viper, replacing it with a VistaJet contract guaranteeing a job for Junko-san and availability anytime anywhere. I had lost my private plane virginity to this sleek beauty, and felt a twinge of guilt every time I entered one of Vista's Bombardier jets, as if I'd traded a faithful companion for a flash concubine.

Once on board, I wondered again at Masa's gamesmanship. While not in a position of strength, Masa was not entirely bluffing. In the Project Nations mix were the cable giants Comcast and Charter Communications. Between them, they provided broadband internet service to over 80 percent of US households.

The cable bundle historically included the "triple play" of video, fixed-line telephony, and broadband. This bundling of services reduces customer churn—the kryptonite of any services business—since people are less likely to switch to a competitor when they purchase multiple services. Additionally, offering multiple services enhances profitability by spreading fixed costs over more "revenue generating units."

But fixed-line telephony had gone the way of the buggy-whip. Offering wireless service was critical for the cable service providers to create a compelling consumer bundle. And "cord-cutting" further disrupted the cable bundle. With the exception of sports and news, entertainment was increasingly streamed on demand rather than transmitted linearly over traditional cable channels. This wasn't all bad news for cable operators since their profitable high-speed broadband product was now a utility as essential as running water.

To offer a mobile telephony product, Comcast and Charter didn't have to own a wireless company. Their alternative was to resell capacity purchased in bulk from the wireless carriers—an MVNO strategy. But MVNO profit margins are razor thin, and no company wants to be accountable to its customers for a service provided by a competitor.

The phone companies came at the bundle from the opposite angle: they had a mobile phone product but craved a video and/or broadband offering. AT&T's disastrous DirecTV acquisition was an attempt to package multichannel video service with its core wireless telephone product, but it failed to anticipate the streaming revolution. Verizon had flirted with the idea of acquiring Charter, but its overtures were rejected. Media reports suggested Verizon's offer was deemed "too low." French media dealmaker Patrick Drahi, who had recently acquired cable operator Altice in the United States and was looking to expand his US footprint, was also rumored to be a suitor.

Charter was in play.

The gatekeeper to Charter was the man who controlled 31 percent of the company via his Liberty Broadband vehicle—the cable cowboy John Malone. Now in his seventies, the libertarian and moneyed Malone had strung together a global media empire over forty years, starting with cable consolidation in the United States. While his kingdom included the Formula One franchise and SiriusXM satellite radio, John Malone was down to earth in a very literal way: his 2.2 million acres made him the largest private landowner in the United States. The landed John Malone was to media dealmaking what Adam Neumann was to salesmanship—the GOAT.

We concocted a merger between Charter and Sprint in a deal that would leave SoftBank in control. The enterprise value (sum of equity value and outstanding debt) of the combined "New Charter," based on the reported $540 acquisition price, would exceed $200 billion, making it the largest M&A transaction in history.[5]

Since Sprint was less than a third of the value of Charter, simply merging Charter and Sprint would leave SoftBank as an inconsequential minority shareholder. SoftBank's bid to be in control required a substantial slug of cash. $65 billion of this would be acquisition debt provided by a syndicate of bank lenders and the balance would be equity from SoftBank's own balance sheet.[6]

The final piece of the deal was the most complicated. SoftBank needed Liberty to "roll over" the 31 percent of Charter shares it controlled into New Charter shares while giving SoftBank a proxy to vote such shares. The proxy allowed SoftBank to control New Charter without buying Liberty's shares, thereby limiting the total cash required to consummate the deal. Moreover, the influencer Malone's willingness to remain as a committed shareholder would be seen as an endorsement for New Charter.

If the Arm acquisition felt like Maverick's F-14 Tomcat in a 4G inverted dive with a MiG, this merger was the equivalent of Maverick's host USS *Enterprise* doing a cartwheel over Marko Ramius's *Red October*. But while the proposition was gigantic, intricate, and financially precarious, the industrial logic was impeccable. In addition to capital and cost efficiency, the merged Charter/Sprint could uniquely offer a compelling "quadruple play," including wireless telephony over an owned network, one up on the traditional cable triple play.

As always, Masa's thinking had an original fourth dimension. Sprint's spectrum assets meant that alone among wireless operators, it had theoretically unlimited network capacity. By offering near-free wireless service as part of its bundle, a SoftBank-controlled New Charter could offer a compelling value proposition to households in the parts of the country served by Old Charter. This was vintage Masa Son—his adolescent "free coffee for all" loss-leader model upending the US communications landscape.

In this game of bluff and counterbluff, information and disinformation, there was another compelling reason to engage with Charter—Kabuki theater for our German audience.[7]

My colleague Alex Clavel was by my side in this and every other major deal. Alex (tall, bespectacled, scholarly) was a Princeton graduate who spoke Mandarin and Japanese. I had recruited him into Morgan Stanley in 1994 and hired him away from Morgan Stanley in 2015. Alex and I had already made a trip to Denver and met with Malone's team led by Greg Maffei, CEO of Liberty Media and a former CFO of Microsoft. Maffei was urbane, silver-haired, and firm in his insistence on a sweetheart deal for Liberty, guaranteeing a minimum return regardless of how "New Charter" performed.

While we did not have an agreement, an offer on the table was tangible progress. But then on July 30, two days after *The Wall Street Journal* published a story about merger talks between Charter and Sprint, our collective excitement was extinguished by a cold shower in the form of an icily dismissive public statement from Charter.

"We understand why a deal is attractive to SoftBank, but Charter has no interest in acquiring Sprint."[8]

Perhaps Charter's management team had genuine concerns about the deal. Maybe CEO Tom Rutledge felt his job was threatened. Or was it a masterful negotiating ploy by the GOAT? Because now the only person who might swing the deal for Masa was John Malone.

■

Masa's meeting with Malone was scheduled for 5 P.M. on August 23 at Liberty's headquarters in Englewood, Colorado. On the morning of August 21, I jettisoned the red paisley bandana and the pendant necklace in favor of that equally absurd candy-stripe sleeper suit laid out for me on the VistaJet bound for Denver via New York. I was wired when I boarded, and after speed-reading *American Psycho*, even more wired when I arrived.

After a day of frantic preparation at Raine's office on Seventh Avenue, Alex and I, along with Jeff and his apprentice Chris Donini (genial, precise, ex-Goldman) departed Teterboro Airport at 0630 the following morning for Denver. As the four of us huddled over breakfast on the Vista plane, Alex received a text message from Tanaka-san.

Son-san's plane has a mechanical problem. A replacement part was required, and he would be delayed.

We weren't alarmed. The stakes were high, schedules would be reworked.

We should have known better. Our hero was a man who wanted to land on Stuart Chambers's boat in a chopper to deliver his bid for Arm.

Another message followed. No problem. On way to Denver via Chicago. Economy Class on United Airlines.

At 2 P.M., Masayoshi Son shuffled into the lobby of the Hilton Inverness Denver, a substantial garment bag slung over a slumped left shoulder, counterbalanced by briefcase held in his right hand, with the grim air of a man who might charge a windmill, his faithful and indefatigable squire Tanaka by his side.

While Masa showered and changed, Tanaka-san regaled us with the hilarious image of his beloved master curled up in his seat while Tanaka politely, desperately, and ultimately unsuccessfully warded off an overzealous United Airlines stewardess from prodding an unsuspecting Masa awake so he might sample United Airline's award-winning meal service. Perhaps much was lost in translation, but there is a reasonable chance that she responded to Tanaka's strenuous objections by assuring him that the meal service was not merely award winning, but free.

■

"How much do we owe if Charter share price is six hundred dollars?" asked Masa.

"Nine billion," was the immediate response from the very precise Chris Donini, his eyes fixated on his laptop screen, primed for the next question.

We were in John Malone's waiting room, with Masa looking straight ahead at a jet that seemed no more than a seven iron away, taxiing on the runway at Denver International Airport. Donini was responding to Masa's questions on SoftBank's exposure as a result of a potential deal guaranteeing a minimum return for Liberty; these were the numbers Masa and I were discussing when I was in Ibiza.

The questions continued.

"How much if it's three hundred dollars?" Masa asked, with intense concentration.

"Twenty-three billion," shot back Donini.

Jeff and I exchanged glances and shook our heads in awe. Our careers combined spanned over sixty years, and we were used to dealing in big numbers. But never before had we heard tens of billions of dollars so familiarly discussed.

Masa liked symmetry when it came to meeting attendees. Since Malone would be accompanied by Maffei, one of Jeff and I needed to drop out. I volunteered. Jeff had dealt with Malone before, and I trusted him to say and do what I might, just better. Besides what was I going to say, ask John how much land was enough?

It was time. Jeff rose, but then paused and gave voice to my thoughts.

"You're going into a meeting with John Malone," he said, addressing Masa. "If you agree to this deal, you're betting the future of SoftBank. If you feel uncomfortable at any point, just walk away."

Masa nodded, but he didn't look at Jeff. He continued to stare at that plane, now no more than a pitching wedge away.

■

The private terminal at Denver International Airport was buzzing that evening. Masa's repaired 650ER had tailed his United Airlines flight from Tokyo, my VistaJet was parked nearby, and Marcelo Claure's Sprint plane was the last to join the gaggle. He had flown in from Kansas City, insisting on meeting us in Denver when I told him the outcome of our negotiations—Masa Son and John Malone had shaken hands on a deal.

Dinner, at an Italian restaurant in a suburban strip mall outside Denver, should have been a celebration. While a glass of the finest Barolo available was raised, Masa seemed circumspect. Was he worried about a winner's curse, or was this a hangover from what must have been a grueling twenty-four hours? Marcelo, Masa's default choice as CEO of the merged entity, seemed understandably apprehensive: the acquisition debt provided no margin for slippage. Ironically, Jeff and I, both previously hawkish, found ourselves in the unusual position of cheerleading. We were both deal junkies, and the idea of pulling off this landmark merger was a high for us.

It didn't matter. After a few weeks of going back and forth, it became clear that CEO Tom Rutledge would not be swayed. Charter had acquired Time Warner Cable for $78.7 billion only a year earlier. Integrating a business of this magnitude was all-consuming, and Rutledge had no appetite to take on a struggling Sprint.

The first signal the deal was off track was when details were leaked to CNBC's David Faber.[9] Manipulating the media to promote your agenda is a common deal tactic, and since Faber was always granted an exclusive annual interview with the otherwise reclusive Malone, there was little doubt as to his source. Realizing the deal was dying, the Liberty team likely wanted to telegraph to the market that someone had been willing not only to pay a rich price for Charter but also to guarantee an even richer price five years forward.

They were talking up their book, as one does in markets.

Faber contacted SoftBank for comment. Denial was pointless—we knew his source. Instead, I played the game, requesting that Faber also report an inconvenient truth his likely source had neglected to share. In the proposed deal, SoftBank would be selling Sprint to New Charter at $10 per share, a hefty 50 percent premium to Sprint's trading value, a detail that Faber would duly report on CNBC. We were packaging our ugly duckling as Snow White, but Liberty didn't care. Malone had his guaranteed return. We, on the other hand, had another agenda—we knew the Germans were watching and listening.[10]

▪

Egos and regulatory hurdles aside, the logic for a Sprint/T-Mobile combination remained compelling. For Sprint it meant survival; for T-Mobile it was a shot at being number one. Meanwhile, with a Republican administration in place, the signals from Washington, DC, continued to blink green.

The next round of negotiations was initiated by the CEOs of the respective companies. Marcelo took his gloves off, Legere shed his snark, and we reengaged with newfound urgency. Over four days of marathon negotiating sessions (two at Morrison & Foerster's offices in San Francisco and another two at Wachtell Lipton in New York) we hammered out the details of a merger, eventually announced in April 2018.

Anticipating the regulatory and political obstacles, New T-Mobile committed to $40 billion of network investment in its first three years of operation, 46 percent more than T-Mobile and Sprint combined in the past three years. The new network was expected to deliver fifteen-times-faster speeds nationwide. Prices would not be raised for three years, and two hundred thousand new jobs would be created as a result of network build-out and retail footprint expansion in rural areas. Cost reductions would run at $6 billion annually, and the new company, led by Legere and headquartered in Seattle, would have a combined enterprise value of $146 billion.[11]

The Germans always had the upper hand in the negotiations, but the outcome was a fair and eventually fruitful culmination of Masa's US telecom adventures, leaving SoftBank with a 24 percent stake in an entity that not only had strong momentum and leadership but would in fact catalyze a massive upgrade in network quality across carriers. The merger promised to be that rarest of phenomena—a win-win outcome where the winners weren't just the fat-cat dealmakers but all shareholders and American consumers at large.

Someone took a photo of me, flanked by Marcelo and Legere with my arms around both, right after we agreed on the deal. Legere, clad in his customary black and magenta, is flashing a V-for-victory sign above my head. Or maybe it's bunny ears, with John you never knew. It was a pic ripe for indulgent self-promotion—megadeal, important people—and one I spontaneously and unashamedly shared on Twitter and LinkedIn.

I liked it, shouldn't everyone?

16

HUNTERS AND COOKS

It is an old investment maxim that when taxi drivers start talking about a stock, it is time to sell.

My driver was piloting a black gull-winged Tesla on the sun-splashed and gridlocked US 101. Billboards for C3.ai and CrowdStrike reminded me I was in Silicon Valley. As always on the 101, I wondered about autonomous flying taxis and levitational hyperloop tunnels. *The smartest people in the world live here, why the fuck don't they solve real problems instead of building silly social networks?*

I looked at my watch anxiously, concerned I was going to be late. I should have planned better, but self-flagellation seemed pointless. Meditation didn't help either, my mind was as cluttered as the freeway. After a few minutes of aimlessly surfing emails, I reluctantly engaged with my Uber driver.

I hate talking to strangers, and when I do, as Maya points out, my mouth has an overly intimate relationship with my feet. However, I'd recently learned that my Uber rating was the lowest in my family. Not that I'm competitive with my kids, it's just that it's nice to be liked. Or maybe it was an obsession with rankings; an Indian education and Wall Street career did that to me.

Samir and Alya were both New Yorkers, so maybe this was

typical American grade inflation? But they both insisted it was because I treat Uber drivers like drivers. "What about tips, can't money buy me love?" I had asked. Maya suggested I listen to the kids, and as always I abided.

At home in London the conversation would have been about the weather or the footie. In the Valley it was usually technology. And when I told my driver I worked for SoftBank, all he wanted to talk about was his Tesla shares.

"Well, Elon's a strange dude, but he is a genius," I responded. "And Tesla is an awesome business. But here's the thing. GM sold 10 million cars and made $12 billion last year. Tesla shipped 100,000 cars and lost $2 billion. Should Tesla be worth more?"

My driver did not react. *Am I not being likable?*

"If you think Tesla rates a tech valuation, a car needs to generate recurring revenue. Like software," I continued, undeterred. "Fully autonomous Teslas rented out by the company when owners don't use them, which is over 90 percent of the time. But when that happens, you'll be out of a gig. So maybe owning Tesla is a hedge against your future income!"

"I don't know, man. I'm buying some more. It keeps going up. Like it's on autopilot!" he finally responded, laughing.

I gave up.

TSLA, along with most tech stocks, was a crowded trade. Buying now seemed as original as discovering the Beatles in 1970. But if you think that makes me smarter than my Uber driver, think again. In the five years following that ride, TSLA was up almost 10X. It's like the Beatles were the next Beatles.

None of which changed the fact that I was going to be late.

■

On that crisp morning in January 2018, my Uber ride was crawling northward to downtown San Francisco.

In the heady eighties, the event that best captured the zeitgeist was Drexel Burnham Lambert's annual convention in

Beverly Hills. It was called the Predators' Ball and its master of ceremonies—Michael Milken. The disrupters of that era were the cannibalistic corporate raiders, and here they mingled with Milken's junk bond investors who bankrolled them.

I wasn't invited to the Predators' Ball, but now I was a keynote speaker at its twenty-first-century equivalent—Morgan Stanley's technology conference in San Francisco.

My agenda was to highlight the disconnect between SoftBank's share price and the value of its underlying assets, a gap as wide as 50 percent. It was a straightforward message—you didn't need a PhD in finance to understand that buying something worth ten dollars for five dollars is a good idea. Masa was SoftBank's largest shareholder, and for him this discount was a constant source of frustration. Why were SoftBank shares on sale? There were technical reasons, like embedded tax liabilities, but for the professional investor community, opacity was a concern. While I always found Masa Son's "crazy guy" self-caricature endearing, fiduciaries managing pension funds for California teachers or New York firemen were understandably wary. And Masa's communication style—the goose laying golden eggs slide was always a favorite—was, well, unconventional.

Buybacks and (at the extreme) privatization are the standard prescriptions for companies with undervalued shares, but both require cash. Buffett's Berkshire Hathaway purchases its stock whenever it trades below asset value, but Berkshire is rated double-A and has greater financial flexibility than SoftBank. Allocating cash between new investments and stock buybacks was a constant debate for us, but meanwhile investor-relations exercises such as this were critical.

The attendees would be analysts and portfolio managers working for the major equity mutual funds or hedge funds. I could tell the difference—American Apparel fleece hoodies and middlebrow observation versus Loro Piana cashmere anoraks and elevated insight.

The featured speakers are, like me, senior executives at listed technology companies. We won't cross the legal lines that seemed so blurry to the Drexel event protagonists, nor is our mission to dismember companies. Unfortunately, some of us really are predators. Your data, increasingly used to train AI models, is the prey. Your mindshare, captured algorithmically and surreptitiously, is the product sold to advertisers.

That doesn't make us evil or even semi-evil. Just greedy, which many believe is good. I know the senior management team at Google; they are fine people, and they help us find information and buy stuff. As a teenager, I once cycled five miles on an infernal Delhi summer afternoon to the US Educational Foundation to research American colleges. The asset plunderers of the eighties, on the other hand, never did anything for me. Moreover, that iconic *Wall Street* villain Gordon Gekko wore two-toned horizontal-stripe monogrammed shirts with French cuffs while Zuckerberg wears T-shirts and hoodies. I get it, but just as the fictional Gekko came to symbolize Wall Street gone rogue, the Zuck caricatured in *The Social Network* epitomizes Silicon Valley excess. And while not as flash, Zuck's wardrobe sends me the same message as Gekko's—fuck you, I'm too busy changing the world, and I'm richer than you besides.

Over a thousand people would see me on stage, and I had wondered what to wear that morning. I tried on my hoodie—navy, baby cashmere, twelve hundred dollars—but decided against it, settling for a vaguely presidential look offered by a fitted navy sport coat. That hoodie always felt like I was trying too hard.

It was an uncomfortably familiar feeling.

■

I made it in time for my presentation—barely.

The conference venue was the grand Grand Ballroom at the palatial Palace Hotel in downtown San Francisco. With its vaulted ceilings and crystal chandeliers, the ten-thousand-square-foot room is the kind of baroque setting where Otto von Bismarck might have proclaimed a unified German state on behalf of his kaiser. But here in the Valley the kaiser was Google, its flag-bearer that morning its CFO Ruth Porat. I admire Ruth. We worked together at Morgan Stanley, and I saw her confidently navigate convoluted deals and demanding clients while dealing with cancer and three young children.

And then there was Evan Spiegel, representing a new breed of tech entrepreneur, peddling Snap's smart glasses with built-in cameras. We associate the Valley with harmless nerdy virginal dorks who channel their harmless nerdy virginal dorkitude into cool inventions like flying cars. But the tech entrepreneur of the times was a millennial tech bro who dates models and ridicules the boomer banker's $300 Hermès tie while sporting a $350 Brunello Cucinelli T-shirt. He may not obsess about an annual bonus, but he knows he is only as cool as the current valuation of his start-up.

I hurriedly made my way to the stage, where another former colleague, Morgan Stanley's head of global technology banking Drew Guevara, was going to interview me in a "fireside chat" format.

Drew and I had pre-agreed the questions, most fitting my agenda promoting SoftBank shares as a value proposition. The people in this room controlled trillions of dollars, and my pitch was delivered in the jargony lingo they understood—sum-of-the-parts valuation, return on equity, loan-to-value ratios. But they were not here for my oracular wisdom—I didn't have any. Everyone wanted to know what Masayoshi Son was thinking and what he might do next. I could see the dollar signs flashing in their eyes when I highlighted the power of the embedded leverage in the Vision Fund, how a $2 billion investment in high-flying Nvidia generated an $8 billion profit within a few months.

Following our dialogue, Drew invited investor questions, of

which there were many—the prospects for a Sprint and T-Mobile merger, SoftBank's share buyback program. But the questions not asked screamed out the loudest. Nobody brought up inflated tech valuations or risk management. Nobody seemed concerned about the tenuous economics of ridesharing. SoftBank's $4.4 billion WeWork deal was the largest slug of capital ever committed to a start-up, but nobody asked what WeWork had to do with technology. Because nobody asks tough questions in a bull market.

I'd lived through the eighties' leveraged buyout boom, the internet bubble of 1999, the housing blowout of 2008, and it's always the same story. We watch fools dancing, and feel like greater fools for watching. But when we join the party, the music stops.

In 1999 Morgan Stanley let its senior bankers create an in-house technology investment fund. It was intended as a retention tool so overpaid bankers wouldn't go work for venture capitalists or tech start-ups where we might make even more money. The plan worked, but in a tragic-ironic sort of way. When the bubble burst, it was a financial Waterloo—we lost 90 percent of our capital. For some, a few more years of toil would be required to pay for that house in the Hamptons. For all, feeling totally fucking stupid hurt as much as losing money.

People like me are supposed to know better. I'd read books like Charles Mackay's nineteenth-century treatise *Extraordinary Popular Delusions and the Madness of Crowds*. But Mackay himself failed miserably in identifying the one major bubble of his own lifetime, that, too, in his own backyard. In the 1840s, Britons were enchanted by the emerging disruptive technology of the times—railways. Mackay dismissed any parallels between railways and Dutch tulip mania, then watched value destruction equivalent to over $400 billion (in today's terms) dwarfing any of the storied bubbles he so vividly chronicled.

I never learn, and neither will the rock star hedge fund managers, because when it comes to irrational exuberance, we are no better than Uber drivers punting on Tesla stock, beholden to market momentum the way Tolstoy's great men and kings were slaves to history. Because FOMO rules in a bull market, more potent than any psychedelic, catalyzing the transformation of individual brilliance into collective insanity.

■

My day ended with an animated conversation over dinner in a private room at the nearby Taj Campton Place Hotel. Among the attendees were celebrated hedge fund managers, including Chase Coleman, the unassuming founder of New York–based Tiger Global.

Toward the end of the meal, a tall bespectacled Asian gentleman who had been seated across from me on the last seat to my right raised a hesitant hand. He introduced himself. I don't remember the name or affiliation, but recall the accent—clipped, Oxbridge, unexpected.

"That was an interesting discussion," he said. "You know, I was looking at your website, and Masa's "Happiness for Everyone" mission. Tell me, does he mean it, the techno-utopia stuff? Or is it really just about world domination?"

"Great question," I responded. "But let me ask you this—why can't it be both?"

Everyone laughed. It's what people do in a bull market.

■

Tiger Global was the one fund that rivaled SoftBank for chutzpah when it came to technology investing, and went on to take a significant position in SoftBank stock. As did its accomplished counterpart Coatue Management.

A few weeks following the Morgan Stanley event, I was in New York to meet with Scott Shleifer, partner and cofounder of Tiger Global's private investing business.

The north-facing views from Tiger Global's office on 9 West

57th in New York may well be the most spectacular urban vistas anywhere. Private equity behemoths KKR and Apollo also had their offices in this modern Olympus. On that clear morning, I could see down the length of Central Park, the George Washington Bridge in the distance, the morning sun bouncing off the twin-towered Century, Majestic, and San Remo on Central Park West.

Scott (youthfully intense, jocular, piercing black eyes) asked me to run through my pitch on SoftBank, but interrupted as I started to discuss Arm.

"I don't care about Arm. Assume it's a bagel," he said, dismissively.

Bagel? It took a moment to register that he was suggesting Son-san's most prized asset was worthless.

He repeated the comment when I got to Sprint, this time even more dismissive.

"Sprint's a fucking bagel. That one I know for sure."

How did the understated Chase and the uproarious Scott survive under the same roof?

The only SoftBank assets Scott cared about were the Vision Fund investments. When you factored in the leverage and the 20 percent carried interest (the profit share all investors had to pay SoftBank) every dollar of appreciation in Vision Fund assets was worth over five dollars to SoftBank. My "deep-value" thesis—buying something worth ten dollars for five—was boring for Scott. On the other hand, SoftBank as a highly leveraged bet on private technology investments was the stuff of priapic fantasies.

Ironically, Tiger Global and Coatue are "Tiger Cubs," both spun out of renowned value investor Julian Robertson's Tiger Management. Robertson's success was based on buying cheap, and in 1998 he made a losing bet against what he perceived to be overpriced technology stocks. He was wrong and yet so right. Investors deserted Robertson as tech stocks zoomed, eventually forcing him to liquidate his fund in March 2000—right before the internet bubble burst. At the time, Chase Coleman and Philippe

Laffont (founder of Coatue) would have been twentysomething apprentices at Tiger Management and must have witnessed their mentor's trauma. Did this explain their decision to run with the bulls? I have no idea, but regardless, "smart money"—the guys who summer in waterfront estates on Meadow Lane and own Gulfstreams—was now along for the ride. They hunt in packs, and when you see them buying, it is the opposite of stock tips from taxi drivers. Investors scour their quarterly Form 13F filings with the SEC for ideas, and the momentum builds, like a snowball gathering mass as it rolls down a hill.

As my favorite poet says, "you don't need a weatherman to know which way the wind blows." As in 2000 and 2008, there would soon be a reckoning. There always is.

■

In our family—which is how Masa frequently described his senior ranks—an intervention was called for, and the natural person to lead this was the man who had been by his side for two decades. But when I raised the subject with him, Ron Fisher shrugged his shoulders in the international gesture for resignation.

I asked for a private chat with Masa regardless. Not just to appease my conscience but to ponder my future. We met in Masa's new home on Mountain Home Road in Woodside.

Masa had always wanted a permanent stead in the Valley, and so he purchased nine acres in California horse country in 2012, down the road from his septuagenarian friend Larry Ellison. Larry's property was twenty-three acres. *Something to do with chromosome pairs in a human cell? Valley founders are weird about sciencey symbolism.* The lakeside home was a replica of a sixteenth-century Japanese imperial estate, and it had taken Larry nine years, $200 million, and ten million pounds of rock to create the desired effect.

When Nikesh and I joined Masa for lunch in Larry's home a

couple of years prior, Larry explained that each lakeside structure was based on a different period of Japanese imperial history and intended to house his collection of Japanese art and artifacts. It was a strange incongruence in an area dominated by equestrian estates. Like bumping into Ryōma in a kimono when you expect to see John Wayne in a Stetson. "Why not buy the real deal in Japan?" I whispered privately to Masa. But of course. Larry also owned two authentic imperial homes in Kyoto.

Masa's new American abode was tastefully grand, which sounds oxymoronic, but pulling this off with peerless panache was yet another of his unacknowledged talents. Oenophiles and curators might experience a warm tingling in the loins when confronted with the wine cellar and art collection, respectively, but my personal highlight was an indigo-veined white Italian Calacatta marble artifact, in a location that forced you to contemplate, at close quarters, the subtle bluish coloration that ran through the brilliant white stone, like Cy Twombly's graffiti-like scribbles on a pearly white canvas. Micturating on an object of such beauty might seem an act of vandalism, but this is exactly what one was expected to do, for it was located in the powder room and it was a urinal.

Tanaka-san greeted me at the door, and after the customary swapping of shoes for indoor slippers I made my way to the living room where Masa was waiting.

I started the conversation by assuring him of my continued loyalty.

"I am so happy to hear that," he responded, smiling warmly. "That is so important."

The smile gradually faded as I started to voice my concerns—the pace of dealmaking, the leverage, the escalating risk.

"Masa, I want you to understand I'm here because of your vision. But some of these investments, I don't understand how they are AI companies, or even technology companies. Maybe we should invest in Google and Microsoft, every time there is a breakthrough in AI, they will buy the technology. Like Deep-Mind," I said. (Founded by wunderkind Demis Hassabis, Deep-Mind's goal was "to solve artificial general intelligence, and then use that to solve everything else." The company was acquired by Google in 2014.)

He listened, expressionless, nodding occasionally, but that last comment got a reaction.

"Yes, maybe we should have another fund. For companies like Google and Microsoft!" he said, suddenly animated.

But then he delivered what sounded like a prepared script.

"You know, in every family there are hunters and cooks. We need the cook, he is important. But for me the hunter is the most important. I always value the hunter more than the cook," he said.

If Masa's mission is to maximize happiness, aren't cooks more valuable? Do hunters make people happy? A good cook puts a smile on anyone's face. The way inventors enrich people's lives, like Gutenberg with his printing press or Edison and his light bulb. And are hunters happier than cooks?

But Masa wasn't inviting a philosophical debate. He was talking about me. *Masa Son is calling me a cook.* Not even a chef—everything sounds nicer in French—but a cook.

The naked Jamie Oliver or the profane Gordon Ramsay had made chefs cool. But the way Masa said it, it hurt. As if I'd been demoted from a glamorous Kshatriya (warrior) status to a journeyman Vaishya (craftsman).

I could have debated the characterization. I'd made it on Wall Street, where you eat what you kill and sometimes kill for sport.

But maybe he had a point. Hunters are hungry for something—money, power, or just the thrill. And I wasn't, at least not anymore. I had enough money, power is an illusion, and reading books that aren't even thrillers was thrilling enough for me.

More importantly, I didn't have his appetite for risk. I wished that I could fail to feel the fear that he failed to feel, but I couldn't.

"You are like family, I always want you with me. I want to talk to you every day. Like Ron, maybe he will retire soon," he continued.

But then he added emphatically.

"You are a smart guy, but you *must* be more like a hunter."

He escorted me to the door, though not before I made what would be my last visit to that magnificent pissoir.

On the way out, before I bowed to him in farewell, I asked him a question.

"Masa, I may be a cook, but can we at least agree I'm Michelin three-star?" I asked.

He threw his head back and laughed. I always made him laugh.

En route to the office in San Carlos (another northbound black gull-winged Tesla on the perma-clogged 101), I emailed Masa to thank him, and suggested a conference call to discuss strategy. In my self-absorbed state, I had failed to highlight the most fundamental point. *The feast is done; the time for hunters and cooks has passed. We need someone a notch lower in that caste system. We need the clean-up crew.*

As always, he responded immediately. With catastrophic confidence, he repeated that together we would change the course of humanity.

Masa Son, like Gatsby, is the single most hopeful person I have ever met and I'm ever likely to meet again.

17

THE BUTTERFLY EFFECT

Mathematics can be an infinite jest. George Boole's algebra reduced all mental activity to simple binary form, while John von Neumann's game theory mathematized human motivation. Chaos theory goes further, explaining cause and effect in the universe. How minor perturbations in one state of a deterministic nonlinear system can predictably create major and unpredictable disorder in another state. The flapping of a monarch butterfly's orange wings, a realignment of Saturn's B ring, a peccadillo in a prior life—apparently this is what makes bad shit happen in our lives. But is this "butterfly effect" a proportional relationship? When the flapping is frantic, does it create a massive shitstorm?

So it seemed in 2017, to an extent that blonde influencers with flawless skin and magenta-clad smooth operators were inconsequential sideshows. It started with that dreaded message. A WhatsApp from my uncle. It was time. Time for that traumatic long-haul flight home.

■

By the time we're fifty, a world without our presence becomes more than a thought experiment. Among aging Silicon Valley venture capitalists and founders, the bragging shifts from massive unicorn valuations to proud medical reports—youthful prostates, low cholesterol, high testosterone. By sixty, the realization dawns that this may not end well. Regardless, death seems an unacceptable compromise. Like the Promethean physicists and chauvinistic mathematicians of a different era, we technologists refuse to accept that life in every form is a wondrous and random dance of frantic complexity. Or pause to wonder, if a flapping butterfly in the Amazon can cause a tornado in Texas, what are the consequences of messing with the circle of life?

Encouragingly, the weed-smoking Nobel laureate physicist Richard Feynman says that "in all of the biological sciences there is no clue as to the necessity of death," while Peter Thiel is convinced that death is a "solvable problem." Ray Kurzweil (of singularity fame) believes that intelligent Wi-Fi-connected nanobots in our bloodstream will routinely repair or replace worn-down cells in our body, while machine versions of our organs will power on forever.[1] Google has a longevity-focused subsidiary called Calico, though its chief scientific officer recently retired, which makes you wonder.

The longevity obsession is not just a Valley phenomenon. David Sinclair is professor of genetics at Harvard Medical School and makes an eloquent case for regulators to classify aging as a treatable disease. (Presumably so his "cure" might be a claim covered by medical insurance.) Sinclair's start-up Tally Health sells you a four-pill daily regimen that purportedly arrests cellular senescence. I'm not convinced it works, but given what's at stake, why take chances? I dutifully pay my $129 monthly subscription while wondering which is the greater travesty—the fact that my biological age increased by four years after three months on the program or that I continue to pay for it.

But is mere life extension a reasonable goal? This was the dilemma I shared with my mother and two brothers, as we sat a prolonged bedside vigil alongside my dying father in the intensive care unit at the Sir Ganga Ram Hospital in Delhi. He was chairman of this charitable hospital, but was now reduced to a catatonic heap. Ironically, in the adjacent glass cubicle was a patient with terminal liver cirrhosis, the type of disease that had been my father's focus as a scientist and practitioner.

I arrived in time. The telling of it strains credibility, but he had waited for me. He raised himself just to hug me and tell me how proud he was of me. He had never embraced me like that before. Then he sank back, exhausted.

If this was a bad Bollywood film, this hospital scene would be when I catch religion and start praying. Instead, my family had to deal with the ultimate mind-bender—when do you switch the machines off? Perhaps the medical profession needs to move beyond a Hippocratic obsession with prolonging life and reflect instead on a graceful and managed exit.

My mother wanted to let him go. While in hospital, she prepared her living will, which I witnessed reflectively and signed sadly. *I should have one too, but what if I change my mind? I still need it though. Otherwise some misguided AI will pick something by Abba as background music for my cremation and where will that leave me? Fucking dead, I guess.*

I read a lot, bedside, before we released him two weeks later. Like Tolstoy's *The Death of Ivan Ilyich* and Atul Gawande's *Being Mortal*, grappling with the metaphysical and physical aspects of dying. But mostly I stared at the series of bright and lively jagged green lines running across the screen above my father's head, as if a story was being written with an anxious electronic beeping as a soundtrack. But all life stories must end, as Richard Feynman tragically discovered when cancer consumed him at age sixty-nine. Soon those lines would flatten, the beeping becoming achingly continuous. For the first time, I appreciated the profundity of needing to believe that those bright jagged lines would continue to illuminate some section of the universe, the beeping heard somewhere in the cosmos.

Will my father's spirit transcend? He had probably earned it.

Mine will be like that of Akaky Akakievich Bashmachkin trolling the alleys of Mayfair, seeking retribution or agitating for my next bonus, or maybe just ripping off that handsome suede-trimmed navy vicuña overcoat in the window display of the Loro Piana store on New Bond Street.

■

The cremation was primeval—open air, wood funeral pyre—in Delhi's Lodhi Road Cremation Ground. I escorted the corpse from the hospital in a rattling ambulance, accompanied by my uncle and two brothers. In a continuing manifestation of the human comedy, our ambulance needed to stop for gas. Diesel, to be precise.

I was back at the crematorium the next morning accompanied by my youngest brother, Nikhil. He is fifteen years younger than me, which makes my feelings equal parts paternal and filial. I took him to see *The Jungle Book* when he was five, but now we were united in a very different cause. We were going to collect our father's mortal remains.

When Hindus die, their ashes are scattered in the sacred waters of the Ganges, usually around the holy cities of Rishikesh or Haridwar in the Himalayan foothills. Or at least I thought it was ashes, but it turns out to be bones. There are contradictory theories around the significance of this ritual. *Does it ease the passage of the soul into its next incarnation, or does it liberate you from this exhausting birth-rebirth cycle?* I asked, and as with many things in India, I found no consensus, only animated opinions, as one might on the equally solemn intergenerational debate of who was the greater test cricketer, Gavaskar or Tendulkar.

En route to the cremation ground, Nikhil and I agreed on the inevitability of being ripped off on an overpriced urn. Instead, we faced macabre reality in the form of a grimy and sympathetic attendant offering us two plastic scoopers and a burlap bag. The scoopers were green polyurethane, faded and scratched, embedded in the visible fissures the DNA of countless saints and sinners. The burlap bag was—well, a fucking burlap bag.

Nikhil and I looked at each other and shook our heads.

"Should we get him to do this?" he suggested, sensing my queasiness.

"No, no, I'll be fine," I lied, managing a tired smile.

We collected the bones. Fragments of charred bones, which we hand washed and placed in the burlap bag. We also found his implanted cardioverter defibrillator (ICD). Metallic, blinking, made in China.

Nikhil picked up the ICD and stared at it intently, as if trying to reverse engineer the inner workings.

"I wonder if it can be reused. Maybe someone's heart can go on," I suggested, fascinated by his fascination.

■

We flew out to Dehradun's Jolly Grant Airport later that morning, en route to Rishikesh, the burlap bag in my black TUMI roll-along whose customary load was a change of clothes and toiletries. *Where does that strange name come from, Jolly Grant?* I asked the stewardess. She giggled, reminding me of Fumiko-san's reaction when I asked about the twenty-seventh floor in Shiodome. Regardless, she promised to ask her colleagues. They stared at me and giggled too. *Even in my motherland, people think I'm strange.*

My subconscious mind must have prescribed "airport name obsession" as trauma therapy; I couldn't let it go. An online source suggested Jolly Grant was a decorated Indian Air Force pilot. Not a conventional Indian name, but then Sikh parents routinely emasculate their male progeny, usually big, turbaned, and hairy, with cutesy names like Sweetie or Happy—why not Jolly? I messaged my friend Rahul who had attended the neighboring Doon School. He said Jolly Grant was not a person but an actual grant from the Nepalese royal family or from the British, he wasn't sure which. I gave up. (In 2023, ChatGPT finally offered a plausible response—an Anglicization of the name of neighboring Jauligrant village.)

We arrived at our destination in the afternoon, a small resort-like collection of private homes a few miles upstream from Rishikesh, and made our way down stone steps leading to the riverbed. Grief-tech is a thing in Silicon Valley. Bay Area start-up HereAfter AI ("where memories live forever") creates a Life Story Avatar of a lost loved one. But avatar comes from Sanskrit, and the ancient Vedic scholars had grief-tech figured out a few thousand years ago. I have not experienced a greater cathartic sensation than gently and lovingly, fragment by fragment, releasing those burnt and washed bones into the icy cold streaming water, watching them spread across the surface and gradually disappear downstream, knowing I had just performed one of the oldest rituals in civilization, humbled by the epiphanous realization that the fundamental nature of human emotions has never changed.

■

Meanwhile, the haters kept on hating, the smearers kept on smearing.

Bradley Hope was an investigative journalist at *The Wall Street Journal* in London. His exposure of the 1MDB scandal involving Goldman Sachs and the Malaysian prime minister made him a celebrity in the world of white-collar crime.[2] In May 2017, Hope sent a series of questions to Finsbury, a London PR firm representing SoftBank, saying he was "preparing an article about an investigation launched in March by the Indian Enforcement Directorate into allegations of improprieties related to SoftBank investments and activities of several of its executives."

The charge was that Nikesh and I, along with our SoftBank team, were perpetrators of a brazen scheme to accept kickbacks in connection with start-up Indian investments made by SoftBank. It was an unsubstantiated allegation, easily disproved. The submission was in Hinglish, accusing me of "having bad character" as if I had smallpox, and circulated widely to journalists. Several news agencies alerted SoftBank, making it clear they saw this scheme for what it was—an invidious smear campaign.

Why would the *The Journal* take this seriously? Their perspective, as explained by editor in chief Gerard Baker, was that the creation of the Vision Fund was a major event in the history of financial markets. Regardless of the substance—or lack thereof—of the allegations, the fact that I had been sidelined from this Vision Fund was newsworthy. They ran the story with the headline "As Allegations Swirl Around SoftBank, It Calls Them Sabotage." SoftBank issued a supportive statement in protest, describing the allegations as "false" and part of a "malicious smear campaign" based on "falsehood and innuendo."

I was at Alya's Columbia College graduation, outdoors on a glorious May morning, when I read Hope's article. My mother had flown in from Delhi and was sitting next to me. It was nice to see her, resilient despite a loss the pain of which I could not fathom. I wish I had been less distracted when she visited. In time, I would forgive the smearers most things, but this was not one of them.

I wrote an impassioned email to the *The Journal*, pointing out that "a slanderous lie when published in *The Wall Street Journal* acquires a patina of respectability" and accusing Hope of an "astonishing compromise to his journalistic integrity."

But the damage was done. While papers like the *Financial Times* steered clear, obscure websites like Janta Ka Reporter in India were happy to publish stories with salacious headlines like "Grave Charges Against SoftBank CFO Alok Sama." If I'd ever dreamed of my name in lights—and I hadn't—it would have been winning a Fields Medal or a Booker. But this? Not that anyone I knew visited these websites, the problem was a butterfly effect in cyberspace. Since my name featured in the headline, the Google search algorithm gleefully and cruelly joined in the conspiracy, ranking the post number one in relevance. Googling myself became a frequent and unhealthy preoccupation. I would stare at the screen, feeling as if someone had taken a shit on my doorstep, but I was powerless to clean up the mess.

I underestimated Hope's persistence. Mark MacDougall told me that the article might be a ploy marking Hope as the go-to person for anyone with information on the scheme. Within a few weeks, Hope reached out to Kroll saying he had some leads, and was determined to "give it the old college try."

■

111.

Cricketers call it "a Nelson" and consider it a terribly unlucky number. It has to do with Lord Nelson, who apparently lost one arm at Tenerife, one eye in Corsica, and one leg before he eventually died at the Battle of Trafalgar in 1805. (One of those darkly humorous tales not entirely substantiated by history.)

I never had problems with Nelsons in my cricketing days, perhaps because I never scored that many runs, not in a single inning anyway. But I was reminded of that curse, one hundred and eleven days after my father died. Another message, another long-haul flight, another bedside vigil. This time it was my mother. No agonizing decisions about ventilators, just inconsolable sobbing when the phone rang at 2 A.M. in my depressingly ornate hotel room at the Leela (I never stayed there again) in Delhi. Maya was with me, and I kept repeating an inane question. *Why does it have to be her?* My father had given up, but after two years of taking care of him, she wanted her life back. She was seventy-six and told me she was looking forward to at least another ten good years.

We were back at the Lodhi Crematorium in the morning, followed by that macabre bone collector routine.

Maya knew how broken I was and asked both Samir and Alya to fly over from New York. Samir accompanied Nikhil and me to the crematorium. I wasn't sure how he would cope; I wasn't sure how I would cope. But he seemed unfazed, joining Nikhil and me in scraping the remains. He found my mother's titanium hip, none the worse for its fiery ordeal.

Same journey flying into that airport with a funny name, onward to that riverside destination outside Rishikesh, except this time Samir accepted the burden of wheeling that same black TUMI roll-along that now housed what was left of my mother. I told him to handle it gently.

Same icy cold water, but less cathartic. Just very sad.

I was too overwhelmed to speak at the prayer meeting after. On the drive to the event venue, I asked Samir to take my place. This was terribly unfair, but he calmly accepted. In an unprepared oration to an audience of over a hundred people, he addressed me directly and told me what remained of my mother wasn't really in that black roll-along. It was in the smiles of her seven grandchildren.

■

My golden retriever Ellie shared a name with that other blonde goddess, Elle Macpherson. A comic highlight of her life was yet another random occurrence that makes one wonder if we really are in a simulation. On a fine summer day in Hyde Park, Ellie decided to chase a jogger, as she often did. Except in this case the runner happened to be Elle Macpherson. It's a thing leggy blondes do, apparently, run in the park. Apologies, introductions, and a mutual display of blonde affection followed.

Ellie was my favorite golfing companion, picking up my divots and barking excitedly when I hooked one into the woods, darting in with the intention of looking for everything except for my ball. Watching her chase down the lush green fairways of Queenwood Golf Club in Surrey made me think of Snoopy's conundrum from *It's a Dog's Life*. "My life has no purpose, no direction, no aim, no meaning, and yet I'm happy. I can't figure it out. What am I doing right?"

For anyone seeking a path to nirvana not involving tracking BMI and net worth or finding that elusive "sense of purpose," dogs offer more clues than any of the 25,000-plus self-help books with "happiness" in the title.

A mysterious autoimmune condition curtailed her already too-short life span in October that year. A heartbroken Maya held her paw as they put her to sleep at the Queen Mother Hospital for Animals in Hertfordshire.

I wasn't around, and I never said goodbye—business trip to Tokyo.

■

Is it appropriate to speak of something as unsightly as death in pretty prose? And why am I able to distill the essence of my dog and my relationship with her in vivid images but my emotions are obscured by clouds when it comes to my parents? It is a haunting paradox, the answer simple and complicated.

My mother's love was the purest kind—unconditional. I could be the criminal mastermind portrayed by the smearers, and she wouldn't care. Nobody would look at me like that again, that wondrous combination of affection and adulation. I needed that energizing self-affirmation, now more than ever. My uncle—her brother—always told me how much she loved hearing from me. Which sounds nice except I was always too busy to call her.

Too much was left unsaid between my father and me. Our relationship changed when I chose not to follow him into the medical profession. I was his firstborn, the clever one, the chosen one. Was he hurt, disappointed, even angry? What did he mean when—on his deathbed—he said he was proud of me? What had I done that I was proud of? Perhaps Obama's observation wasn't so trite. Like Masayoshi Son, maybe I was always trying to live up to my father's expectations, in my case without ever knowing what they were.

With both of them gone, who will remember me as I was?

As a four-year-old, I was denied admission to the Modern School in Delhi. The headmaster, gently and seriously, explained to my distraught twenty-five-year-old mother that her son was "a little bit retarded." Who will know stories like that about me? No matter how old you are, your childhood dies with your parents.

Every immigrant struggles with cultural and national ambivalence, and I am no exception. Under English common law, "domicile" is determined by your father. It is an archaic and patriarchal definition, but it gets at a fundamental truth—where you are from depends on your parents. Where am I from now that they are gone? Therein lies another paradox: I owned three homes, but now I felt homeless.

I think of them often, the way I want to remember them. My mother in a bright yellow sari dancing joyously at my wedding, the self-conscious smile when she saw me looking at her. My father ensconced in an armchair, enjoying the warm orange glow of a portable room heater, a shawl draped around him on a chilly Delhi winter evening, cradling a Scotch and soda, lip-synching his favorite maudlin melodies from *Pakeezah*.

As with most things, I have a song associated with the memory of my parents. "Did I miss the mark or over-step the line, That only you could see?" asks a raspy, melancholic, late-life Dylan in "Shooting Star."

So many questions, so much to say. But while the dead maintain a social media presence, they still won't return phone calls.

18

HOW MUCH LAND DOES A MAN NEED?

Before Meghan Markle, the last American to roil the House of Windsor was Wallis Simpson. But Simpson's paramour was a king who abdicated for her rather than a spare five times removed. And while she didn't have Markle's media savvy, Simpson managed to pack the best of British irony in an unforgettable quote—"You can never be too rich or too thin."

Those words seemed prescient in the Roaring Twenties redux. Warhol's piss painting—he urinated on it for an oxidation effect—of Basquiat sold for a splashy $40 million at Christie's, while semaglutides like Ozempic became as hot as ChatGPT.[1]

Simpson's cynical one-liner may also have been the inspiration for the founders of the Lanserhof Group. Three spa retreats in the Bavarian Black Forest, the Tyrolean Alps, and at Sylt on the North Sea serve up a daily fare of passage salts, purifying teas, and spelt bread. Bread that you must masticate a minimum of thirty times while vigilant sentinels who look ominously like

Nurse Ratched from *One Flew Over the Cuckoo's Nest* watch over you.

Other European spa retreats also peddle this draconian gut-cleansing regime, but Lanserhof, through a combination of sleek, minimalist design and clever marketing, has cemented its place in the annual calendar of the sybaritic jet set. Bang in there between St. Barts and Aspen, or Saint-Tropez and Courchevel. If you're not toxed, wtf is the point of a torturous detox?

There is another dimension to the Lanserhof experience, replicable on a shoestring budget, or no budget at all. It is the novelty of being all dressed down with nowhere to go after being done with "dinner" at 6 P.M., and with it a rare opportunity for reflective fireside reading.

■

It was over a year since I'd lost my father, my mother, and my dog. I was a case study in the consequences of a Shakespearean grief that does not speak, but Mark MacDougall was adamant that a leave of absence would suggest guilt. So there I was, feeling like Hamlet but acting like Caesar.

The saboteurs remained at large, their identity a mystery. I received an anonymous and absurd "gotcha" letter threatening me with public revelation of an obscure conflict unless I resigned within two weeks. The alleged smoking gun was SoftBank's purchase of a small stake in OYO Rooms from an Indian venture fund to which I had committed $100,000, of which a small fraction went into OYO. Setting aside the materiality, I made this investment prior to joining SoftBank, disclosed it, and recused myself from decision-making in respect of OYO. Typical of these tiresome threats, there was no follow-up, but it was spooky, even more so for being postmarked Hamburg?

Following the game of phones, Marcelo Claure took on a new role as chief operating officer of SoftBank Group, and became my friend and partner. While the Vision Fund deal frenzy went on, I tried to get WeWork to collaborate with Airbnb for a grandly scaled WeLive business, but the brawny Brian Chesky was firmly grounded while the reedy Adam Neumann lived in the clouds. Masa had bought Fortress Investment Group, run by the self-described "financial services garbage collector" Peter Briger. Pete and I bonded over our Dylan fandom, and I joined Fortress's board. Shepherding Arm as a board member threw up interesting experiences, including a seat at a charity banquet next to someone whose place card simply said "Andrew" but turned out to be the Duke of York. After I had made a persistent case for IPO'ing SoftBank Corp (SoftBank's Japanese mobile business), we finally did so, following which I helped SoftBank Corp consolidate its control over Yahoo! Japan, a convoluted multiparty deal for which the management team remains grateful. Inspired by its hard-charging CEO, Anthony Noto, I joined the board of SoFi, a Nikesh-era $1 billion SoftBank investment that became a resounding success story. And I finally did get to hang out with Jamie Dimon—an intimate private dinner at Masa's Woodside home, where Jamie described his battle with throat cancer.

All of this was done as if I were a patron of a certain hotel in California, checked out but unable to leave.

■

Maya and I landed at Innsbruck Airport on a chilly January morning in 2019, en route to Lans in Austria, our luggage equal parts loungewear and books. My Lanserhof reading list included a collection of Tolstoy short stories, among them a parable James Joyce called "the greatest story that the literature of the world knows."[2]

Tolstoy's *How Much Land Does a Man Need?* begins with two sisters debating the quality of their respective lives. The older lauds her sophisticated urban lifestyle, while the younger extols her rustic life, devoid of stress and temptation. Pakhom, the younger sister's husband, listens and agrees with his wife, but reveals that "my only grievance is I don't have enough land." (Had I been in a writing workshop with Leo, I would have suggested he introduce a neighbor who had more land than Pakhom.)

The Devil has been listening and now has his hook.

Pakhom kicks off his real estate investment career negotiating a deal with a village woman who owns a three-hundred-acre estate. He sells his foal and his bees, and combined with family savings has enough to make a 50 percent down payment on thirty acres of land, with the balance to be paid over two years. Pakhom has now discovered the heady drug that is leverage. He borrows more to buy seeds, sows the newly bought land, and within a year has a flourishing crop.

A Trumpy New York story follows—rivalries, litigation, regional expansion, and of course, more leveraged deals. Our hero accumulates thirteen hundred acres of land and the trimmings of wealth (lavish home, fine vodka). But he wants more.

Pakhom meets a merchant who tells him of a distant tribe—the Bashkirs—who own fertile land. Intrigued, Pakhom sets off, ready to cajole the Bashkirs into parting with their prime property. The Bashkir elder proposes an unusual deal. Pakhom can have as much land as he can circumnavigate in a day, sunrise to sunset, for a flat payment of 1,000 rubles. There is, however, a catch. Pakhom must return to his starting point by sundown, else he forfeits 100 percent of his deposit.

Energetic and optimistic, Pakhom sets out at sunrise. The land gets better as he goes farther, tempting him to venture beyond what he intended, unwilling to rest for fear of missing out.

When he eventually decides to make the turn home, Pakhom finds the going increasingly tough. Exhausted, dehydrated, and eventually terrified, he wills himself to carry on, even as he sees the sun receding in the distance. He fears ridicule even more than he does death. "If I stop now, after coming all this way, they'd call me an idiot," he tells himself.

In a Tinseltown version, Orff's ominous "O Fortuna" would

play in the background, building up to its thunderous climax as Pakhom makes it to the finish line, just as the sun disappears. But even as he does, Pakhom's legs give way and he falls to the ground, dead.

The story ends with Tolstoy answering the question he poses in the title. Pakhom's worker picks up the spade and digs a grave for his master. Six feet long.

Tolstoy, like Zola or Balzac, understood greed and lost illusions better than I ever did. Just like the Vedic oracles understood stages of life and the letting go of it. His Victorian pomposity notwithstanding, the poet Henley was also onto something. *Fuck those butterflies. I am the master of my fate, I am the captain of my soul.*

EPILOGUE

The Dude Abides

"Schmuck insurance" is a smart option when you sell an asset. In 2003, with the music business reeling from the Napster and YouTube assault, Time Warner divested Warner Music Group. As part of the sale agreement, CEO Dick Parsons negotiated an option to buy back 15 percent of Warner Music at a discounted fixed price. "In case the music industry starts to go like gangbusters, we won't look like schmucks for selling," he explained.[1]

When it pays out, schmuck insurance creates that elusive win-win outcome, at an emotional if not a mathematical level. This was the spirit in which I went long SoftBank shares on my way out. It was a fraction of my exposure while an employee but enough to nudge my monetary dial should the shares take off.

While my separation agreement was fair and the farewell announcement laudatory, my exit was disappointingly uneventful. Like a breakup when your partner's first reaction is to politely and generously inquire if you wish to take that new blender. (I took the Linley desk and the Ricard *Tibetan Monk* portrait that hung behind it in my office.) My timing, on the other hand, seemed inspired.

■

In 2019, the SoftBank story was dominated by the shambolic and comic WeWork saga—chronicled in the Apple TV series *WeCrashed.*

After SoftBank's initial $4.4 billion commitment, Adam attempted to sell Masa on what might have been the wackiest investment proposition ever. Instead of leasing and renting out office space, he wanted to turbocharge the capital intensity of his business by buying buildings. Everything, everywhere, all at once. For this he wanted an additional $70 billion. Masa was in for as much as $20 billion in a deal that would have bought out existing investors, but markets and Goto-san took a hand. Confronted with concerned shareholders and pressure from Japanese lenders, Masa slashed SoftBank's commitment to $2 billion of equity as part of a complex $5 billion package valuing WeWork at a previously agreed $42 billion, more than twice its valuation in 2017.[2]

I had sat through Adam's pitch to Masa in Tokyo, in awe of the man's audacity. This grand illusion was in addition to fantastical sideshows like his wife Rebekah's WeGrow, a school that replaced math and Shakespeare with yoga and soulfulness, or Wavegarden, whose business model was—literally—making waves. Other Adam shenanigans included carrying a stash of marijuana across borders on his Gulfstream G650ER, or selling the rights to the brand "We" to WeWork for $5.9 million. (The latter approved by his board, but later returned following public outrage).[3] All part of the corporate mission, as stated in its Form S-1 SEC filing—a document where misstatements invite legal liability—of "raising the world's consciousness." Without irony, WeWork was saying We intend to get the world high, and sue us if We don't.

Almost as outrageous was the sad spectacle of Wall Street's finest, led by the king Jamie Dimon, competing for the privilege of unloading this hallucinogenic story on public markets, with promises of IPO valuations north of $50 billion. For a company that lost $1.9 billion in 2018 and $905 million in the first half of 2019.[4] As jarring as the fantasy that WeWork was a technology company were comical metrics like "community-adjusted profits," perhaps inspired by the Valley's scammy "adjusted earnings" that exclude stock-based compensation, both akin to household budgets that wish away mortgage payments and taxes.

"Any Wall Street analyst who believes WeWork is worth over $10 billion is lying, stupid, or both," said the outspoken NYU professor Scott Galloway.[5] He was wrong. The bankers were neither lying nor stupid, merely disingenuous. I might have done the same; it's the way the game is played. If a client wants a $50 billion valuation, you promise $50 billion. You can't predict the madness of crowds. Maybe you get away with it, but if not, you blame the markets or (in this case) a client who was smoking weed accompanied by shots of Don Julio 1942.

Following the predictable and embarrassing failure of the IPO, SoftBank took control of WeWork. Adam was paid $770 million for handing the keys to SoftBank's Marcelo Claure and walked away a billionaire.[6] Incredibly, his new yet familiar "community-driven living" venture (Flow) found a backer in Andreessen Horowitz and became a unicorn without a penny in revenue.

Adam did nothing illegal, perhaps not even immoral. He just tickled the comedic underbelly of capitalism. (It would have been funnier if he'd pulled it off with his original big idea—the WeePad.)

Masa did not offer any excuses. He did not blame his team, who for the most part were like Tennyson's fatally dutiful Light Brigade, or even Adam Neumann. "I may be more at fault than Adam, for telling him to be more aggressive," he said, in a classy mea culpa, disarming the media's—unfair and recurring—characterization of him as a one-hit wonder.

■

The December 23, 2019, issue of *Bloomberg Businessweek* featured a bonfire of stacked and bundled one-hundred-dollar notes, with the headline "Season's Greetings from SoftBank." The Vision Fund's Saudi association following the horrific Khashoggi affair was unwelcome baggage, and questions were asked about a "culture of recklessness."

And then came the pandemic.

Like many, I bought into the notion that placing the bulk of humanity in a cryogenically frozen state would lead to permanent lifestyle changes and adoption of technologies such as virtual meetings or telemedicine. There is precedent for this. In China, the 2003 SARS outbreak turbocharged Alibaba's Taobao e-commerce platform. Similarly, India's controversial demonetization in 2016 led to an explosion in electronic payments. A transformation that stuck.

Modern monetary theory—the seductive falsehood that central banks can create money and governments spend without consequences—became fashionable following the pandemic. Free money fueled this ZIRP (zero interest rate policy) bubble, stretching valuations the way molly powers Ibiza dance clubs.

In a stunning reversal, SoftBank's share price doubled from the oh-so-cruel April of 2020. I felt stupid having bailed out, though my schmuck insurance lifted my portfolio and my spirits. Which was the point, of course.

In this collective mayhem, SoftBank invested $38 billion off its own balance sheet into 183 companies.[7] The most by any venture investor in a single year, a pace all the more remarkable for being concentrated in the second half.

For all players, speed of execution, with minimal diligence, became a selling point when growth investors competed for deals in this frenzied "spray and pray" investing market. Tiger Global declined board positions and outsourced postinvestment advice to management consultants.

A new breed of speculator emerged in these Roaring Twenties—the meme investor. *Is this smart money or dumb money?* The oracle of this virtual community went by a delightfully ironic moniker—#DeepFuckingValue. In place of Warren Buffett's fascination with Dairy Queen, #DeepFuckingValue had a juvenile penchant for chicken tenders dipped in champagne while celebrating his latest "stomp" on his Roaring Kitty YouTube channel. He traded from his basement and favored a bandana while doing so. I had no clue why—it looked cool I guess? These "diamond hand" investors declared that fundamentals do not matter and claimed to have different ways of making money. Like Dogecoin. The creator of the WallStreetBets forum—where #DeepFuckingValue held virtual court—described it as follows: "The boomer says to the millennial, 'What are you, growth or value?' and he goes 'I'm a meme investor, and I'm kicking your ass.'"[8]

I blogged in February 2021, warning that #DeepFuckingValue might suffer the same fate as that Miami stripper from *The Big Short,* who owned six properties bought with 95 percent leverage and became a symbol for the madness of the times. And when the unlikely pairing of Ted Cruz and Alexandria Ocasio-Cortez united on an asinine cause—the unfettered ability of kids to hang themselves speculating the same way a hedge fund manager could—I didn't need conversations with Uber drivers to tell me this was a world gone mad. When you see guns and sharp swords in the hands of young children, you know a hard rain's a-gonna fall. I sold what I could except my schmuck insurance, because, well, it was schmuck insurance. That and one Bitcoin. Because you never really know.

The NASDAQ was up 46.6 percent in 2020 and another 26.6 percent in 2021. Private and public markets tend to work reflexively. Accordingly, venture capitalists spawned 596 unicorns in 2021, up from 198 in 2020 and 64 in (pre–Vision Fund) 2016.[9]

The following year was predictably calamitous—not just for crypto-punting kids but also my big-boy friends at Tiger Global, which lost an aggregate $41 billion across its public and private funds. Chase Coleman avoided the mistake that his guru Julian

Robertson made in 1999–2000, when Robertson was run over by bulls. Instead, Coleman made the mistake Robertson was so determined to avoid, and was mauled by the bear. (His partner Scott Shleifer, after delivering returns substantially south of "a fucking bagel," announced his decision to step down in 2023.)[10]

You don't recover from a year like that, maybe ever. When you're down 56 percent, as Tiger's flagship hedge fund was in 2022, you need to be up 127 percent just to make up your losses. This is not portfolio theory, it's elementary arithmetic. Net of fees, it might take ten years to recover, and that's in a bull market and assuming the money sticks. Because investors typically and tragically exit at market bottoms. Moreover the worst years for star money managers invariably coincide with the highest volume of assets under management. Investors chase performance, which in and of itself means greater size. Simple rate of return calculations take no account of the fact that in their bad years managers frequently destroy more absolute wealth than in all their up years combined. So it was with Long-Term Capital Management (with two Nobel laureates in their ranks, perhaps the smartest guys ever in any room) in 1998.

The caricature of smart money and dumb money is classist, reductionist, and false. In bull markets all money is smart money, but every decade or so we are reminded that speculative markets are mostly a case of dumb and dumber.

■

In August 2022, with a keen appreciation of the spirit if not the actual texts of Greek tragedy, a contrite Masa pronounced that "I am ashamed of myself for being elated by the profits of the past."[11] His Vision Fund had announced a staggering $23 billion loss for the quarter, and he declared this earnings presentation would be his swan song. (For the fiscal year ended March 31, 2023, the loss widened to $32 billion.)[12] As always, an idiosyncratic slide accompanied his message. A brooding samurai. Not Ryōma, but the first shogun, Tokugawa Ieyasu, seated in a reflective pose, left elbow anchored to his knee, chin resting on hand. Like Rodin's *Thinker*, except the facial expression suggested painful constipation instead of deep contemplation. The self-admonishing portrait was commissioned by the shogun following a humiliating defeat at the Battle of Mikatagahara in 1573. A penitent Masa added, "We have lost six trillion yen in six months. I always want to reflect on this, and have it serve as a reminder."[13]

In victory and in defeat, always that neat mathematical symmetry. Money raised at a billion dollars a minute in 2016, money lost at a trillion yen a month in 2022.

The irony in Masa Son stepping back, as with Julian Robertson in 2000, is that he was right. ChatGPT-3 was launched in 2022, and with it a universal validation of his early conviction that AI would be the catalyst for the next wave of technology innovation. As big as the Intel 8080 chip, the internet, or the iPhone. In another testament to his trend-spotting ability, on May 24, 2023, NVDA, identified by Masa as his "bet the house" trade more than five years earlier, ripped 25 percent higher in a single day to become the fifth trillion-dollar tech beast. By February 2024, Nvidia was worth $2 trillion, more than either Amazon or Google. (Here's a sobering fact for momentum investors—if you bought Cisco at its peak in 2000, twenty-four years later you'd still be losing money).

Masa Son's idea of superman was Leonardo da Vinci; I agree. That AI will outsmart da Vinci is a foregone conclusion, but will "it" match him for creativity? Seemingly virtuosic models like ChatGPT work by predicting what word, symbol, or pixel comes next based on analyzing what came next before. But this is a process that by definition precludes originality, for "like Hockney" is not the same as "the next Hockney." Can an image of "cats kissing in the style of Klimt" generated by Dall-E inspire the hypnotic immersion I felt in front of da Vinci's *The Last Sup-*

per in Milan? Or the head-scratching wonderment provoked by Masa Son's slideshows or Warhol's piss paintings? Originality, even when it flirts with absurdity, is always thrilling. In the race against the machines, it may be our last stand.

■

The Vision Fund didn't pan out the way Mohammed bin Salman might have liked, but as crude oil prices catapulted to $120 a barrel in 2022, I'm not sure he cared that much.

In 2016, Mohammed went to Silicon Valley. Now the Valley comes to Mohammed. After snubbing him, the great and the greater of Silicon Valley flock to his annual "Davos in the Desert" extravaganza. PIF no longer needs hand-holding from SoftBank to navigate the world of technology: ironically, it will almost certainly surpass Masa's goal of a trillion under management. In March 2024, the media reported a PIF initiative that seemed Masa-inspired—a gigantic $40 billion AI fund.[14] And despite being labeled "scary motherfuckers" by its star recruit Phil Mickelson,[15] PIF is positioning itself to own global golf. Forget buying football teams, the oligarchs and Emiratis already did that, why not own an entire sport? Cricket could be next—invented in England, appropriated by the Indians, owned by the Saudis?

Like my man said, money doesn't talk, it swears.

■

SoftBank portfolio companies fared less well, making poor use of their benefactor's unprecedented largesse.

WeWork attempted a revival after an IPO in October 2021 but eventually filed for bankruptcy in November 2023—$47 billion of value destruction in four years,[16] with SoftBank's losses exceeding $10 billion, record territory for a single private investment. Bizarrely, a couple of months later, the master of grand illusions—does it get grander than "first trillionaire" and "president of the world"?—stepped forward to buy the company out of bankruptcy. If he pulls it off, Adam Neumann can add master of grand irony to his grand résumé.

Zume "pivoted" from robots making pizza to sustainable packaging, before finally shutting down in June 2023.[17] Katerra, the "technology-driven" construction company, also folded, a hit of over $1 billion for the Vision Fund.[18] Once Beijing decided that to be rich wasn't so glorious, DiDi's stock plunged from over $15 to under $3; the Vision Fund had invested over $11 billion in the company. OYO restructured and scaled back its misplaced international ambitions, laying off several thousand people in the process.[19] Greensill Capital filed for bankruptcy, wiping out the Vision Fund's $1.5 billion investment.[20] Sam Bankman-Fried's FTX blew up in November 2022, with SoftBank a prominent casualty.[21] Messaging start-up IRL had received a $150 million investment at a valuation of $1.2 billion.[22] I'd never heard of IRL, and for good reason. In June 2023 came the startling revelation that 95 percent of its purported 20 million user base was fake. Mortgage lender Better Home, which received $1.8 billion from SoftBank, saw its share price crash 95 percent from IPO. Bizarrely, in its SEC filings, the company warned that its founder and CEO, Vishal Garg, "detrimentally affected our productivity and financial results and has disrupted certain third party relationships."[23] "Smart glass" startup View, once valued at $2 billion after raking in $1.1 billion from the Vision Fund, laid off a quarter of its workforce in 2023 before filing for bankruptcy in April 2024.[24]

Vivek Ramaswamy, whose Roivant Technologies had received $1.1 billion from the Vision Fund, ran for president. I won't comment on his neo-Trumpian politics, but I like that he insisted Vivek be pronounced to rhyme with "cake." (Alok, just so we're clear, rhymes with "coke".)

Herman Narula's Improbable Worlds shifted its focus to "the convergence of AI, metaverse and blockchain technologies." Since one metaverse is not enough, it has a plan for a "network of interoperable Web3 metaverses."

The hunters, it would seem, did not deliver for Son-san.

■

The investment world wondered if we had seen the last of Son-san's marvelously profligate Apple Pencil and delightfully quirky slides. I got that a lot, and responded by pointing out that I still believed and—more tangibly—owned SoftBank stock. It helped that Masa promoted my former deputies Alex Clavel and Navneet Govil to oversee the Vision Fund. History was also in Masa's favor. Aside from his own comeback, shogun Tokugawa Ieyasu's best years came after his most famous defeat.

Not surprisingly, on the summer solstice of 2023, the *Financial Times* proclaimed that "we're weeping, laughing, cheering and dancing." At SoftBank's annual general meeting, after a period during which "the tears didn't stop for days," Masayoshi Son announced that "the time has come to shift to offense mode." With $35 billion from the disposition of that once sacred Alibaba stake (at one point worth $200 billion, but eventually disposed for an estimated cumulative gain of $72 billion[25]) that Apple Pencil was locked and loaded, ready to make another dent in the universe. Otherwise why else even be here?

Masa's latest enigmatic slide featured a goldfish, in a bowl, staring quizzically at a question mark. "Do you want to be a goldfish?" asked Son-san of the AI doubters in the world. His latest project—with typical whimsical flair codenamed Izanagi, after the Japanese god of creation—was a chip venture to challenge Nvidia. The size? One hundred billion dollars.[26]

No matter the results, I will always be inspired by the colossal vitality of Masa Son's visions.

■

The resurrection began with "New" T-Mobile, which lived up to its commitment to challenge the duopoly and shake up the US wireless industry. Shares rose over 50 percent in the three years following the Sprint merger, and in December 2023 SoftBank received an additional $7.6 billion windfall after T-Mobile shares exceeded pre-agreed performance benchmarks.[27] The deal team worked this provision into the merger agreements: the cooks, it would seem, outdid the hunters.

Arm thrived. After the IoT story disappointed—connected toasters weren't nearly as cool as we expected—Masa attempted to merge Arm with Nvidia in a deal always doomed from an antitrust perspective. But with relentless strategic and operational focus—again, Masa's most underrated talent—he pivoted Arm to reposition its business to ride the explosive demand for energy-efficient AI processors at the edge of networks. In September 2023, the company went public in the biggest IPO of the year, the stock up almost 25 percent on the first day of trading, the value double what SoftBank paid in 2016. Nobody cheered louder than me, and not just because of my schmuck insurance.

But the best was yet to come. On February 8, 2024, after reporting stellar results and revising outlook, Arm stock exploded like a supernova. A three-day gain of 90 percent, $72 billion in absolute terms, making up for many WeWorks and many Zumes and many Wags and many Katerras. Arm's equity value exceeded $150 billion, almost quintuple what SoftBank paid in 2016—a stunning albeit unrealized gain of over $100 billion.

And so it goes.

■

As for Zuck, he displayed encouraging maturity and self-awareness. "I've failed and been embarrassed so many times in my life, it's a core competence," he said. Impressively, he claimed to have completed the Murph Challenge—a one-mile run, one hundred pull-ups, two hundred push-ups, three hundred squats, followed by another one-mile run, all while wearing a weighted vest—in under forty minutes. About the time for my morning constitutional around the Serpentine in Hyde Park.

I always thought Zuck's defense should be that if Facebook is as powerful as people believe, he would be more popular than the Beatles. Social media's influence says more about our collective frailty (what Zadie Smith describes as our "falsely jolly, fake-friendly, self-promoting and slickly disingenuous" behavior online[28]) than it does about Facebook. But perhaps Zuck has no desire to live in the hearts and minds of people. Perhaps he would rather live in the metaverse.

Fortunately for Zuck, Elon Musk displaced him as the most pilloried tech billionaire. I've always been a fan of Elon's focus on solving our biggest problems, and it made me sad to see his puerile antics. Following Instagram's launch of a Twitter competitor, the self-proclaimed Technoking bizarrely and publicly challenged Zuck to a cage fight. Musk's ballsy attitude, presumably along with his member, hardened in his next tweet as he proposed "a literal dick measuring contest"[29] while concurrently launching his "pro-humanity" AI start-up.

With Silicon Valley Man reduced to his pair of dangling appendages as the primary neural processor, women are our only hope in this race against AI.

If validation of Neumann's (the math guy, not the WeWork dude—*what would the former have thought of the latter?*) prediction that technologists will become our new gods was required, I got it in April 2024. It was the wondrous spectacle of Margot Robbie and Bradley Cooper, on stage in Hollywood, presenting $3 million and the Breakthrough Prize in Fundamental Physics to atomic clockmakers Hidetoshi Katori and Jun Ye at Yuri Milner's annual "Oscars for nerds" gala. It made me wonder how my life might have changed had I, as a teenager, seen Farrah Fawcett and John Travolta present a Breakthrough math prize to some shlubby geek for cracking an obscure differential geometry problem. It is a marvelous thing Yuri has done, glamorizing science in this fashion, but there is the sobering Sebaldian view, enunciated by Musk at the Breakthrough event. "Technology is what moves civilization forward, and saves lives, and makes life interesting," said Musk. "Hopefully it doesn't kill us all."[30]

Not that I'm overly concerned about AI destroying the world. As with self-driving cars, when it comes to damaging humanity, we seem to set the bar higher for machines than we do for humans. My pet peeve with AI is the worms inside my brain telling me what to read or listen to next. A Spotify algo would never have fed the street music of Soweto ("township jive") to Paul Simon, but this was the inspiration for his masterpiece *Graceland.* Dilute intellectual curiosity, and the machines will win in any conspiracy to dumb down the human race.

(Warning: If an AI algo recommends *Memories of an Aging Financier* by Dick Money as your next read, ignore it. Tell it to put a sock in it, zip it, can it, muzzle it, drop dead, fuck off. Read Tolstoy or Gogol instead.)

■

In March 2023, after five years of blistering performance led by a brilliant new CEO, the cybersecurity firm Palo Alto Networks reached a milestone perhaps only I noticed; its equity value exceeded that of SoftBank. Its chairman and CEO is Nikesh Arora, and he is doing just fine. His projected compensation—all performance based—will likely set a new record for nonfounder executives. And so it goes.

I quipped that it was a matter of time before a headline in Janta Ka Reporter accused Nikesh of starting the Ukraine war just to dial up paranoia about Russian cyberattacks. Neither of us laughed. Five years on, it was still too soon.

■

In February of 2020, Maya and I were in Delhi, hosting a small dinner to celebrate her birthday. I was distracted, checking my iPhone frequently. When *The Wall Street Journal* app notified the story was live, Maya and I read it together.

It was Bradley Hope's whodunit exposé, splashed on the front page, describing in lurid detail the "dark arts campaign of personal sabotage" directed at Nikesh and me.

Hope had reached out seeking comments—I had none—so I knew the broad outline of his story. Even so, it was startling to see it in print. Anyone who says truth is stranger than fiction hasn't read *Benjamin Button,* but in my world, this is as weird as it gets—a mercenary Italian "businessman" who wasn't paid what was promised, his self-righteous apprentice in Geneva, the London arm of a global investigative firm, dodgy Indian operatives, sharpshooting American lawyers, computer hackers, an attempt at sexual blackmail.

Disappointingly, there was no recognition of my quiet heroism in the line of fire.

I had a question for Maya after we finished reading.

"How come only Nikesh got a honey trap? I mean, what the fuck, I wasn't important enough?"

We both laughed. She had lived this frightening story with me, and now it felt nice to share a joke about it.

According to *The Journal*, this was no racist conspiracy, nor was it a corporate vendetta or business dispute. Instead, *The Journal* accused an individual who vigorously denied the allegations. I won't name him because I cannot verify the facts and I've been the target of fake news myself, but more importantly, it doesn't matter. (Yes, I know—such ambiguity in a work of fiction would be unacceptable. Reality, however, is annoyingly complicated.) I didn't need redemption: everyone I cared about knew the truth. Besides, my Apple Watch and Oura ring confirmed that life was good. I missed Viper, La Tâche, and Tanaka-san, but I finished at least a book a week and started many more, the only billionaires I encountered were on *Succession,* my iPhone no longer convulsed with furtive messages from secret agents, and my facial skin remained tight without Botox. While I remained in awe of his splendid handle, I had no desire to mutate into Akaky Akakievich Bashmachkin's vengeful, covetous, and coat-stealing apparition. Instead, I want to be released, my washed bones floating downstream in the Ganges. Because one life is enough.

■

On a balmy early September evening in 2021, I arrived at a handsome red brick townhouse on West Tenth Street in Greenwich Village.

The earnest millennial poets and storytellers lounging on the stoop eyed me curiously as I grappled with the oddity of an entrance door that opened outward. *Who is this dude?* they must have wondered, while puffing on their cigarettes, for their writerly minds an intriguing prompt for a story. One of them wore a beret: I later learned he was a street poet from Vermont and an ardent Trotskyite. Which makes him seem weird, but the real oddity, like Don Henley's Deadhead sticker on a Cadillac, was me.

Fortunately, the electronic latch responded to my student ID, which made me seem less of a nervous impostor. That and the backpack.

Once inside, the black-and-white portraits of American writers—Toni Morrison, Saul Bellow—reminded me why we were all here. Like Sappho, to write words more naked than flesh, stronger than bone, more sensitive than nerve. Which sounds grand, but the terrifying part of this writing business—the poetry racket is worse—is that unlike finance, you never know if your stuff is any good. But the young ones taught me that it didn't matter. Writing was our way of inhabiting and observing the world, with no reasonable expectation of tangible reward.

I was at the Lillian Vernon Creative Writers House, a holdout from the Village's bohemian past and home to NYU's MFA program, and my launching pad for a second act. Late in life perhaps, but I was counting on David Sinclair magic pills to help me in that search for lost time.

My class, a seminar with the formidable Hari Kunzru, was in an interior room on the first floor. Nothing like a wood-paneled Wall Street boardroom with oil canvases of grumpy old men, or the minimalist Valley equivalent with framed Apple ads from the eighties. Instead, the room was furnished with rickety metallic chairs with faux wood seats and four rectangular tables with scratched Formica tops arranged in a square. The carpet was gray and stained; on the cream-colored walls more monochromatic images of writers.

The bereted Trotskyite was sitting across from the door, and I caught his eye. Maybe he smiled, I couldn't tell under the mask.

I took a seat next to him.

"Hi, I'm Ben," he said.

"You a first-year?" I inquired, assuming this still worked as a student icebreaker.

"Second . . . you just starting?"

"Well, it's thirty-five years since I was last in a classroom. As a student anyway," I responded.

"Ha! I didn't want to ask. But that's cool."

He asked what I had been doing. I considered a fuzzy answer, like "corporate executive" but that sounded lame. Besides, one mask was bad enough.

When I told him I was an investment banker he looked away, and started chatting with the person seated on his other side. Meanwhile, I fidgeted with my iPad.

After a couple of minutes Ben addressed me again.

"But you're here now, and you want to be a writer. That's cool," he said. "Are you working on something, like a project?"

"Not yet. I mean, I've seen a lot. I want to write to help me make sense of it, maybe figure out what it all means?"

"I get it, I get it!" he said, nodding vigorously. "That's cool. Yeah, kind of what everyone's doing."

Everyone? What about dudes who create robots that make pizza in trucks and schemers who set honey traps and the jokerman who looks like Jesus and invented baby clothes with kneepads?

No, Ben. In my world the only reason people examine their lives is to figure out ways to make more money.

ACKNOWLEDGMENTS

The biggest challenge in plagiarizing one's own life is that real people are involved. Moreover, executive memoirs tend to be shamelessly self-aggrandizing, annoyingly didactic, and breathtakingly boring. I was determined not to go there, but in my NYU writing workshops I was persuaded by my fellow students that mine was a human story worth telling. So to them, first and foremost, I owe a debt of gratitude. Being part of this community is a memory I will always cherish.

A special shoutout to my inspiring teachers—Hari Kunzru, Jonathan Foer, Darin Strauss, Parul Sehgal, Leigh Newman, and the indefatigable David Lipsky—all of whom contributed meaningfully to this project.

Thanks also to my editor, Tim Bartlett, for his patience and insight; my agent Lynn Johnston for believing; Kevin Reilly, Gabrielle Gantz, Michelle Cashman, Laura Clark, Ginny Perrin, Hannah Dragone, Lauren Riebs, and Meryl Levavi for making it all come together; and my family for providing real-time support and feedback.

I still have no clue if my stuff is any good, but without their collective support, I know it could have been a lot worse.

NOTES

Prologue

1. Benjamin Labatut, *The Maniac* (New York: Penguin Press, 2023), 250.

1. Born to Run

1. Lawrence Malkin, "Procter & Gamble's Tale of Derivatives Woe," *The New York Times,* April 14, 1994.
2. Neil Weinberg, "Master of the Internet," *Forbes,* July 5, 1999, https://www.forbes.com/forbes/1999/0705/6401146a.html?sh=5056042c1e17.
3. Bruce Einhorn, "Masayoshi Son's $58 billion Payday on Alibaba," *Bloomberg,* May 9, 2014.
4. Pavel Alpeyev and Takashi Amano, "SoftBank President Arora Receives Pay Package of $73 Million," *Bloomberg,* May 26, 2016.

2. I Took a Pill in Ibiza

1. Emily Glazer and Kirsten Grind, "Elon Musk Has Used Illegal Drugs, Worrying Leaders at Tesla and SpaceX," *The Wall Street Journal,* January 6, 2024.
2. Kirsten Grind and Katherine Bindley, "Magic Mushrooms. LSD. Ketamine. The Drugs That Power Silicon Valley," *The Wall Street Journal,* June 27, 2023, https://www.wsj.com/articles/silicon-valley-microdosing-ketamine-lsd-magic-mushrooms-d381e214.

3. The Airport Test

1. James Barton, "SoftBank May Acquire America Movil's Mexican Assets," *Developing Telecoms,* November 3, 2014, https://developingtelecoms.com/telecom-business/telecom-investment-mergers/5539-softbank-may-acquire-america-movil-s-mexican-assets.html.
2. Brooks Barnes and Michael J. de la Merced, "In SoftBank, DreamWorks Animation May Have A Suitor," *The New York Times,* September 29, 2014, https://www.nytimes.com/2014/09/29/business/media/japanese-company-is-said-to-bid-for-dreamworks-animation.html.
3. "SoftBank and Legendary to Form Strategic Partnership," *PR Newswire,* October 2,

2014, https://www.prnewswire.com/news-releases/softbank-and-legendary-to-form-strategic-partnership-277892671.html.
4. SoftBank Annual Report, 2000.
5. Rishi Iyengar, "Warren Buffett Is Investing in Paytm, His First Indian Company," *CNN Business,* August 27, 2018, https://money.cnn.com/2018/08/27/technology/paytm-warren-buffett/index.html.
6. Jon Russell, "SoftBank Snaps Up Korean Global Video Site DramaFever to Increase Its Entertainment Focus," *TechCrunch,* October 14, 2014, https://techcrunch.com/2014/10/14/softbank-snaps-up-korean-video-site-dramafever-to-increase-its-entertainment-focus/.
7. James B. Stewart, "Was This $100 billion Deal the Worst Merger Ever?" *The New York Times,* November 19, 2022, https://www.nytimes.com/2022/11/19/business/media/att-time-warner-deal.html?smid=nytcore-ios-share&referringSource=articleShare.

4. Happiness for Everyone

1. Allan Weber, "Japanese-Style Entrepreneurship: An Interview with Softbank's CEO, Masayoshi Son," *Harvard Business Review,* January–February 1992, https://hbr.org/1992/01/japanese-style-entrepreneurship-an-interview-with-softbanks-ceo-masayoshi-son.
2. SoftBank Group Website, https://group.softbank/en.
3. Guinness Book of World Records, https://www.guinnessworldrecords.com/world-records/94151-largest-loss-of-personal-fortune.
4. Charlie Rose, March 10, 2014, https://charlierose.com/videos/23495.
5. Martin Fackler, "SoftBank to Buy Vodafone's Japan Cellphone Unit for $15 Billion," *The New York Times,* March 18, 2016, https://www.nytimes.com/2006/03/18/business/worldbusiness/softbank-to-buy-vodafones-japan-cellphone-unit-for.html.
6. SoftBank Group Website, "SOFTBANK to Acquire Vodafone K.K., to Establish Mobile Communications Business Alliance with Yahoo! JAPAN," press release, March 17, 2006, https://group.softbank/en/news/press/20060317.
7. Kana Inagaki and Leo Lewis, "SoftBank Mobile Arm to Be Valued at Almost $63 Billion in IPO," *Financial Times*, November 30, 2018.

5. Strawberry Fields Forever

1. SoftBank Group Website, "Origin of Our Brand Name and Logo," https://group.softbank/en/philosophy/identity.
2. Elon Musk, Twitter, February 6, 2020.
3. Mike Wall, "Elon Musk Floats 'Nuke Mars' Idea Again," *Space.com,* August 17, 2019, https://www.space.com/elon-musk-nuke-mars-terraforming.html.

6. FaceTime

1. Meta Website, "Facebook Receives Investment from Digital Sky Technologies," May 26, 2009, https://about.fb.com/news/2009/05/facebook-receives-investment-from-digital-sky-technologies/.
2. "Bytedance Is Said to Secure Funding at Record $75 Billion Value," *Bloomberg*, October 26, 2018.
3. Elon Musk, *Saturday Night Live,* NBC, May 8, 2021.
4. Scott Galloway, "America's False Idols," *The Atlantic,* September 22, 2022.

7. City of Djinns

1. Walter Isaacson, *Elon Musk* (New York: Simon & Schuster, 2023), 354.
2. "Vanguard Cuts IPO-Bound Ola's Valuation by 52% to $3.5 Billion," *Fortune*

India, August 2, 2023, https://www.fortuneindia.com/enterprise/vanguard-cuts-ipo-bound-olas-valuation-by-52-to-35-bn/113597.

3. Alex Sherman, "Blind Optimism and Masa's Yes-Men Led SoftBank to Overvalue WeWork, Sources Say," *CNBC,* September 25, 2019.

8. Show Me the Money

1. Tim Brugger, "SoftBank Taps 19 Banks For $20 Billion Loan to Pay for Sprint Deal," *The Motley Fool,* September 12, 2013, https://www.fool.com/investing/general/2013/09/12/softbank-taps-19-banks-for-20-billion-loan-to-pay.aspx.
2. Will Partin, "The 2010s Were a Banner Decade for Big Money and Tech—and Esports Reaped the Rewards" *The Washington Post,* January 28, 2020, https://www.washingtonpost.com/video-games/esports/2020/01/28/2010s-were-banner-decade-big-money-tech-esports-reaped-rewards/#.
3. Sophie Knight, Ritsuko Ando, and Malathi Nayak, "SoftBank Buys $1.5 Billion Stake in Finnish Mobile Games Maker Supercell," *Reuters,* October 16, 2013, https://www.reuters.com/article/idUSBRE99E0ID/.
4. Ingrid Lunden, "SoftBank Ups Its Stake In Supercell to 73% as Sole External Shareholder," *TechCrunch,* June 1, 2015, https://techcrunch.com/2015/06/01/softbank-buys-another-23-of-supercell-shares-now-owns-73-of-the-mobile-gaming-giant/.
5. SoftBank Group Website, "Tencent to Acquire Majority Stake in Supercell from SoftBank," press release, June 21, 2016, https://group.softbank/en/news/press/20160621.
6. Maggie Hiufu Wong, "25 Years On: Remembering the Glory Days of Hong Kong's Old Kai Tak Airport," *CNN Travel,* June 23, 2023, https://edition.cnn.com/travel/article/hong-kong-kai-tak-airport/index.html.
7. Alyssa Abkowitz and Rick Carew, "Uber Sells China Operations to Didi Chuxing," *The Wall Street Journal,* August 1, 2016, http://www.wsj.com/articles/china-s-didi-chuxing-to-acquire-rival-uber-s-chinese-operations-1470024403.
8. Reed Stevenson and Takashi Amano, "SoftBank Proceeds from Alibaba Selldown Rise to $10 Billion," *Bloomberg,* June 3, 2016, https://www.bloomberg.com/news/articles/2016-06-03/softbank-proceeds-from-alibaba-selldown-rises-to-10-billion.

9. This Aggression Will Not Stand, Man

1. R. G. Grant, "Bombing of Tokyo," *Britannica,* last updated January 4, 2024, https://www.britannica.com/event/Bombing-of-Tokyo.
2. "SoftBank President Arora to Buy $480 Million of Company's Shares," *Reuters*, August 19, 2015, https://www.reuters.com/article/idUSL3N10U34Q/.
3. Peter Elstrom and Pavel Alpeyev, "SoftBank Investors Call for Internal Probe of No. 2 Arora," *Bloomberg,* April 21, 2016, https://www.bloomberg.com/news/articles/2016-04-21/softbank-investors-call-for-internal-probe-of-president-arora-in9tcg8v.

10. Curveball

1. Mitsuru Obe, "Japan Banks Lend to SoftBank While Selling Its Bonds to Baseball Fans," *Nikkei Asia,* December 23, 2019, https://asia.nikkei.com/Business/SoftBank2/Japan-banks-lend-to-SoftBank-while-selling-its-bonds-to-baseball-fans; Robert Smith, "SoftBank Has Become Whale of Japan's Retail Bond Market," *Financial Times,* May 21, 2019, https://www.ft.com/content/24c4a8a8-7885-11e9-bbad-7c18c0ea0201.
2. Soulaima Gourani, "Pain and Suffering Are Crucial For Your Growth And Success," *Forbes,* March 14, 2024.
3. Barack Obama, *The Audacity of Hope: Thoughts on Reclaiming the American Dream* (New York: Crown, 2006).
4. "SoftBank's Son Stands Up to Anti-Korean Bigotry in Japan," *Nikkei Asia,* August

27, 2015, https://asia.nikkei.com/NAR/Articles/SoftBank-s-Son-stands-up-to-anti-Korean-bigotry-in-Japan.

5. Jayson Derrick, "Remember When Yahoo Turned Down $1 Million to Buy Google?" *Yahoo! Finance*, July 25, 2016, https://finance.yahoo.com/news/remember-yahoo-turned-down-1-132805083.html.
6. "Yahoo's Billion Dollar Blunders with Google, Facebook, Microsoft, and Netflix," *YourStory.com*, May 9, 2023, https://yourstory.com/2023/05/yahoos-billion-dollar-blunders-google-facebook-microsoft-netflix; Chris Gaithers and Dawn Chmielewski, "In YouTube Deal, Google Beats Yahoo at Its Own Media Game," *Los Angeles Times*, October 11, 2006.
7. Erin Griffith, "Nikesh Arora Resigns at SoftBank," *Fortune*, June 21, 2016, https://fortune.com/2016/06/21/nikesh-arora-resigns-at-softbank/.

11. The Crystal Ball

1. Anita Raghavan, "SoftBank-ARM Deal Brings Together Morgan Stanley Alumni," *The New York Times*, July 19, 2016, https://www.nytimes.com/2016/07/19/business/dealbook/softbank-arm-deal-brings-together-morgan-stanley-alumni.html.
2. Arash Massoudi, "How Masayoshi Son Brought Arm into SoftBank's Embrace," *Financial Times*, July 19, 2016, https://www.ft.com/content/cf6c0be0-4dd4-11e6-8172-e39ecd3b86fc.

12. That's Far Out, Man

1. Lewis Page, "Suicide Bum Blast Bombing Startles Saudi Prince," *The Register*, September 21, 2009, https://www.theregister.com/2009/09/21/bum_bombing/.
2. "Industry Diversification and Job Growth in Saudi Arabia," *Harvard Kennedy School Growth Lab*, https://growthlab.hks.harvard.edu/applied-research/saudi-arabia.
3. "Saudi Budget Looks Positive but Deficit Will Stay Large," *FitchRatings*, January 5, 2016, https://www.fitchratings.com/research/sovereigns/saudi-budget-looks-positive-but-deficit-will-stay-large-05-01-2016.
4. Bradley Hope and Justin Scheck, *Blood and Oil* (London: John Murray, 2020), 109.
5. Masayoshi Son, interview with Carlyle cofounder David Rubinstein, Bloomberg TV, *Bloomberg*, October 11, 2017.
6. Eric Johnson, "Benchmark's Bill Gurley Says He's Still Worried About a Bubble," *Vox.com*, September 12, 2016, https://www.vox.com/2016/9/12/12882780/bill-gurley-benchmark-bubble-venture-capital-startups-uber.
7. "Ex-Citi CEO Defends 'Dancing' Quote to U.S. Panel," *Reuters*, April 8, 2010, https://www.reuters.com/article/idUSN08198108/.
8. "Masayoshi Son Prepares To Unleash His Second $100 billion Tech Fund," *The Economist*, March 23, 2019, https://www.economist.com/business/2019/03/23/masayoshi-son-prepares-to-unleash-his-second-100bn-tech-fund.
9. Arash Massoudi, Kana Inagaki, and Leslie Hook, "SoftBank Uses Rare Structure for $93 Billion Tech Fund," *Financial Times*, June 12, 2017.
10. "Japanese Billionaire Masayoshi Son, Larry Ellison, Apple, Saudi Arabia All Bet On $100 Billion Vision Fund," *Forbes*, April 5, 2017.
11. Madhav Chanchani and Archana Rai, "India will get at least $10 billion investment from SoftBank: Masayoshi Son," *The Economic Times*, December 6, 2016, https://economictimes.indiatimes.com/small-biz/startups/india-will-get-at-least-100-billion-investment-from-softbank-masayoshi-son/articleshow/55803071.cms?-from=mdr.
12. Ryan Knutson and Alexander Martin, "When Billionaires Meet: $50 Billion Pledge from SoftBank to Trump," *The Wall Street Journal*, December 7, 2016, http://www

.wsj.com/articles/donald-trump-says-softbank-pledges-to-invest-50-billion-in-u-s-1481053732?st=36zigyjzs8a5cld&reflink=article_copyURL_share.

13. Donald J. Trump, Twitter, December 7, 2016.

13. First Blood

1. Seth Hettena, "The Cleaner," *The American Lawyer,* October 1, 2008.
2. John le Carré, *Tinker, Tailor, Soldier, Spy* (New York: Knopf, 1974).

14. Let Me Roll It

1. Mayumi Negishi, "SoftBank Sells Entire Nvidia Stake," *The Wall Street Journal,* February 6, 2019, https://www.wsj.com/articles/softbank-sells-entire-nvidia-stake-11549462246?st=f3ji6zsbh0e9lkj.
2. Nick Friedell, "Curry's 61-foot 3-pointer Longest FG This Season," *ABC News,* March 19, 2019, https://abc7news.com/sports/currys-61-foot-3-pointer-longest-fg-this-season/5204323/.
3. Jeremy Kahn, "SoftBank Leads $502 Million Investment in U.K. Tech Startup," *Bloomberg,* May 11, 2017, https://www.bloomberg.com/news/articles/2017-05-11/softbank-leads-502-million-investment-in-u-k-tech-startup.
4. PitchBook Data.
5. Eliot Brown and Maureen Farrell, *The Cult of We* (London: Mudlark, 2021), 167.
6. Brown and Farrell, *Cult of We,* 167.
7. Alex Konrad, "WeWork Confirms Massive $4.4 Billion from SoftBank and Its Vision Fund," *Forbes,* August 24, 2017, https://www.forbes.com/sites/alexkonrad/2017/08/24/wework-confirms-massive-4-4-billion-investment-from-softbank-and-its-vision-fund/?sh=5875c4ad5b3c.
8. "WeWork Receives $4.4 billion Investment from SoftBank Group and SoftBank Vision Fund," *Business Wire,* https://www.sttinfo.fi/tiedote/62863473/wework-receives-44-billion-investment-from-softbank-group-and-softbank-vision-fund?publisherId=58763726.
9. Eliot Brown and Maureen Farrell, *The Cult of We* (London: Mudlark, 2021), 174.
10. PitchBook Data.
11. Saritha Rai, "Paytm Raises $1.4 Billion from SoftBank to Expand User Base," *Bloomberg,* May 18, 2017, https://www.bloomberg.com/news/articles/2017-05-18/paytm-raises-1-4-billion-from-softbank-to-expand-user-base.
12. Jon Russell, "Budget Hotel Pioneer OYO Raises $250M Led by SoftBank's Vision Fund," *TechCrunch,* September 7, 2017, https://techcrunch.com/2017/09/07/oyo-raises-250m/.
13. Alex Wilhelm, "SoftBank's Vision Fund Leads $1B Investment into Indian Hotel Company OYO," *Crunchbase,* September 25, 2018, https://news.crunchbase.com/venture/softbanks-vision-fund-leads-1b-for-indian-hotel-company-oyo/.
14. Tad Friend, "Tomorrow's Advance Man," *New Yorker,* May 11, 2015, https://www.newyorker.com/magazine/2015/05/18/tomorrows-advance-man.
15. Raymond Zhong, "Wag, the Dog-Walking Service, Lands $300 Million from SoftBank Vision Fund," *The New York Times,* January 13, 201, https://www.nytimes.com/2018/01/30/business/dealbook/softbank-vision-fund-wag.html.
16. Katie Roof, "SoftBank Deal Values Food Startup Zume at $2.25 Billion," *The Wall Street Journal,* November 1, 2018, https://www.wsj.com/articles/zume-a-food-robotics-and-logistics-startup-cooks-up-2-25-billion-valuation-in-softbank-deal-1541099560.
17. "Compass Attracts $450 Million Investment from the SoftBank Vision Fund," *PR Newswire,* December 7, 2017, https://www.prnewswire.com/news-releases/compass-attracts-450-million-investment-from-the-softbank-vision-fund-300568288.html.

18. "Roivant Sciences Raises $1.1 Billion in Equity Investment Led By SoftBank Vision Fund," *PR Newswire,* August 9, 2017, https://www.prnewswire.com/news-releases/roivant-sciences-raises-11-billion-in-equity-investment-led-by-softbank-vision-fund-300501758.html.
19. Giles Turner, "SoftBank Said to Write Down $1.5 Billion Greensill Holding," *Bloomberg,* March 1, 2021, https://www.bloomberg.com/news/articles/2021-03-01/softbank-is-said-to-write-down-1-5-billion-greensill-investment.
20. Jackie Wattles, "SoftBank-Backed Satellite Startup OneWeb Files for Bankruptcy," *CNN Business,* March 28, 2020, https://www.cnn.com/2020/03/28/tech/oneweb-softbank-bankruptcy-scn/index.html.
21. Elizabeth Howell and Tereza Pultarova, "Starlink Satellites," Space.com, n.d., https://www.space.com/spacex-starlink-satellites.html.
22. Jon Russell, "Grab Confirms $1.46B Investment from SoftBank's Vision Fund," *TechCrunch,* March 5, 2019, https://techcrunch.com/2019/03/05/grab-vision-fund/.
23. Seth Fiegerman, "Uber Sells 15% Stake to SoftBank," *CNN Business,* December 28, 2017, https://money.cnn.com/2017/12/28/technology/uber-softbank-investment/index.html.
24. Theodore Schleifer, "Uber's Dara Khosrowshahi Sums Up Perfectly How CEOs Feel About Taking Money from SoftBank," *Vox,* February 14, 2018, https://www.vox.com/2018/2/14/17014762/uber-softbank-dara-khosrowshahi-goldman-sachs.
25. Zheping Huang and Jane Zhang, "ByteDance Offers Investors a Buyback at $268 Billion Valuation," *Bloomberg,* December 6, 2023, https://www.bloomberg.com/news/articles/2023-12-06/bytedance-offers-to-buy-back-5-billion-worth-of-shares-scmp.
26. Jon Russell, "SoftBank Invests $1B in Korean E-commerce Firm Coupang at a $5B Valuation," *TechCrunch,* June 3, 2015, https://techcrunch.com/2015/06/02/coupangzillion/; Eliot Brown, "DoorDash Is Set to Deliver SoftBank a Big Hit," *The Wall Street Journal,* December 2, 2020, https://www.wsj.com/articles/doordash-is-set-to-deliver-softbank-a-big-hit-11606906803.
27. Tripp Mickle and Liz Hoffman, "Web Retailer Fanatics Raises $1 Billion from SoftBank's Vision Fund," *The Wall Street Journal,* August 8, 2017, https://www.wsj.com/articles/web-retailer-fanatics-raises-1-billion-from-softbanks-vision-fund-1502219551.
28. David Welch and Sarah McBride, "GM Buys SoftBank's $2.1 Billion Stake in Cruise Self-Driving Unit," *Bloomberg,* March 18, 2022, https://www.bloomberg.com/news/articles/2022-03-18/gm-buys-2-1-billion-softbank-stake-in-cruise-self-driving-unit.
29. Sebastian Mallaby, *The Power Law* (New York: Penguin Press, 2022), 347.
30. Polina Morinova, "Sequoia Capital Is on Track to Raise $8 Billion for Its Monster Fund," *Fortune,* April 27, 2018, https://fortune.com/2018/04/27/sequoia-capital-global-fund/.
31. Jessica E. Lessin, "'Pressures Remain': Coatue Prepares Tech Founders for the Road Ahead," *The Information,* June 29, 2023, https://www.theinformation.com/articles/pressures-remain-coatue-prepares-tech-founders-for-the-road-ahead.

15. Game of Phones

1. Mike Isaac, "AT&T Drops Its T-Mobile Merger Bid in $4B Fail," *Wired,* December 19, 2011, https://www.wired.com/2011/12/att-tmobile-merger-ends/.
2. SoftBank Group Website, "Completion of Acquisition of Sprint," press release, July 11, 2013, https://group.softbank/en/news/press/20130711.
3. Michael J. De La Merced, "The Biggest Champion of a Sprint-T-Mobile Deal: SoftBank Chief," *The New York Times,* June 5, 2014, https://archive.nytimes.com/dealbook.nytimes.com/2014/06/05/the-biggest-champion-of-a-sprint-t-mobile-deal-softbanks-chief/.

4. John Legere, Twitter, July 24, 2015.
5. David Faber, "SoftBank Willing to Re-engage Charter Communications on Deal, Sources Say," *CNBC*, November 6, 2017.
6. Alex Sherman, "SoftBank Said to Have $65 Billion in Funds for Charter Deal," *Bloomberg*, July 31, 2017.
7. Ryan Knutson and Dana Cimilluca, "Sprint Proposes Merger with Charter Communications," *The Wall Street Journal*, July 28, 2017, https://www.wsj.com/articles/sprint-proposes-merger-with-charter-communications-1501284899.
8. Greg Roumeliotis and Liana Baker, "Charter Communications Says 'No Interest' in Buying Sprint," *Reuters*, July 31, 2017, https://www.reuters.com/article/us-charter-commns-m-a-sprint-corp-idUSKBN1AG066/.
9. "Faber Report: What to Make of Sprint, Charter and Masa Son," *CNBC*, July 31, 2017, https://www.cnbc.com/video/2017/07/31/faber-report-what-to-make-of-sprint-charter-and-masa-son.html.
10. Faber, "SoftBank Willing to Re-engage Charter Communications."
11. Edmund Lee, "T-Mobile Absorbs Sprint After Two-Year Battle," *The Wall Street Journal*, April 1, 2020, https://www.wsj.com/articles/t-mobile-absorbs-sprint-after-two-year-battle-11585749352.

17. The Butterfly Effect

1. Richard P. Feynman, *The Pleasure of Finding Things Out: The Best Short Works of Richard P. Feynman* (New York: Perseus Books, 1999), 100; Kamelia Angelova, "Peter Thiel: Death Is a Problem That Can Be Solved," *Business Insider*, Feb. 9, 2012, https://www.businessinsider.com/peter-thiel-death-is-a-problem-that-can-be-solved-2012-2; Tim Newcomb, "Humans Are on Track to Achieve Immortality in 7 Years, Futurist Says," *Popular Mechanics*, March 13, 2023, https://www.popularmechanics.com/science/health/a43297321/humans-will-achieve-immortality-by-2030/.
2. Bradley Hope and Tom Wright, *Billion Dollar Whale* (New York: Hachette 2018).

18. How Much Land Does a Man Need?

1. Sebastien Raybaud, "Warhol's Portrait of Basquiat Garners US$40 Million at New York Sale," *The Value*, Nov. 15, 2021, https://en.thevalue.com/articles/christies-new-york-20th-century-art-evening-sale-andy-warhol-basquiat.
2. Donna Tussing Orwin, *The Cambridge Companion to Tolstoy* (Cambridge: Cambridge University Press, 2002), 209.

Epilogue

1. Shira Ovide, "The Benefits of Deal 'Schmuck Insurance,'" *The Wall Street Journal*, June 13, 2011, https://www.wsj.com/articles/BL-DLB-33622.
2. David Gelles, "SoftBank Bets Big on WeWork. Again," *The New York Times*, January 7, 2019, https://www.nytimes.com/2019/01/07/business/softbank-wework.html.
3. Eliot Brown, "How Adam Neumann's Over-the-Top Style Built WeWork," *The Wall Street Journal*, September 18, 2019, https://www.wsj.com/articles/this-is-not-the-way-everybody-behaves-how-adam-neumanns-over-the-top-style-built-wework-11568823827; Annie Palmer, "WeWork CEO Returns $5.9 Million the Company Paid Him for 'We' Trademark," *CNBC*, September 4, 2019, https://www.cnbc.com/2019/09/04/wework-ceo-returns-5point9-million-the-company-paid-for-we-trademark.html.
4. Samantha Sharf, "WeWork Files IPO Plan, Showing First-Half Losses Grew 25%," *Forbes*, August 14, 2019, https://www.forbes.com/sites/samanthasharf/2019/08/14/wework-ipo-sec-s1/?sh=1a40c7444f08.
5. Scott Galloway, "NYU Professor Calls WeWork 'WeWTF,' Says Any Wall Street

Analyst Who Believes It's Worth over $10 Billion Is 'Lying, Stupid, or Both,'" *Business Insider,* August 21, 2019, https://www.businessinsider.com/nyu-professor-calls-wework-wewtf-and-slams-bankers-2019-8.

6. Rohan Goswami, "Here's How Much WeWork Co-founder Adam Neumann Made Before Company's Bankruptcy," *CNBC,* November 6, 2023.
7. Eliot Brown, "SoftBank Emerges as a Big Loser of the Tech Downturn. Again," *The Wall Street Journal,* August 2, 2022, https://www.wsj.com/articles/softbank-tech-downturn-startups-losses-vision-fund-masayoshi-son-11659456842.
8. Jack Hough, "Reversion to the Meme: GameStop, WallStreetBets, and the New Rules for Stock Trading," *Barron's,* January 28, 2021, https://www.barrons.com/articles/reversion-to-the-meme-gamestop-wallstreetbets-and-the-new-rules-for-stock-trading-51611861219.
9. Jordan Rubio, "Charting How the Unicorn Baby Boom Turned Bust in 2022," *Pitchbook*, December 14, 2022.
10. Hema Parmar and Gillian Tan, "Tiger Global's Scott Shleifer Steps Down as Head of Private Investing," *Bloomberg,* November 2023.
11. Leo Lewis and Eri Sugiura, "Masayoshi Son 'Ashamed' of Focus on Profits After SoftBank Logs Record $23Bn Loss," *Financial Times,* August 8, 2022, https://www.ft.com/content/8d84b488-8f97-4742-ab46-154d3b312a82.
12. Arjun Kharpal, "SoftBank Posts Record $32 Billion Loss at its Vision Fund Tech Investment Arm," *CNBC,* May 11, 2023, https://www.cnbc.com/2023/05/11/softbank-full-year-2022-earnings-vision-fund-posts-32-billion-loss.html.
13. Gearoid Reidy, "SoftBank's Shogun Has a Rare Moment of Contrition," *Bloomberg,* August 8, 2022, https://www.bloomberg.com/opinion/articles/2022-08-08/softbank-ceo-masayoshi-son-has-a-rare-moment-of-contrition.
14. Maureen Farrell and Rob Copeland, "Saudi Arabia Plans $40 Billion Push Into Artificial Intelligence," *The New York Times,* March 19, 2024, https://www.nytimes.com/2024/03/19/business/saudi-arabia-investment-artificial-intelligence.html.
15. Dylan Dethier, "Mickelson Claims His 'Scary M-f-' Chat Was Off the Record. Here's What We Know," *Golf Magazine,* October 13, 2022, https://golf.com/news/phil-mickelson-alan-shipnuck-interview-saudi-comments/.
16. Rohan Goswami, "WeWork, Once Valued at $47 Billion, Files for Bankruptcy," *CNBC,* November 6, 2023, https://www.cnbc.com/2023/11/07/wework-files-for-bankruptcy.html.
17. Sarah McBride, "Fallen Pizza Startup Zume Shuts Down After Raising Millions," *Bloomberg,* June 2, 2023, https://www.bloomberg.com/news/articles/2023-06-03/fallen-pizza-startup-zume-shuts-down-after-raising-millions.
18. Cory Weinberg, "Bankrupt Startup That Blew $2 Billion from SoftBank Sues Ex-CEO, Board Directors over 'Self-Dealing,'" *The Information,* April 25, 2022, https://www.theinformation.com/articles/bankrupt-startup-that-blew-2-billion-from-softbank-sues-ex-ceo-board-directors-over-self-dealing.
19. ET Bureau, "Oyo to Shut Doors on 2400 Indian Staffers, May Let More Go in March," *The Economic Times,* January 15, 2020, https://economictimes.indiatimes.com/small-biz/startups/newsbuzz/oyo-to-shut-doors-on-2400-indian-staffers-may-let-go-more-in-march/articleshow/73237497.cms.
20. Eshe Nelson, Jack Ewing, and Liz Alderman, "The Swift Collapse of a Company Built on Debt," *The New York Times,* March 28, 2021, https://www.nytimes.com/2021/03/28/business/greensill-capital-collapse.html.
21. Min Jeong Lee, "SoftBank Is Said to Expect About $100 Million Loss on FTX Stake," *Bloomberg,* November 11, 2022, https://www.bloomberg.com/news/articles/2022-11-11/softbank-is-said-to-expect-about-100-million-loss-on-ftx-stake.

22. Rohan Goswami, "SoftBank Sues Social Media Startup It Invested in, Alleges It Faked User Numbers," *CNBC,* August 4, 2023, https://www.cnbc.com/2023/08/04/softbank-sues-social-media-startup-irl-alleging-fake-user-numbers.html.
23. Ortenca Aliaj and Eric Platt, "How SoftBank's Bet on US Mortgage Lender Better Backfired," *Financial Times,* December 21, 2023.
24. "Smart Glass Startup View to Go Private and Declare Bankruptcy," *The Real Deal,* April 3, 2024.
25. Eliot Brown, "SoftBank's Gain on Alibaba over 23 Years: $72 billion," *The Wall Street Journal,* May 11, 2023, https://www.wsj.com/livecoverage/stock-market-today-dow-jones-05-11-2023/card/softbank-s-gain-on-alibaba-over-23-years-72-billion-mUstxx3qn5K41CZbFAvm.
26. Gillian Tan, Min Jeong Lee, and Ian King, "Masayoshi Son Seeks to Build a $100 Billion AI Chip Venture," *Bloomberg,* February 16, 2024.
27. Sam Nussey, "SoftBank Gets $7.6 Billion T-Mobile Stake Windfall, Shares Soar," *Reuters,* December 27, 2023, https://www.reuters.com/business/finance/softbank-shares-jump-6-after-exercising-t-mobile-option-2023-12-27.
28. Zadie Smith, "Generation Why?" *The New York Review,* November 25, 2010, https://www.nybooks.com/articles/2010/11/25/generation-why/.
29. Bess Levin, "If You've Got The Ruler, Elon Musk Has the Dick," *Vanity Fair,* July 10, 2023, https://www.vanityfair.com/news/2023/07/elon-musk-mark-zuckerberg-dick-measuring-contest.
30. Sarah McBride, "Kim Kardashian and the Scientists," *Bloomberg Tech Daily,* April 16, 2024.

INDEX